# MOBILE COMMUNICATION AND NETWORK



AUTHOR

**Dr. Vimal Bhatia**
*Professor,*
*Department of Electrical Engineering,*
*Indian Institute of Technology Indore*

REVIEWER

**Dr. Upasani Dhananjay Eknath**
*Professor*
*Department of Electronics & Telecommunication Engineering*
*Principal,*
*Samarth Group of Institutions College of Engineering, Belhe, Pune*

KHANNA BOOK PUBLISHING CO. (P) Ltd.
4C/4344, Ansari Road, Darya Ganj, New Delhi, India

All India Council for Technical Education
Nelson Mandela Marg, Vasant Kunj, New Delhi, India

Dear Readers,

To prevent the piracy, this book is secured with HIGH SECURITY HOLOGRAM on the front title cover. In case you don't find the hologram on the front cover title, please write us to at contact@khannabooks.com or whatsapp us at +91-99109 09320 and avail special gift voucher for yourself.

Specimen of Hologram on front Cover title:

Moreover, there is a SPECIAL DISCOUNT COUPON for you with EVERY HOLOGRAM.

How to avail this SPECIAL DISCOUNT:

Step 1: Scratch the hologram

Step 2: Under the scratch area, your "coupon code" is available

Step 3: Logon to www.khannabooks.com

Step 4: Use your "coupon code" in the shopping cart and get your copy at a special discount

Step 5: Enjoy your reading!

**ISBN:** 978-93-5538-916-9

**Book Code:** UG491EN

**Mobile Communication And Network**

*by* Dr. Vimal Bhatia

**First Edition:** 2026

*Originally Published by:*
**All India Council for Technical Education, Ministry of Education, GOI**

*Exclusively Published & Distributed by:*
**Khanna Book Publishing Co. (P) Ltd.**
4C/4344, Ansari Road, Daryaganj,
New Delhi (INDIA)

Visit us at: **www.khannabooks.com**
Write us at: **contact@khannabooks.com**

To view complete list of books, Please scan the QR Code: KPH

*Printed in Bharat.*

प्रो. टी. जी. सीताराम
अध्यक्ष
Prof. T. G. Sitharam
Chairman

सत्यमेव जयते

आज़ादी का अमृत महोत्सव

अखिल भारतीय तकनीकी शिक्षा परिषद्
(भारत सरकार का एक सांविधिक निकाय)
(शिक्षा मंत्रालय, भारत सरकार)
नेल्सन मंडेला मार्ग, वसंत कुंज, नई दिल्ली–110070
दूरभाष : 011–26131498
ई–मेल : chairman@aicte-india.org

ALL INDIA COUNCIL FOR TECHNICAL EDUCATION
(A STATUTORY BODY OF THE GOVT. OF INDIA)
(Ministry of Education, Govt. of India)
Nelson Mandela Marg, Vasant Kunj, New Delhi-110070
Phone : 011-26131498
E-mail : chairman@aicte-india.org

# FOREWORD

Engineers are the backbone of any modern society. They are the ones responsible for the marvels as well as the improved quality of life across the world. Engineers have driven humanity towards greater heights in a more evolved and unprecedented manner.

The All India Council for Technical Education (AICTE), have spared no efforts towards the strengthening of the technical education in the country. AICTE is always committed towards promoting quality Technical Education to make India a modern developed nation emphasizing on the overall welfare of mankind.

An array of initiatives has been taken by AICTE in last decade which have been accelerated now by the National Education Policy (NEP) 2020. The implementation of NEP under the visionary leadership of Hon'ble Prime Minister of India envisages the provision for education in regional languages to all, thereby ensuring that every graduate becomes competent enough and is in a position to contribute towards the national growth and development through innovation & entrepreneurship.

One of the spheres where AICTE had been relentlessly working since past couple of years is providing high quality original technical contents at Under Graduate & Diploma level prepared and translated by eminent educators in various Indian languages to its aspirants. For students pursuing 2nd year of their Engineering education, AICTE has identified 87 books, which shall be translated into 12 Indian languages - Hindi, Tamil, Gujarati, Odia, Bengali, Kannada, Urdu, Punjabi, Telugu, Marathi, Assamese & Malayalam. In addition to the English medium, books in different Indian Languages are going to support the students to understand the concepts in their respective mother tongue.

On behalf of AICTE, I express sincere gratitude to all distinguished authors, reviewers and translators from the renowned institutions of high repute for their admirable contribution in a record span of time.

AICTE is confident that these outcomes based original contents shall help aspirants to master the subject with comprehension and greater ease.

(Prof. T. G. Sitharam)

# Acknowledgment

The authors are grateful to the authorities of AICTE, particularly Prof. (Dr.) T G Sitharam, Chairman; Dr. Abhay Jere, Vice-Chairman, Prof. Rajive Kumar, Member-Secretary, Dr. Sunil Luthra, Director and Reena Sharma, Hindi Officer Training and Learning Bureau Cell for their planning to publish the books on Mobile Communication and Networks. We sincerely acknowledge the valuable contributions of the reviewer of the book Dr. Upasani Dhananjay Eknath, Department of Electronics & Telecommunication Engineering, Principal, Samarth Group of Institutions College of Engineering, for making it students' friendly and giving a better shape in an artistic manner. This book is an outcome of various suggestions of AICTE members, experts and authors who shared their opinion and thought to further develop the engineering education in our country. Acknowledgements are due to the contributors and different workers in this field whose published books, review articles, papers, photographs, footnotes, references and other valuable information enriched us at the time of writing the book.

**Dr. Vimal Bhatia**

# Preface

The book "Mobile Communication and Networks" is the culmination of our extensive experience teaching fundamental of digital communication and networking courses. Its inception stemmed from the desire to impart foundational knowledge of mobile communication and networks concepts to engineering students, equipping them with a comprehensive understanding of the subject matter. To ensure a thorough grasp of the fundamentals and to offer essential supplementary information, we meticulously integrated topics recommended by AICTE throughout the book in a systematic and structured manner. Our aim was to provide wide coverage while maintaining clarity and coherence. Throughout the book, efforts were dedicated to elucidating complex concepts in the simplest and most accessible manner possible, facilitating effective learning for students at all levels of proficiency.

Throughout the manuscript preparation process, we meticulously consulted various standard textbooks to ensure comprehensive coverage of the subject matter. As a result, we developed sections containing critical questions, solved problems, and supplementary exercises. In crafting these sections, particular attention was given to defining key terms, presenting theorems, and providing a comprehensive synopsis of formulas for quick reference and revision of fundamental principles. The book encompasses a diverse range of medium to advanced level problems, meticulously organized in a logical and systematic manner. These problem sets have been rigorously tested over numerous years of teaching, catering to a broad spectrum of students and ensuring their effectiveness in facilitating learning and understanding.

In addition to incorporating illustrations and examples where necessary, we have augmented the book with a multitude of solved problems in each unit to enhance comprehension of the associated topics. It is noteworthy that, across all editions, we have integrated pertinent laboratory practical experiments to provide readers with hands-on training in the subjects covered. This distinctive feature sets our book apart and reinforces practical application alongside theoretical understanding.

Regarding the current book, "Mobile Communication and Networks" aims to offer a comprehensive understanding of mobile communication engineering topics covered within. This book is designed to equip engineering students with a solid foundation in mobile communication and networking, enabling them to tackle future challenges and explore advanced topics such as 5G and beyond, Signal Propagation, OFDM, Multipath Fading, Antennas, MIMO and more. The subject matter is presented in a structured manner, ensuring that students are prepared to work across various sectors or in national laboratories at the forefront of technological advancements.

We sincerely anticipate that this book will motivate students to engage with and delve into the fundamental principles of engineering physics, thus fostering a robust understanding of the subject. We are grateful for any constructive comments and suggestions that will aid in enhancing future editions of the book. It brings us great joy to offer this resource to both teachers and students, and we take pride in the comprehensive coverage of various aspects included within its pages.

**Dr. Vimal Bhatia**

# Outcome Based Education

For the implementation of an outcome based education the first requirement is to develop an outcome based curriculum and incorporate an outcome based assessment in the education system. By going through outcome based assessments evaluators will be able to evaluate whether the students have achieved the outlined standard, specific and measurable outcomes. With the proper incorporation of outcome based education there will be a definite commitment to achieve a minimum standard for all learners without giving up at any level. At the end of the programme running with the aid of outcome based education, a student will be able to arrive at the following outcomes:

**PO1. Engineering knowledge**: Apply the knowledge of mathematics, science, engineering fundamentals, and an engineering specialization to the solution of complex engineering problems.

**PO2. Problem analysis**: Identify, formulate, review research literature, and analyze complex engineering problems reaching substantiated conclusions using first principles of mathematics, natural sciences, and engineering sciences.

**PO3. Design / development of solutions**: Design solutions for complex engineering problems and design system components or processes that meet the specified needs with appropriate consideration for the public health and safety, and the cultural, societal, and environmental considerations.

**PO4. Conduct investigations of complex problems**: Use research-based knowledge and research methods including design of experiments, analysis and interpretation of data, and synthesis of the information to provide valid conclusions.

**PO5. Modern tool usage**: Create, select, and apply appropriate techniques, resources, and modern engineering and IT tools including prediction and modelling to complex engineering activities with an understanding of the limitations.

**PO6. The engineer and society**: Apply reasoning informed by the contextual knowledge to assess societal, health, safety, legal and cultural issues and the consequent responsibilities relevant to the professional engineering practice.

**PO7. Environment and sustainability**: Understand the impact of the professional engineering solutions in societal and environmental contexts, and demonstrate the knowledge of, and need for sustainable development.

**PO8. Ethics**: Apply ethical principles and commit to professional ethics and responsibilities and norms of the engineering practice.

**PO9. Individual and team work**: Function effectively as an individual, and as a member or leader in diverse teams, and in multidisciplinary settings.

**PO10. Communication**: Communicate effectively on complex engineering activities with the engineering community and with society at large, such as, being able to comprehend and write effective reports and design documentation, make effective presentations, and give and receive clear instructions.

**PO11. Project management and finance**: Demonstrate knowledge and understanding of the engineering and management principles and apply these to one's own work, as a member and leader in a team, to manage projects and in multidisciplinary environments.

**PO12. Life-long learning**: Recognize the need for, and have the preparation and ability to engage in independent and life-long learning in the broadest context of technological change.

# Course Outcomes

After completion of the course the students will be able to:

**CO-1**: Understand the fundamentals of mobile communication systems, including cellular architecture and networking.

**CO-2**: Analyze the performance and characteristics of various wireless communication technologies (e.g., GSM, CDMA, LTE, 5G).

**CO-3**: Design and simulate basic mobile communication systems, considering factors such as channel modeling, interference, and modulation techniques.

**CO-4**: Explain the concepts of mobility management, handover techniques, and resource management in mobile networks.

**CO-5**: Critically analyze and compare different generations of mobile networks (2G, 3G, 4G, and 5G) in terms of performance, capabilities, and deployment considerations.

**CO-6**: Investigate emerging trends and ethical issues in mobile communication technologies.

| Course Outcomes | Expected Mapping with Programme Outcomes<br>*(1- Weak Correlation; 2- Medium correlation; 3- Strong Correlation)* | | | | | | | | | | | |
|---|---|---|---|---|---|---|---|---|---|---|---|---|
| | PO-1 | PO-2 | PO-3 | PO-4 | PO-5 | PO-6 | PO-7 | PO-8 | PO-9 | PO-10 | PO-11 | PO-12 |
| CO-1 | 3 | 1 | 2 | 1 | 1 | 1 | - | - | - | – | - | - |
| CO-2 | 3 | 2 | 2 | 2 | 2 | 1 | - | - | - | – | - | - |
| CO-3 | 2 | 1 | 3 | 1 | 1 | 2 | - | - | - | – | - | - |
| CO-4 | 2 | 2 | 1 | 1 | 1 | 1 | - | - | - | – | - | - |
| CO-5 | 2 | 2 | 1 | 2 | 2 | 2 | - | - | - | – | - | - |
| CO-6 | 1 | 2 | 3 | 2 | 2 | 3 | - | - | - | – | - | - |

# Guidelines for Teachers

To implement Outcome Based Education (OBE) knowledge level and skill set of the students should be enhanced. Teachers should take a major responsibility for the proper implementation of OBE. Some of the responsibilities (not limited to) for the teachers in OBE system may be as follows:

- Within reasonable constraint, they should manoeuvre time to the best advantage of all students.
- They should assess the students only upon certain defined criterion without considering any other potential ineligibility to discriminate them.
- They should try to grow the learning abilities of the students to a certain level before they leave the institute.
- They should try to ensure that all the students are equipped with the quality knowledge as well as competence after they finish their education.
- They should always encourage the students to develop their ultimate performance capabilities.
- They should facilitate and encourage group work and team work to consolidate newer approach.
- They should follow Blooms taxonomy in every part of the assessment.

## Bloom's Taxonomy

| Level | Teacher should Check | Student should be able to | Possible Mode of Assessment |
|---|---|---|---|
| Create | Students ability to create | Design or Create | Mini project |
| Evaluate | Students ability to justify | Argue or Defend | Assignment |
| Analyse | Students ability to distinguish | Differentiate or Distinguish | Project/Lab Methodology |
| Apply | Students ability to use information | Operate or Demonstrate | Technical Presentation/ Demonstration |
| Understand | Students ability to explain the ideas | Explain or Classify | Presentation/Seminar |
| Remember | Students ability to recall (or remember) | Define or Recall | Quiz |

# Guidelines for Students

Students should take equal responsibility for implementing the OBE. Some of the responsibilities (not limited to) for the students in OBE system are as follows:

- Students should be well aware of each UO before the start of a unit in each and every course.
- Students should be well aware of each CO before the start of the course.
- Students should be well aware of each PO before the start of the programme.
- Students should think critically and reasonably with proper reflection and action.
- Learning of the students should be connected and integrated with practical and real life consequences.
- Students should be well aware of their competency at every level of OBE.

# List of Abbreviations

| Abbreviation | Full form | Abbreviation | Full form |
|---|---|---|---|
| ACI | Adjacent Channel Interference | BS | Base Station |
| AFD | Average Fade Duration | BSC | Base Station Controller |
| AMC | Adaptive Modulation and Coding | BW | Bandwidth |
| AM | Amplitude Modulation | CAI | Co-antenna Interference |
| ASK | Amplitude Shift Keying | CCI | Co-channel interference |
| ASCI | Advanced Speech Call Features | CDMA | Code Division for Multiple Access |
| AWGN | Additive White Gaussian Noise | CDF | Cumulative Distribution Function |
| BER | Bit Error Rate | CIR | Channel Impulse Response |
| BFSK | Binary Frequency Shift Keying | CR | Communication Resource |
| BIP | Bit Interleaved Parity | CRC | Cyclic Redundancy Check |
| BLAST | Bell Laboratories Layered Space-Time | CSI | Channel State Information |
| BoS | Bandwidth on Demand | CVR | Communication between Vehicles and Roadside infrastructure |
| BPSK | Binary Phase Shift Keying | CVV | Vehicle-to-Vehicle Communication |

| | | | |
|---|---|---|---|
| DCA | Dynamic Channel Assignment | FCA | Fixed Channel Assignment |
| DFE | Decision Feedback Equalization | FDD | Frequency Division Duplex |
| DOA | Direction-of-Arrivals | FDTD | Finite Difference Time Domain |
| DS-CDMA | Direct-Sequence Code Division Multiple Access | FDMA | Frequency Division for Multiple Access |
| DSL | Digital Subscriber Line | FEC | Forward Error Correction |
| DSRC | Dedicated Short-Range Communication | FEM | Finite Element Method |
| DQPSK | Differential Quadrature Phase Shift Keying | FM | Frequency Modulation |
| EBG | Electromagnetic Bandgap | FSK | Frequency Shift Keying |
| ECSD | Enhanced Circuit Switched Data | GMSK | Gaussian Minimum Shift Keying |
| EDGE | Enhanced Data for GSM Evolution | 3GPP | 3rd Generation Partnership Project |
| EGC | Equal Gain Combining | GPS | Global Positioning System |
| EGPRS | Enhanced GPRS | GPRS | General Packet Radio Service |
| EIRP | Effective Isotropic Radiated Power | GSM | Global System for Mobile Communication |
| EMC | Electromagnetic Compatibility | HSDPA | High-Speed Downlink Packet Access |
| E/O | Electrical-to-Optical | HSUPA | High-Speed Uplink Packet Access |
| ESA | Electrically Small Antennas | IDFT | Inverse Discrete Fourier Transform |
| ETC | Electronic Toll Collection | IFFT | Inverse Fast Fourier Transform |

| | | | |
|---|---|---|---|
| IMT-2000 | International Mobile Telecommunications—2000 | MLSE | Maximum Likelihood Sequence Estimators |
| ISDN | Integrated Services Digital Network | MMSE | Minimum Mean Square Error |
| ISI | Inter Symbol Interference | mMTC | Massive machine-type communication |
| ITS | Intelligent Transport System | MoM | Method of Moments |
| ITU-R | The International Telecommunications Union-Radio Communication | MS | Mobile Station |
| LCR | Level Crossing Rate | MSC | Mobile Switching Center |
| LMS | Least Mean Squares | MSK | Minimum Shift Keying |
| LOS | line-of-sight | MRC | Maximal Ratio Combining |
| LTE | Long-Term Evolution | MT | Mobile Terminals |
| MCA | Multichannel Access | NLOS | non-line-of sight |
| MCM | Multi Carrier Modulation | NFC | Near Field Communication |
| MEMS | Microelectromechanical Systems | O/E | Optical-to-Electrical |
| MIMO | Multiple-Input Multiple-Output | OFDM | Orthogonal Frequency Division Multiplexing |
| MLC | Maximum Likelihood Combining | OFDMA | Orthogonal Frequency Division Multiple Access |
| OQPSK | Offset Quadrature Phase Shift Keying | RF | Radio Frequency |

| PCB | Printed Circuit Boards | RLS | Recursive Least Squares |
|---|---|---|---|
| PCM | Pulse-Code Modulation | RMS | Root Mean Square |
| PEC | nonperfect Electric Conductor | RTT | Radio Transmission Technology |
| PDF | Probability Density Function | SAR | Specific Absorption Rate |
| PIFA | Planar Inverted-F Antenna | SDMA | Space Division Multiple Access |
| PSK | Phase Shift Keying | SINR | Signal-to-Interference-Noise Ratio |
| P/S | Parallel-to-Serial converter | SISO | Single-Input Single-Output |
| PTM | Point-to-Multipoint | SIR | Signal-to-Interference Ratio |
| PTP | Point-to-Point | SNR | Signal-to-Noise Ratio |
| PWB | Printed Wiring Board | S/P | Serial-to-Parallel converter |
| QAM | Quadrature Amplitude Modulation | STSP | Space-Time Signal Processing |
| QCELP | Qualcomm 9600 bps Code Excited Linear Predictive | SVD | Singular Value Decomposition |
| QoS | Quality of Service | TDMA | Time Division for Multiple Access |
| QPSK | Quadrature Phase Shift Keying | TDD | Time Division Duplex |
| | | | |
| TIA | Telecommunications Industry Association | WiMAX | Worldwide Interoperability for Microwave Access |

| | | | |
|---|---|---|---|
| UMTS | Universal Mobile Telecommunications Services | WIN | Wireless Intelligent Networking |
| UTRA | Universal Terrestrial Radio Access | WLAN | Wireless Local Area Networks |
| UWB | Ultra-Wideband | WMAN | Wireless Metropolitan Area Networks |
| V-BLAST | Vertical-Bell Laboratories Layered Space-Time | WMS | Wireless Mobile Systems |
| VBS | Voice Broadcast Service | WPAN | Wireless Personal Area Networks |
| VCO | Voltage-Controlled Oscillator | WWAN | Wireless Wide Area Networks |
| VGCS | Voice Group Call Service | ZFE | Zero Forcing Equalizer |
| VSWR | Voltage Standing Wave Ratio | | |

# List of Figures

# Table of Content

## UNIT 5 RECEIVER STRUCTURE



## UNIT 6 MULTIPLE-INPUT MULTIPLE-OUTPUT

# 1 Cellular Concepts

## UNIT SPECIFICS

*We will be discussing following aspects in this Unit:*

- *Understanding the basic architecture of cellular networks;*
- *Reusing frequency channels in various cells to optimize bandwidth in cellular networks;*
- *Cell splitting and channel assignment involve dividing larger cells into smaller ones;*
- *Handoff, interference management, and capacity enhancement, power control;*
- *Overview of cellular standards.*

*The practical applications of the topics are discussed for generating further curiosity and creativity as well as improving problem solving capacity.*

*Besides giving a large number of multiple choice questions as well as questions of short and long answer types marked in two categories following lower and higher order of Bloom's taxonomy, assignments through a number of numerical problems, a list of references and suggested readings are given in the unit so that one can go through them for practice. It is important to note that for getting more information on various topics of interest some QR codes have been provided in different sections which can be scanned for relevant supportive knowledge.*

*After the related practical, based on the content, there is a "Know More" section. This section has been carefully designed so that the supplementary information provided in this part becomes beneficial for the users of the book. This section mainly highlights the initial activity, examples of some interesting facts, analogy, history of the development of the subject focusing the salient observations and finding, timelines starting from the development of the concerned topics up to the recent time, applications of the subject matter for our day-to-day real life or/and industrial applications on variety of aspects, case study related to environmental, sustainability, social and ethical issues whichever applicable, and finally inquisitiveness and curiosity topics of the unit.*

## RATIONALE

*This unit on cellular networks and wireless communication provides foundational knowledge on cell structure, frequency reuse, and cell splitting, essential for understanding cellular network design and optimization. It elucidates key concepts like channel assignment, handoff mechanisms for maintaining call continuity, and strategies for interference mitigation to ensure network quality. Moreover, it addresses capacity considerations, pivotal for meeting user demands and facilitating network expansion, alongside power control techniques vital for enhancing communication quality.*

*Delving into wireless standards, the unit offers an overview of 2G and 3G technologies, marking significant advancements in cellular communication. These standards illustrate the evolution from basic voice services to the incorporation of high-speed data transmission, underscoring the dynamic nature of wireless communication technology. Through this exploration, students gain insights into the complexities of modern cellular networks, the challenges of maintaining robust and efficient communication channels, and the technological innovations that drive the mobile communication industry forward. This comprehensive approach not only highlights the operational principles of cellular networks but also connects these concepts to the broader context of wireless communication, showcasing its impact on global connectivity and the technological landscape.*

## PRE-REQUISITES

*Basic knowledge of Mathematics &*

*Communication Systems*

## UNIT OUTCOMES

*After completion of this Unit students will be able to:*

*U1-O1: Describe cellular networks*

*U1-O2: Describe the frequency reuse*

*U1-O3: Explain cell splitting and channel assignment*

*U1-O4: Explain the roll of handoff, inference management and capcity*

*U1-O5: Overview of 2G and 3G cellular standards*

| Unit-1 Outcomes | EXPECTED MAPPING WITH COURSE OUTCOMES (1- Weak Correlation; 2- Medium correlation; 3- Strong Correlation) | | | | | |
|---|---|---|---|---|---|---|
| | CO-1 | CO-2 | CO-3 | CO-4 | CO-5 | CO-6 |
| U1-O1 | 3 | 3 | 3 | - | 3 | 1 |
| U1-O2 | 1 | 1 | 2 | 2 | 1 | - |
| U1-O3 | 2 | 1 | 3 | 1 | 2 | 1 |
| U1-O4 | - | - | 3 | 1 | 2 | 2 |
| U1-O5 | 3 | 3 | 3 | - | 3 | 1 |

## 1.1 CELLULAR CONCEPTS

A cellular system provides wireless communication to the public telephone network for any location within the radio range of the system. The cellular system accommodates a huge number of users within the limited available spectrum over a large area. In a cellular radio system, high capacity is achieved within small areas around the base stations, known as cells, allowing the same radio resources to be reused by another base station located some distance away.

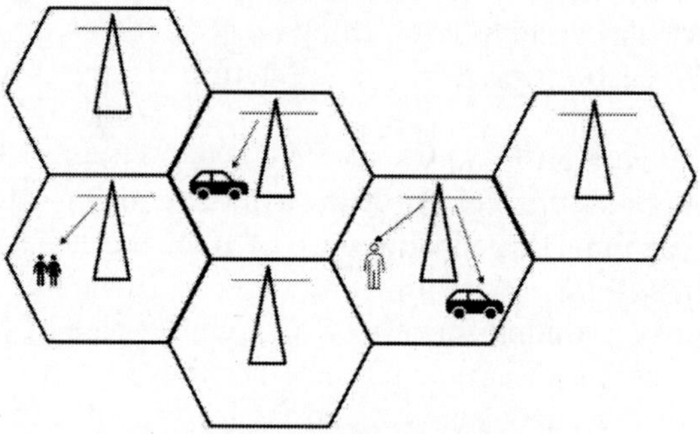

Fig. 1.1: An illustration of cellular system

Fig. 1.1 shows a basic cellular system which consist of mobile station, base station and mobile switching center. The power of radio signals transmitted by the base station diminishes as the signals travel away from the BS. To be detected by the mobile user, whether they are hand-held personal units or installed in vehicles, a minimum signal strength (let's say x dB) is required. The region where the signal strength surpasses this threshold value of x dB is defined as the coverage area of a base station. Considering the base station as an isotropic radiator, this coverage area takes the form of a circular region. The circle that represents the actual radio coverage is referred to as the footprint of a cell. In some cases, there may be overlap between adjacent circles or a gap between the coverage areas of two adjacent circles, as depicted in Fig. 1.1. Consequently, the circular geometry is unsuitable for describing cells in a regular manner. For efficient cellular design over a territory, regular polygons such as equilateral triangles, squares, and regular hexagons are more suitable. These shapes can cover the entire area without any overlap or gaps.

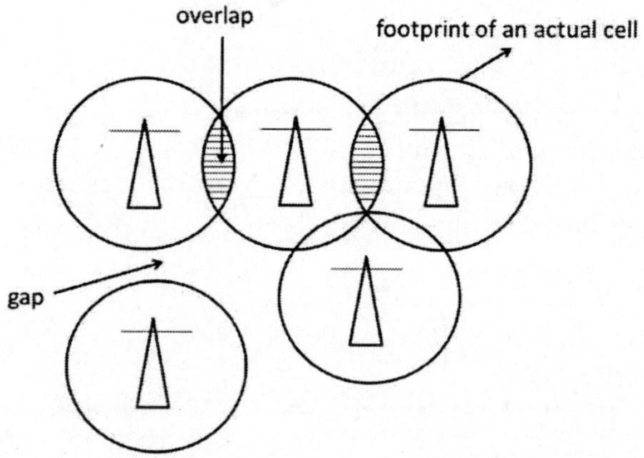


Fig 1.2 An illustration of cell with gaps and overlaps

### 1.1.1 Frequency Reuse

Frequency reuse, also known as frequency planning, is a technique employed in communication systems to enhance capacity and spectral efficiency by reusing frequencies and channels. This fundamental concept forms the basis of commercial wireless systems, particularly those that involve dividing an RF radiating area into cells.

The increased capacity in a commercial wireless network, compared to a network with a single transmitter, arises from the ability to reuse the same radio frequency in different areas for distinct transmissions. In mobile cellular systems, frequency reuse involves allocating frequencies to services in a regular pattern of cells, each covered by a base station. This repeating regular pattern of cells is referred to as a cluster.

Within a cluster, each cell uses radio frequencies exclusively within its boundaries, allowing the same frequencies to be reused in other cells not far away without causing interference, in separate clusters. These cells are termed "co-channel" cells. The reuse of frequencies facilitates the handling of a large number of calls in a cellular system with a limited number of channels.

Fig. 1.1 illustrates a frequency planning scenario with a cluster size of 7, showcasing co-channel cells in different clusters labeled with the same letter. The proximity between co-channel cells in different clusters is determined by the chosen cluster size and the layout of the cell cluster.

Consider a cellular system with S duplex channels available, let N represent the number of cells in a cluster. If each cell is assigned K duplex channels, all in unique and disjoint channel groups, the S = KN holds under normal circumstances.

Now, if the clusters are repeated M times within the total area, the total number of duplex channels (T) or users in the system becomes T = MS = KMN. Clearly, if K and N remain constant, then T is directly proportional to M. Similarly, if T and K remain constant, then N is inversely proportional to M. The capacity gain achieved is directly proportional to the number of times a cluster is repeated, as shown in equation. For a fixed cell size, a smaller N (e.g., N=25) reduces the cluster size, leading to an increase in the number of clusters and, consequently, the capacity. However, smaller N values result in co-channel cells being located closer together, leading to increased interference.

The choice of N is crucial, as it impacts interference levels and, consequently, communication quality. The smallest N value that keeps interference below the tolerated limit is selected. However, the cluster size N is not arbitrary and is determined by the following equation:

$$N = i^2 + ij + j^2 \tag{1.1}$$

where $i,\ j = 0, 1, 2, ...$ are integer numbers and represent the coordinates of the cell layout in a hexagonal grid pattern. Hence, possible values of N are 1, 3, 4, 7, 9, 12, 13, 16, 19, 21, and so on. This equation guides the selection of an appropriate N value based on interference considerations and ensures optimal cellular system performance.

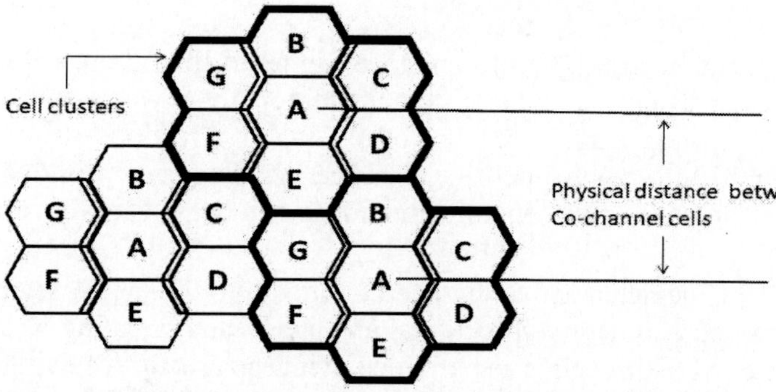


Fig. 1.3 Cellular system with frequency reuse technique.

### 1.1.2 Cell Splitting

Cell splitting is a strategy based on reducing the cell radius to minimize the need for modifying existing cell parameters. This technique involves subdividing a congested cell into smaller cells, each equipped with its own base station, leading to a proportional reduction in antenna size and transmitting power. The primary objective of cell splitting is to enhance the capacity of a cellular system by increasing the number of times channels are reused.

In the cell splitting process, new cells, often referred to as microcells due to their smaller radii, are inserted between existing cells. This insertion results in an augmented capacity because of the additional channels per unit area. However, there are challenges associated with increasing capacity by reducing the cell radius. The introduction of smaller cells, or microcells, necessitates the deployment of additional base stations in the system to cover the expanded number of cells. One challenge lies in incorporating these new base stations without relocating existing base station towers. Another challenge involves addressing the fluctuating demand in different geographical areas of the system. For example, densely populated city areas may require cells with the smallest radius to support high demand. In contrast, as one moves from urban to suburban areas, the radius of cells generally increases due to a decrease in user density. Effectively managing these challenges is crucial for optimizing the capacity and performance of the cellular network.

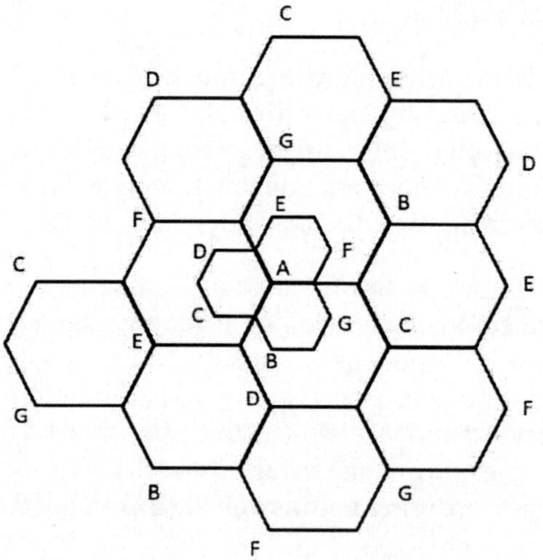

Fig. 1.4 Splitting of congested seven cell cluster

**Sectoring**

Sectoring is a technique designed to enhance Signal-to-Interference Ratio (SIR) without the need to increase the cluster size in a cellular system. Traditionally, it was assumed that the base station, located at the center of a cell, transmitted uniformly in all directions using an omnidirectional antenna. However, to mitigate co-channel interference, it has been discovered that replacing a single omnidirectional antenna with several directional antennas, each covering a specific sector, can be beneficial.

In Fig. 1.4 a cell is depicted as having been divided into three 120-degree sectors. The base station is equipped with three 120-degree directional antennas, each radiating into one of the three sectors. The channel set assigned to this cell is also divided, with each sector receiving one-third of the available cell channels. This approach, known as "sectoring," reduces co-channel interference by utilizing directional antennas. This means that a given cell receives interference and transmits with only a fraction of the available co-channel cells.

In a seven-cell-cluster layout with 120-degree sectored cells, it becomes apparent that mobile units in a particular sector of the center cell will experience co-channel interference from only two of the first-tier co-channel base stations, as opposed to interference from all six. This targeted reduction in interference enhances the overall performance and efficiency of the cellular network.

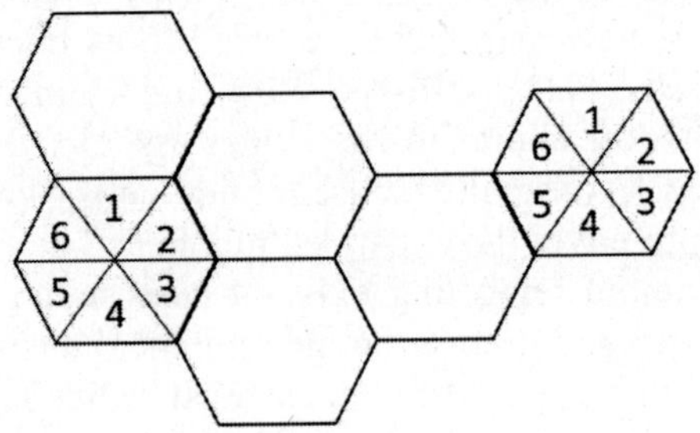


Fig. 1.5 Sectoring

## 1.1.3 Channel Assignment

With the exponential growth in the number of mobile users, mobile service providers have been compelled to adopt strategies ensuring the efficient use of the limited radio spectrum. Aimed at enhancing capacity while minimizing interference, a frequency reuse scheme has proven instrumental in meeting these goals. Various channel assignment strategies have been employed to support these objectives, classified into two categories: fixed and dynamic, as detailed below.

Fixed Channel Assignment (FCA): In the fixed channel assignment strategy, each cell is assigned a predetermined number of voice channels. Communication within a cell is restricted to the specific unused channels allocated to it. Should all channels be occupied, calls are blocked, necessitating subscriber wait times. While this approach requires basic circuitry, it results in suboptimal channel utilization. An alternative method allows channels to be borrowed from adjacent cells if all designated channels are in use, known as the borrowing strategy. In such cases, the Mobile Switching Center (MSC) oversees the borrowing process, ensuring uninterrupted calls in progress.

Dynamic Channel Assignment (DCA): In the dynamic channel assignment strategy, channels are temporarily allocated to cells for the duration of calls. When a call attempt is initiated from a cell, the corresponding BS requests a channel from the MSC, which then assigns one to the requesting BS. Upon call completion, the channel is returned to a central pool. To prevent co-channel interference, a channel in use in one cell can only be reassigned simultaneously to another cell if the distance between them exceeds the minimum reuse distance. Compared to FCA, DCA reduces the likelihood of call blocking and enhances network trunking capacity, offering improved quality of service as all channels are available to all cells. However, this assignment strategy places a heavier load on the switching center during periods of high traffic.

### 1.1.4 Handoff

When a user transitions from one cell to another, maintaining communication between the user pair requires shifting the user channel from one Base Station (BS) to another without interrupting the call. In other words, as a Mobile Station (MS) moves into a new cell while a conversation is ongoing, the Mobile Switching Center (MSC) seamlessly transfers the call to a new Frequency Division Duplexing (FDD) channel without disrupting the conversation. This process is known as handoff or handover. Ensuring successful and imperceptible handoffs is crucial in any cellular system. Handoffs must be executed smoothly to avoid user perception of the transition.

Once a signal level is established as the minimum acceptable for good voice quality ($P_{h,min}$), a slightly stronger level is selected as the threshold ($P_{h,H}$) at which handoff should occur. This threshold is illustrated in Fig. 1.6. A parameter known as the power margin ($\Delta$) plays a significant role during the handoff process, as given below,

$$\Delta = P_{h,H} - P_{h,min} \tag{1.2}$$

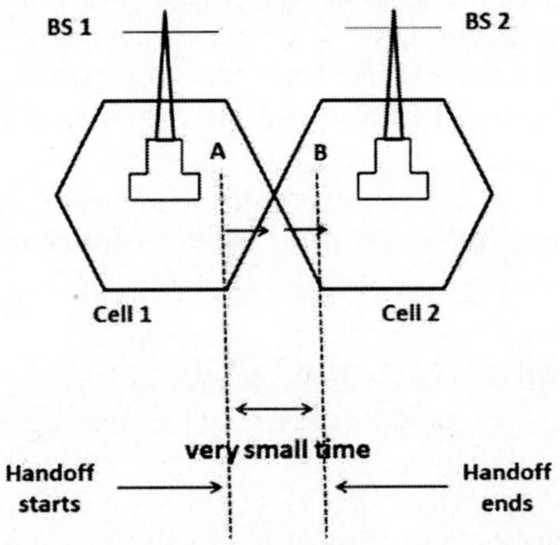


Fig. 1.6 Handoff process

The power margin must be carefully chosen, as it should neither be too large nor too small. If $\Delta$ is too small, there may not be sufficient time to complete the handoff, potentially resulting in call loss as the user crosses the cell boundary. Conversely, if $\Delta$ is too high, the MSC may be burdened with unnecessary handoffs, as the MS may not intend to enter the neighboring cell. Therefore, $\Delta$ should be selected judiciously to ensure imperceptible handoffs while meeting other operational objectives.

Further, handoff can be classified into three main types: hard handoff, soft handoff, and softer handoff. Hard handoff can be further categorized into intra-frequency and inter-frequency hard handoffs. During a hard handoff, the old connection is terminated before establishing the new one. In inter-frequency hard handoff, the carrier frequency of the new radio access differs from the old one to which the mobile station (MS) was connected. Conversely, an intra-frequency handoff occurs when the new carrier frequency remains the same as the original carrier. Inter-frequency handoffs may occur between distinct radio access networks, such as between GSM and Universal Mobile Telecommunications Services (UMTS), and are also known as intersystem handoffs. These handoffs always involve different frequencies.

Soft handoff refers to establishing the new connection before releasing the old one. In 3G systems, most handoffs are intra-frequency soft handoffs. A soft handoff between sectors of different base stations, not necessarily the same Base Station Controller (BSC), is termed a 2-way soft handoff. If more than two sectors are involved in the handoff process, it's called a multi-way soft handoff. In softer handoff, the BS transmits through one sector but receives from multiple sectors. This setup allows the MS to have active uplink radio connections with the network through multiple sectors of the same BS. When both soft and softer handoffs occur simultaneously, it's referred to as a soft-softer handoff.

## 1.1.5 Interference, System Capacity and Power Control

The susceptibility and interference issues encountered in mobile communications equipment stem due to time congestion within the electromagnetic spectrum. This congestion serves as a critical constraint on the performance of cellular systems. Interference may arise from various sources, including clashes between mobile devices within the same cell or due to calls in neighbouring cells. Additionally, interference can occur between base stations operating within the same frequency band or from unintended energy leakage from non-cellular systems into the frequency band of the cellular network.

When interference occurs in voice channels, users may experience cross-talk, which manifests as noise during communication. Similarly, interference in control channels can result in missed or erroneous calls due to digital signalling disruptions. Urban areas tend to experience more severe interference due to higher levels of Radio Frequency (RF) noise and increased densities of mobile devices and base stations.

Interference can generally be categorized into two types: co-channel interference, where signals from the same frequency band interfere with each other, and adjacent channel interference, where signals from neighboring frequency bands cause disruption.

### 1.1.5.1 Co-channel Interference (CCI)

To effectively utilize the available spectrum, it is essential to employ frequency bandwidth reuse across relatively small geographical areas. However, as frequency reuse increases, so does interference, leading to decreased system capacity and service quality. Cells that employ the same set of frequencies are termed co-channel cells. Co-channel Interference (CCI) occurs when two different radio transmitters using the same frequency experience cross-talk, as is the case with co-channel cells. CCI may arise due to adverse weather conditions, poor frequency planning, or an overcrowded radio spectrum.

If the cell size and transmitted power at base stations remain constant, CCI becomes independent of transmitted power and relies on the cell radius (R) and the distance between interfering co-channel cells (D). Increasing the D/R ratio enlarges the effective distance between co-channel cells and reduces interference. The parameter Q, known as the frequency reuse ratio, is linked to cluster size (N) as,

$$Q = \frac{D}{R} = \sqrt{3N} \tag{1.3}$$

In hexagonal geometry, a smaller Q implies a smaller cluster size and increases cellular capacity. Conversely, a larger Q decreases system capacity but enhances transmission quality. Selecting appropriate values for N is crucial. The Signal-to-Interference Ratio (SIR) for a mobile receiver monitoring the forward channel can be calculated as,

$$\frac{S}{I} = \frac{S}{\sum_{i=1}^{N_c} I_i} \tag{1.4}$$

where $N_c$ is the number of cells corresponding to CCI interference, $S$ refers to the desired signal power from the BS and $I_i$ corresponds to the interference power from the $i^{th}$ interfering co-channel BS. The received power in the mobile radio channel decreases according to a power law based on the distance between the transmitter and receiver. The same is expressed as,

$$P_r = P_o * (\frac{d}{d_o})^{-n}$$

$$P_r(dB) = P_o(dB) - 10 * n * \log(\frac{d}{d_o}) \tag{1.5}$$

where $P_o$ represents the received power at a nearby reference point located in the far field region, at a short distance do away from the transmitting antenna. The variable $n$ denotes the path loss exponent. Assuming $D_i$ represents the distance of the $i^{th}$ interferer from the mobile, the received power at a given mobile due to the $i^{th}$ interfering cell is directly proportional to $(D_i)$ raised to the power of $n$, where the value of $n$ typically ranges between 2 and 4 in urban cellular systems. Assuming a consistent path loss exponent across the coverage area and uniform transmitted power, the SIR can be approximated as follows

$$\frac{S}{I} = \frac{R^{-n}}{\sum_{i=1}^{N_c} D_i^{-n}} \tag{1.6}$$

$$\frac{S}{I} = \frac{(\sqrt{3N})^n}{N_c} \tag{1.7}$$

In this scenario, the MS is presumed to be positioned at a distance of $R$ from the center of the cell. If we focus solely on the initial layer of interfering cells and make the assumption that the interfering base stations are evenly spaced from the reference base station, with the distance between their respective cell centers denoted as $D$, then the preceding equation can be transformed into the following:

$$\frac{S}{I} = \frac{(D/R)^n}{N_c} \tag{1.8}$$

This serves as an approximate indication of the SIR. Empirical assessments conducted on the AMPS cellular system, utilizing FM and 30 kHz channels, demonstrate that satisfactory voice quality is achieved when the SIR exceeds or equals 18 dB. Assuming $n = 4$, the value of $N$ can be computed as 6.49, thus establishing the minimum $N$ as 7. These equations are formulated based on hexagonal geometry, and the distances from the nearest interfering cells may vary with different frequency reuse strategies. For a more rough estimate of co-channel SIR, one can opt for a different way to calculate.

This example illustrates a case of 7-cell reuse, where the mobile is situated at a distance of D-R from the two nearest interfering cells, and approximately D+R/2, D, D-R/2, and D+R distance from other interfering cells in the first tier. By substituting $n = 4$ into the aforementioned equation, the SIR can be approximately determined as,

$$\frac{S}{I} = \frac{R^{-4}}{2 * (D-R)^{-4} + (D+R)^{-4} + (D)^{-4} + (D+R/2)^{-4} + (D-R/2)^{-4}} \tag{1.9}$$

$$\frac{S}{I} = \frac{1}{2 * (Q-1)^{-4} + (Q+1)^{-4} + (Q)^{-4} + (Q+1/2)^{-4} + (Q-1/2)^{-4}} \tag{1.10}$$

By selecting a value of N as 7 (resulting in Q = 4.6), the calculation reveals that the worst-case Signal-to-Interference Ratio (SIR) reaches 53.70 (equivalent to 17.3 dB). This indicates that in a scenario involving 7-cell reuse, the lowest achievable SIR is slightly below 18 dB. The most challenging situation arises when the mobile device is positioned at the corner of a cell, known as a vertex, as depicted in Fig. 1.7 Consequently, it is recommended to utilize a cluster size of N = 12, although this choice leads to a reduction in capacity by 7/12. Hence, effective management of co-channel interference is crucial for optimizing link performance, which in turn influences the frequency reuse plan and the overall capacity of the cellular network. Strategies to minimize co-channel interference include optimizing base station frequency assignments and transmit powers, as well as adjusting the antenna tilt to control signal propagation.

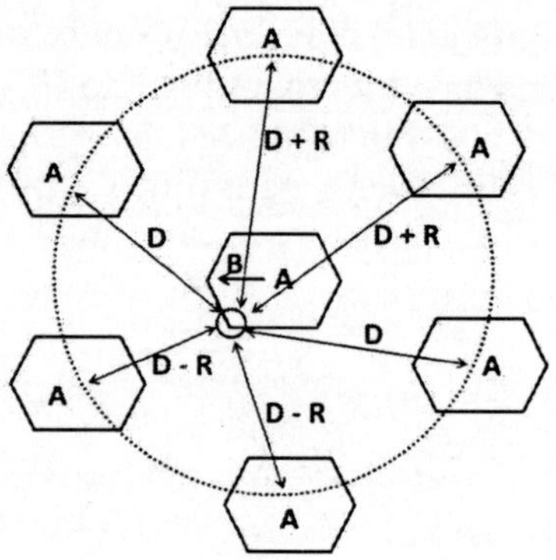


Fig. 1.7 First tier of CCI affected cells.

### 1.1.5.2 Adjacent Channel Interference (ACI)

ACI represents a distinct form of interference arising from adjacent channels, namely, channels located in neighbouring cells. It manifests as signal degradation on one frequency due to the presence of another signal on a nearby frequency. This occurs when imperfect receiver filters permit nearby frequencies to infiltrate the passband. This issue is exacerbated when a nearby channel user transmits in close proximity to the subscriber's receiver while attempting to receive a base station signal on the same channel, known as the near-far effect. Packing more adjacent channels into the channel block increases spectral efficiency, provided that the resulting performance degradation can be tolerated within the system's link budget. Moreover, this effect may arise if a mobile device near a base station transmits on a channel close to one used by a weaker mobile device. This scenario may occur if the base station struggles to distinguish the mobile user from the "bleed over" caused by the nearby adjacent channel mobile device. Adjacent channel interference is more common in small cell clusters and heavily utilized cells. Mitigating this interference to some extent is achievable by maintaining a significant frequency separation between channels. Therefore, channel assignments are structured to prevent the formation of a contiguous band of frequencies within a single cell, maximizing frequency separation. Effective assignment strategies are crucial for minimizing interference. However, if the frequency factor is small, the distance between adjacent channels may fail to keep the interference level within tolerance limits. For instance, if a mobile device is ten times closer to the base station than another mobile device and experiences energy spillage from its passband, the SIR for the weaker mobile device is approximately.

$$\frac{S}{I} = 10^{-n} \tag{1.11}$$

This can be readily derived from the previous SIR equations. When the path loss exponent equals 4, the resulting SIR amounts to 52 dB. Optimal performance demands precise filtration mechanisms, particularly when both nearby and distant users operate within the same cell. Typically, each base station receiver is equipped with a high-quality cavity filter to effectively eliminate the ACI. Additionally, power control plays a critical role in extending the battery life of subscriber units while also mitigating reverse channel SIR within the system. This entails adjusting the transmission power of each mobile device to the minimum level required for maintaining a satisfactory link quality on the reverse channel.

## 1.2 OVERVIEW OF WIRELESS STANDARD

In the recent decades, wireless communications technologies has undergone revolutionary advancements, fundamentally altering the landscape of modern telecommunications. What began modestly with only a few hundred users has evolved into a technology accessible to a significant portion of the world's population. The emergence of the Internet of Things based networks has spurred a growing need for ubiquitous data access across wireless networks. This shift has propelled wireless communications forward, transitioning from traditional voice-centric networks to encompass Internet, multimedia, and video services. Here are the key wireless standards for each generation of the wireless revolution, ranging from second generation (2G) to the fifth generation (5G)

### 1.2.1 2G Wireless Standards

The 2G wireless standards were originally designed to offer essential wireless voice communication capabilities to users using mobile cellular devices. Additionally, they represented the first generation of fully digital wireless communication devices, a significant advancement from the analog nature of 1G systems. The broad set of 2G standards are as follows:

- 2G – Global System for Mobile Communication (GSM) - One of the most widely adopted 2G standards globally, GSM offered digital voice communication along with text messaging and provide a data rate of 10kbps.
- 2G – IS-95 (CDMA) - IS-95 are based on Code Division for Multiple Access (CDMA) and provide data rate of 10kbps.
- 2.5G – General Packet Radio Services (GPRS) - To increase the data rate GPRS is proposed with the idea to provide a data access. The data rate achieved is 50 kbps.
- 2.5G – Enhanced Data for GSM Evolution (EDGE) – EDGE also provide both data and voice communication and achieve data rate of 200kbps.

The increasing demand for higher data rates over mobile devices led to the development of the 3G cellular standards.

### 1.2.2 3G Wireless Standards

Around the year 2000, the third generation of wireless standards, known as 3G, emerged. These standards predominantly relied on CDMA technology for multiple access, leveraging its superior properties compared to other access technologies like Time Division for Multiple Access (TDMA) and Frequency Division for Multiple Access (FDMA). Additionally, 3G standards are often referred to as wideband wireless technologies due to their utilization of spectral bandwidth typically exceeding 5 MHz. The various 3G standards are given below.

- 3G – Wideband Code Division for Multiple Access (WCDMA)/ Universal Mobile Telecommunications System (UMTS) - Provided higher data speeds and greater capacity for multimedia applications. UMTS is capable to support data rate of 384kbps.
- 3G – CDMA 2000 - Enhanced data transmission rates and supported advanced features like video calling and mobile internet access. CDMA-200 is also able to support data rate of 384kbps.
- 3.5G – HSDPA/HSUPA - The increasing demand for higher data rates prompted the integration of HSDPA and HSUPA, additions to the WCDMA standard. These additions bolstered the capabilities of the WCDMA suite of 3G standards, extending their range to deliver speeds of 5–30 Mbps, thereby enabling a wider array of services.
- 3.5G – 1x Evolution Data Optimized (1xEVDO) -Rev. A, B - The CDMA 2000 suite was also expanded to incorporate the 1xEVDO standard, along with subsequent revisions designated as rev. A and rev. B. These revisions aimed to boost data rates, achieving speeds nearing 30 Mbps.

These rates are expected to further increase manifold in 4G cellular networks.

### 1.2.3 4G Wireless Standards

The 4G wireless standards are founded on the groundbreaking technology of Orthogonal Frequency Division Multiplexing (OFDM). The multiple access scheme derived from OFDM is known as Orthogonal Frequency Division Multiple Access (OFDMA). Additionally, another significant advancement in 4G wireless systems is Multiple-Input Multiple-Output (MIMO) technology, which involves utilizing multiple antennas at both the transmitter and receiver ends of the system.

- 4G – (Long-Term Evolution) LTE- Offered significantly faster data speeds, low latency, and improved spectral efficiency compared to previous generations. LTE offers peak download speeds of up to 100 Mbps and upload speeds of up to 50 Mbps. However, real-world speeds may vary depending on network conditions and other factors.
- 4G – Worldwide Interoperability for Microwave Access (WiMAX) - Provided high-speed wireless internet access over a wide area.
- 4G – LTE Advanced - LTE-Advanced, often marketed as 4G LTE-A, further improves data rates with peak download speeds of up to 1 Gbps and upload speeds of up to 500 Mbps.

### 1.2.4 5G Wireless Standards

The 5G standard, or 5G NR (New Radio), enables transformative use cases such as autonomous vehicles, augmented reality, remote surgery, smart cities, and massive IoT deployments, due to its ultra-fast speeds, low latency, and high capacity.

- 5G- 5G New Radio (NR) - 5G NR offers significantly higher data rates compared to 4G technologies. Depending on the deployment scenario and spectrum used, 5G can achieve peak download speeds ranging from 1 Gbps to 10 Gbps or even higher. Upload speeds are also significantly improved, typically ranging from 100 Mbps to several Gbps.

## UNIT SUMMARY

The overview provides a comprehensive understanding of cellular concepts including coverage, frequency reuse, cell splitting, sectoring, and channel assignment. It explores techniques like handover and addresses interference management, system capacity, and power control. Furthermore, it outlines the evolution of wireless standards from 2G to 5G, showcasing their technological advancements and data rate capabilities.

Cellular systems ensure widespread wireless communication by dividing areas into cells, each served by a base station. Frequency reuse optimizes spectrum usage, allowing multiple cells to share frequencies without interference. Cell splitting subdivides congested cells into smaller ones, enhancing capacity and channel reuse. Sectoring further boosts capacity by dividing cells into sectors served by directional antennas, reducing interference and improving efficiency. Channel assignment strategies, both fixed and dynamic, optimize channel utilization while minimizing interference.

The evolution of wireless standards illustrates the progression from basic voice communication in 2G to high-speed data and multimedia services in 4G and 5G. 5G, with its ultra-fast speeds, low latency, and high capacity, enables transformative applications like autonomous vehicles and smart cities. Overall, these advancements reflect the continual innovation driving the wireless industry towards more efficient and capable communication technologies.

## EXERCISE

**Multiple Choice Questions (MCQs)**

1. What is the main function of a BS in a cellular network?
   a) To provide a connection between mobile devices and the core network
   b) To allocate IP addresses to devices
   c) To route calls between different networks
   d) To encrypt data for secure transmission
2. Which of the following is a characteristic of the 4G LTE network compared to 3G?
   a) Lower data rates
   b) Higher latency
   c) Higher data rates
   d) Limited to voice services

3. What does the term "handoff" refer to in a cellular network?
   a) The process of transferring an active call or data session from one cell to another
   b) The initial connection establishment between a mobile device and the network
   c) The process of disconnecting a call due to signal loss
   d) The allocation of a new IP address to a mobile device
4. Which technology is primarily used for short-range communication between devices, such as in contactless payments?
   a) LTE
   b) NFC
   c) WiMAX
   d) GSM
5. What does the term "frequency reuse" refer to in cellular networks?
   a) Using the same frequency channel in multiple cells separated by a sufficient distance
   b) Recycling used frequencies for different applications
   c) Allocating new frequencies for each call
   d) Avoiding the use of the same frequency in any two cells
6. What is the primary purpose of the subscriber identity module (SIM) card in mobile devices?
   a) To store user contacts and messages
   b) To identify and authenticate the subscriber to the network
   c) To enhance signal strength
   d) To provide additional storage for apps
7. Which generation of cellular technology introduced the concept of mobile broadband?
   a) 1G
   b) 2G
   c) 3G
   d) 4G
8. What is the main advantage of using code division multiple access (CDMA) over frequency division multiple access (FDMA)?
   a) Higher spectral efficiency
   b) Easier implementation
   c) Lower power consumption
   d) Compatibility with all types of networks
9. Which of the following is a key feature of 5G technology?
   a) Limited device connectivity
   b) Low data transfer rates
   c) Massive machine-type communication (mMTC)
   d) Exclusive support for voice calls
10. What does "MIMO" stand for in wireless communication?
    a) Multiple Input Multiple Output
    b) Mobile Internet Mobile Operator
    c) Multi Interface Multi Operation
    d) Master Input Master Output

11. What is CCI in cellular networks?
    a) Interference caused by adjacent frequencies in neighboring cells
    b) Interference from distant cells using the same frequency channel
    c) Interference from the same frequency within a single cell
    d) Interference caused by hardware malfunctions in the base station
12. Which factor primarily affects the level of CCI?
    a) The power of the transmitted signal
    b) The distance between cells using the same frequency
    c) The number of users in a cell
    d) The type of modulation used
13. Which of the following is a challenge associated with handoff in high-speed mobile environments?
    a) Decreased battery life of mobile devices
    b) Increased interference from adjacent cells
    c) Rapidly changing signal strength and quality
    d) Increased network congestion

**Answers:**

1. a) To provide a connection between mobile devices and the core network
2. c) Higher data rates
3. a) The process of transferring an active call or data session from one cell to another
4. b) NFC
5. a) Using the same frequency channel in multiple cells separated by a sufficient distance
6. b) To identify and authenticate the subscriber to the network
7. c) 3G
8. a) Higher spectral efficiency
9. c) Massive Machine-Type Communication (mMTC)
10. a) Multiple Input Multiple Output
11. b) Interference from distant cells using the same frequency channel
12. b) The distance between cells using the same frequency
13. c) Rapidly changing signal strength and quality

**KNOW MORE**

***For more information related to this topic scan the QR code.***

**OR**

***Type this link in your browser***

**https://archive.nptel.ac.in/courses/117/102/117102062/**

## REFERENCE


1. T. S. Rappaport, "Wireless Communications Prentice Hall PTR." New York, 1996.
2. K. Feher, Wireless Digital Communications: Modulation and Spread Spectrum Applications. Upper Saddle River, NJ: Prentice Hall, 1995.
3. J. H. Schiller, "Wireless and Mobile Communications." Handbook of Research on Ubiquitous Computing Technology for Real Time Enterprises. IGI Global, 2008.
4. R. Steele, Mobile Radio Communications, IEEE Press, New York, 1992.
5. AJ Viterbi, CDMA: Principles of Spread Spectrum Communications, Addison Wesley, 1995.
6. VK Garg & JE Wilkes, Wireless & Personal Communication Systems, Prentice Hall, 1996.
7. J. G. Proakis, Digital Communications, 4th ed. NY: McGraw Hill, 2000.
8. WCY Lee, Mobile Cellular Telecommunications Systems, McGraw Hill, 1990.
9. WCY Lee, Mobile Communications Design Fundamentals, Prentice Hall, 1993.
10. R. Pandya, Mobile and Personal Communication Systems and Services, 4th ed. New Delhi: PHI, 2004.
11. G. T. Stüber, Principles of mobile communications, KAP, 2001.

# 2 Signal Propagation

## UNIT SPECIFICS

*In this Unit we will be discussing the following aspects:*

- *Reflection, refraction, diffraction, and scattering,*
- *Large scale signal propagation and lognormal shadowing.*
- *Fading channels- Multipath and small-scale fading- Doppler shift,*
- *Statistical multipath channel models, narrowband and wideband fading models,*
- *Power delay profile, average and rms delay spread,*
- *Coherence bandwidth and coherence time,*
- *Flat and frequency selective fading,*
- *Slow and fast fading,*
- *Average fade duration and level crossing rate.*

*The practical applications of the topics are discussed for generating further curiosity and creativity as well as improving problem solving capacity.*

*Besides giving a large number of multiple-choice questions as well as questions of short and long answer types marked in two categories following lower and higher order of Bloom's taxonomy, assignments through a number of numerical problems, a list of references and suggested readings are given in the unit so that one can go through them for practice. It is important to note that for getting more information on various topics of interest some QR codes have been provided in different sections which can be scanned for relevant supportive knowledge.*

*After the related practical, based on the content, there is a "Know More" section. This section has been carefully designed so that the supplementary information provided in this part becomes beneficial for the users of the book. This section mainly highlights the initial activity, examples of some interesting facts, analogy, history of the development of the subject focusing the salient observations and finding, timelines starting from the development of the concerned topics up to the recent time, applications of the subject matter for our day-to-day real life or/and industrial applications on variety of aspects, case study related to environmental, sustainability, social and ethical issues whichever applicable, and finally inquisitiveness and curiosity topics of the unit.*

## RATIONALE

*This fundamental unit on signal propagation mechanism helps students to get a primary idea about the different types of propagation mechanism and their application in wireless communication process. The chapter covers various aspects of wireless channel propagation, including reflection, refraction, diffraction, and scattering phenomena. It explores large-scale signal propagation and lognormal shadowing effects. Additionally, it delves into fading channels, encompassing multipath and small-scale fading, such as Doppler shift, and introduces statistical multipath channel models, narrowband, and wideband fading models. Other key concepts discussed include the power delay profile, average and root mean square (rms) delay spread, coherence bandwidth, and coherence time. Moreover, the chapter distinguishes between flat and frequency-selective fading, slow and fast fading, and examines metrics such as average fade duration and level crossing rate.*

## PRE-REQUISITES

*Fundamental knowledge of Mathematics: Calculus (Class XII) & Physics: Basic of Communication (Class XII)*

## UNIT OUTCOMES

*After completion of this Unit students will be able to:*

*U2-O1:* *Describe basics of channel fading.*

*U2-O2:* *Explain fading channels and statistical multipath channel models.*

*U2-O3:* *Describe the power delay profile, average and rms delay spread.*

*U2-O4:* *The importance of coherence bandwidth and coherence time is explained.*

*U2-O5:* *Flat and frequency selective fading.*

*This table below need to be filled after discussion as marked with red.*

| **Unit-2: Outcomes** | **EXPECTED MAPPING WITH COURSE OUTCOMES** (1- Weak Correlation; 2- Medium correlation; 3- Strong Correlation) | | | | | |
|---|---|---|---|---|---|---|
| | **CO-1** | **CO-2** | **CO-3** | **CO-4** | **CO-5** | **CO-6** |
| **U2-O1** | 3 | 3 | 3 | - | 3 | 1 |
| **U2-O2** | 1 | 1 | 2 | 2 | 1 | - |
| **U2-O3** | 2 | 1 | 3 | 1 | 2 | 1 |
| **U2-O4** | - | - | 3 | 1 | 2 | 2 |
| **U2-O5** | 3 | 3 | 3 | - | 3 | 1 |

## 2.1 INTRODUCTION

The transfer of electromagnetic waves from a transmitter to a receiver is known as signal propagation, and it is an essential component in wireless communication. Signals propagate through a variety of medium, each medium having its own properties.

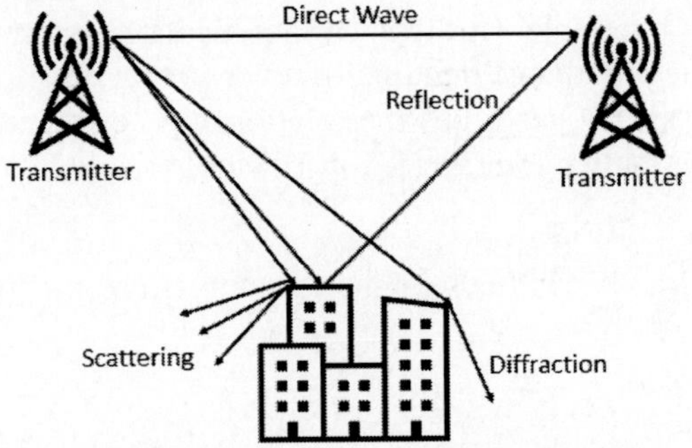


Fig. 2.1 Signal Propagation

### 2.1.1 Reflection

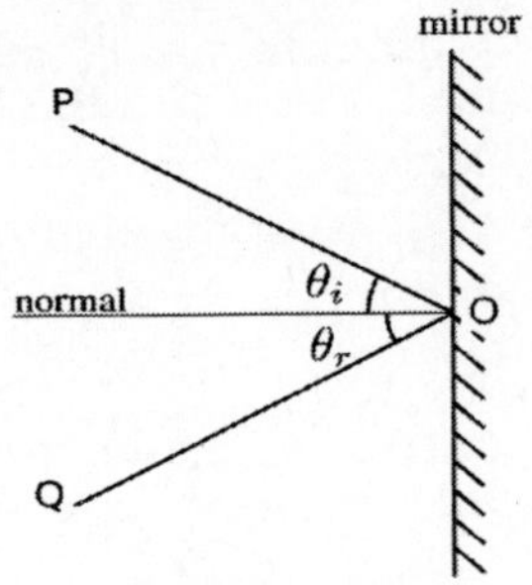


Fig. 2.2 Specular reflection

In the context of wireless communication, reflection is a phenomenon which occurs when electromagnetic waves, such as radio signals, strike an obstacle, and a portion of the wave energy returns in the opposite direction There are two essential laws of reflection, according to which the angle of incidence and the angle of reflection made by the light wave on the smooth reflecting surface are equal. Also, the incident ray, normal, reflected ray, incident angle, and reflected angle, all lie on the same plane Reflection can either strengthen or weaken the signal, depending factors like the material and angle of the reflecting surface. Understanding and managing reflections are crucial for optimizing wireless communication system performance. This phenomenon can lead to signal multipath, where multiple versions of the signal arrive at the receiver at different times due to various reflection paths. First law of reflection is described by the following mathematical equation:

$$\theta_i = \theta_r \tag{2.1}$$

where $\theta_i$ is the angle of incidence and $\theta_r$ is the angle of reflection. This equation states that the angle at which the incoming wave hits the surface is equal to the angle at which the reflected wave departs from the surface.

### 2.1.2 Refraction

Refraction is the bending of a signal as it passes through different materials with varying optical densities, such as air and glass. This bending occurs because the speed of the signal changes when it moves from one medium to another. Refraction can lead to signal distortion, shifting the path of the waves and affecting the coverage and quality of wireless signals. Understanding refraction helps in designing more efficient and reliable wireless communication systems. Snell's Law provides a quantitative description of the amount of bending of a wave, that depends on the refractive index of the two mediums. The Snell's Law describes the relationship between the angles of incidence ($\theta_i$) and refraction ($\theta_r$) and the refractive indices ($n_1, n_2$) of the Air and Glass mediums:

$$n_1 sin\,(\theta_i) = n_2 sin(\theta_r) \tag{2.2}$$

where $n_1$ and $n_2$ are the refractive indices of the Air and Glass mediums, and $\theta_i$ is the angle of incidence, $\theta_r$ is the angle of refraction.

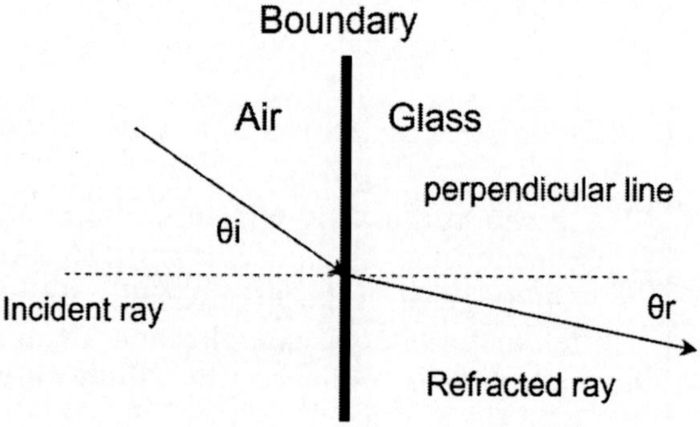


Fig.2.3 Refraction of a signal

### 2.1.3 Diffraction

Diffraction in wireless communication refers to the bending of radio waves around obstacles, such as buildings, hills, or other large objects, that are in their path. When radio waves encounter an obstacle, they spread out and curve around the edges of the obstacle, allowing them to reach areas that would otherwise be obstructed. This phenomenon is similar to how water waves bend around a rock in a stream. Diffraction helps extend the coverage area of wireless signals, allowing them to reach beyond obstacles and into areas that are not in direct line of sight with the transmitter. Understanding diffraction is important for designing effective wireless networks with better coverage and connectivity. The mathematical expression for the angular position of diffraction maxima (bright spots) for a single slit diffraction pattern is given by:

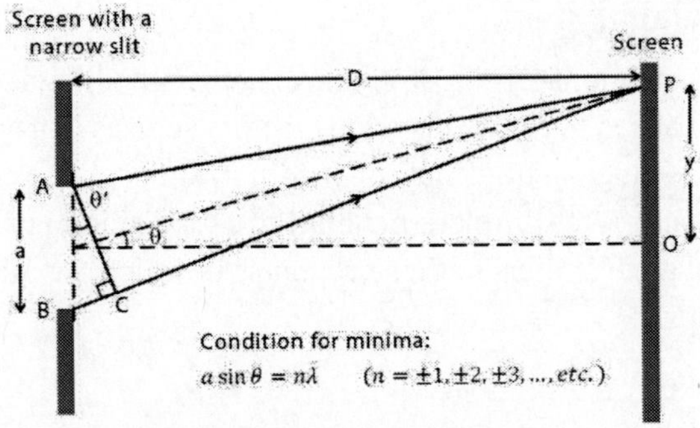


Fig.2.4 Single Slit Diffraction

$$asin\,(\theta)\ = m\,\lambda \tag{2.3}$$

where $\theta$ is the angle of observation, $m$ is the order of the diffraction maximum ($m = 0, \pm1, \pm2, ...$), $\lambda$ is the wavelength of the signal, and $a$ is the width of the slit.

### 2.1.4 Large-Scale Signal Propagation

As we know the behaviour of wireless signals over large distances, including effects like route loss, shadowing, and fading, is referred to as large-scale signal propagation. Large-scale signal propagation encompasses the behaviour of electromagnetic waves over extended distances in wireless communication. It addresses signal attenuation, path loss, and coverage area influenced by factors like distance, terrain, and obstacles. Path loss increases with distance, following models like Friis' equation, while shadowing introduces fluctuations due to environmental obstacles. Fading, classified into small and large-scale, results from interference during signal reflection and scattering. Understanding large-scale propagation aids in designing efficient wireless systems, considering factors like antenna placement and power levels to ensure reliable coverage and optimize performance over diverse environments.

### 2.1.5 Lognormal Shadowing

Lognormal shadowing is a statistical model used to describe the variability in signal strength caused by environmental obstacles and irregularities. The lognormal shadowing model is often expressed as:

$$P_r(dB) = P_{r0}(dB) - 10n\left(\frac{d}{d_0}\right) + X \tag{2.4}$$

where $P_r$ in decibels ($dB$) is the received power, $P_{r0}$(in $dB$) is the reference received power in dB at a reference distance, $n$ is the path loss exponent, $d$ is the distance, $d_0$ is the reference distance, $X$ is a Gaussian-distributed random variable representing lognormal shadowing. In another words we can also say Lognormal shadowing is a way to describe how wireless signals weaken as they travel through obstacles like buildings or trees. Imagine shining a flashlight through a foggy room; sometimes the light is brighter, and other times it's dimmer due to the fog. Similarly, wireless signals can vary in strength due to obstacles in their path. The lognormal part refers to a mathematical model used to understand this variation. It's like predicting how bright the flashlight will be at different points in the room based on the fog's density. This helps in designing better wireless communication systems.

## 2.2 FADING CHANNELS

Fading is defined as the fluctuations of the strength of transmitted signal due to propagation in a wireless medium. It can be caused because of various factors such as change in distance between the transmitter and the receiver, change in transmission medium, atmospheric condition and also because of obstacles in the environment. This wireless medium of propagation is called as a fading channel. In communication, fading channels refers to those channels in which the quality of transmitted signal can fluctuate over time or space.

### 2.2.1 Multipath Fading

A signal propagating through the wireless channel reaches the receiver after traveling through a number of different paths known as multipath. The signals take these multiple paths due to interaction with objects such as buildings, trees, and other obstacles in the propagation environment such as reflections, diffractions and scattering as is shown in Fig. 2.5. The multiple signal paths can cause the signal to experience varying phase shifts, delays, and amplitudes, leading to constructive and destructive interference at the receiver. Due to these interactions, there is fluctuation in power of signal and also its phase. Pathloss is another word for the drop-in signal power. There are three things that can cause signal power to drop: mean transmission pathloss, macroscopic fading, and microscopic fading.

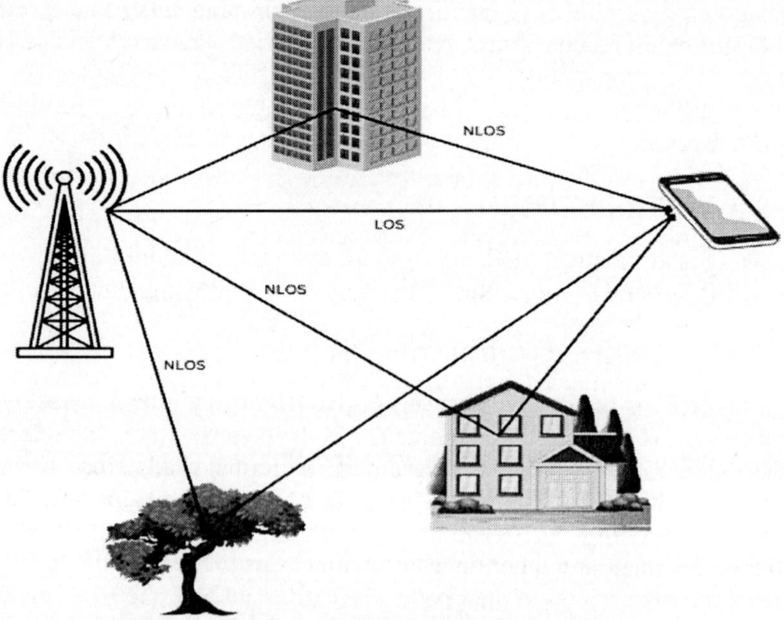


Fig. 2.5 Multipath Fading

Let us assume a passband signal defined as,

$$s(t) = Re\{s_b(t)e^{j2\pi f_c t}\} \tag{2.5}$$

where $Re(x)$ depicts the real part of complex variable $x$. The linear time varying ($\tau$) channel impulse response of any single $i^{th}$ path can be defined as

$$h_i(\tau) = a_i\delta(\tau - \tau_i) \tag{2.6}$$

where, $a_i$ is the attenuation factor and $\tau_i$ is the path delay. The wireless channel can be assumed to have $L$ propagation paths consisting of one line-of-sight (LoS) component and other non-line-of-sight (NLOS) components. This Channel Impulse Response (CIR) can be defined as

$$h(\tau) = \sum_{i=0}^{L-1} a_i\delta(\tau - \tau_i) \tag{2.7}$$

The received wireless signal is given as

$$y(t) = s(t) * h(t) = \int_{-\infty}^{\infty} h(\tau)\, s(t-\tau)\, d\tau \tag{2.8}$$

On inserting the L tapped channel, we obtain,

$$y(t) = \sum_{i=0}^{L-1} a_i \int_{-\infty}^{\infty} \delta(\tau - \tau_i)\, s(t-\tau)\, d\tau = \sum_{i=0}^{L-1} a_i s(\tau - \tau_i) \tag{2.9}$$

This can further be written in the form of transmitted baseband signal $s_b(t)$ as

$$\begin{aligned} y(t) &= Re\left\{\sum_{i=0}^{L-1} a_i s_b(t - \tau_i) e^{j2\pi f_c(t-\tau_i)}\right\} \\ &= Re\{\textstyle\sum_{i=0}^{L-1} a_i e^{-j2\pi f_c \tau_i} s_b(t - \tau_i) e^{j2\pi f_c(t-\tau_i)}\} \end{aligned} \tag{2.10}$$

From the above equation, we can find the equivalent complex baseband received signal as

$$y_b(t) = \sum_{i=0}^{L-1} a_i e^{-j2\pi f_c \tau_i} s_b(t - \tau_i) \tag{2.11}$$

### 2.2.2 Small scale fading

Small scale fading refers to the fading of a signal over a short period of time (in microseconds or less) or short distance (in order of a few centimetres or meter). It occurs due to multiple paths between transmitter and receiver causing constructive or destructive interference. So, we can say that it is caused due to multipath propagation, speed of the moving receiver and surrounding objects where the received signal amplitude and phase depends on the path that it took between the transmitter and receiver. It is a very common phenomenon in wireless communication.

### 2.2.3 Doppler shift

It is the basic idea behind how electromagnetic radio waves travel. Doppler shift of an electromagnetic wave is the change in frequency that is thought to be caused by the relative motion between the transmitter and the receiver. It is defined by

$$f_d = v\cos(\theta)(f_c/c) \tag{2.12}$$

Where $v$ is the velocity of receiver towards the transmitter in the direction of motion, θ is the angle of arrival of the received signal with respect to the direction of motion, and $f_c$ is the carrier frequency and $c$ is the speed of light.

The range of frequencies in which doppler shift occurs is called doppler spread. It is the inverse of coherence time which is the time for which the channel remains constant.

It is thought that the frequency is higher than it really is when the receiver is moving toward the emitter and lower when it is not.

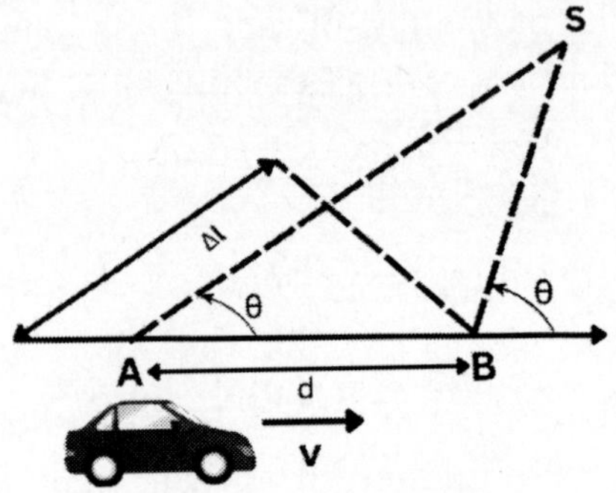


Fig.2.6 Doppler shift

## 2.3 STATISTICAL MULTIPATH CHANNEL MODELS

As we know, when a signal is transmitted from a transmitter, it reaches the receiver through multiple paths. In this section, we will discuss modeling this multipath channel with the help of a random time-varying impulse response. There are two main characteristics of multipath channel:

- First is the time delay spread which means the time difference between the arrival of the first and the last received signal component for the same transmitted pulse. There is minimal time spreading in the received signal if the delay spread is tiny in relation to the inverse of the signal bandwidth. On the other hand, a large delay spread causes the received signal to spread out much in time, which significantly distorts the signal.
- Second is the time-varying nature of the multipath channel due to the relative movement between the transmitter and the receiver. This may cause constructive or destructive interference of the multipath components, which causes a change in the amplitude and phase of the received signal.

### 2.3.1 Narrowband fading models

Narrowband fading, which depends on both signal bandwidth and channel delay spread, is the scenario when the channel's delay spread is significantly less than the inverse of bandwidth of transmitted signal which means, for all t,

$$T_m(t) < \frac{1}{B} \tag{2.13}$$

where B denotes the bandwidth of transmitted signal and $T_m(t)$ denotes the delay spread of the channel given by,

$$T_m(t) = max(\tau_n(t)) - min(\tau_n(t)) \tag{2.14}$$

where $max(\tau_n(t))$ denotes the time at which the last significant impulse response in channel was observed and $min(\tau_n(t))$ denotes the time at which the first significant impulse response in the channel was observed.

### 2.3.2 Wideband fading models

Another distortion that can occur due to multipath fading is when the duration of the signal that is received increases. In this scenario the channel's delay spread becomes more than the inverse of bandwidth of transmitted signal i.e. for all t,

$$T_m(t) > \frac{1}{B} \tag{2.15}$$

As the bandwidth of transmitted signals increases, these multipath components interfere with the other transmitted pulses and we observe Inter Symbol Interference (ISI).

## 2.4 POWER DELAY PROFILE

It is used to describe the distribution of average received signal power with respect to the multipath delay. It shows the time-varying nature of the channel as the average power is varying with time delay. This could be due to the multipath fading that occurs due to reflection, diffraction and scattering of the transmitted signal.

In Fig. 2.7, there is an L = 8 tap channel, where we can observe the average power at each time delay. Also, we can observe that the average power decreases with the time delay increasing as the signal component that suffers more attenuation arrives with more delay.

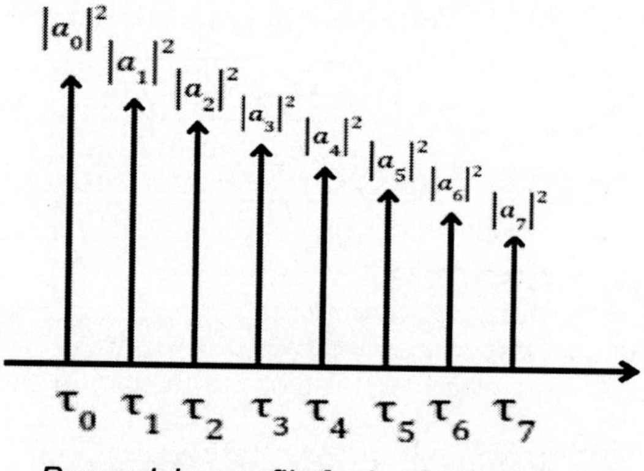


*Power delay profile for L = 8 tap channel*

Fig.2.7 Power delay profile

The power delay profile can be defined as:

$$\Phi(t) = \sum_{i=0}^{L-1} g_i \delta(t - \tau_i) \tag{2.16}$$

where $g_i$ denotes the gain at each delay as

$$g_i = |a_i|^2 \tag{2.17}$$

where $a_i$ is the attenuation associated with the $i^{th}$ path. Power delay profile can be used for calculating average and RMS delay spread.

### 2.4.1 Average delay spread

In most of the multipath wireless communication scenarios, it is observed that the components that arrive much later have very insignificant values of average power as compared to the initial components due to a lot of attenuation. So, maximum delay spread is not a reliable measure of the delay spread as it only considers the time delay and not the gain of the component. To obtain a more reliable measure, we calculate average delay spread. It is expressed as

$$\mu_{avg} = \frac{\int_0^{\infty} \tau A_c(\tau) d\tau}{\int_0^{\infty} A_c(\tau) d\tau} \tag{2.18}$$

where $A_c(\tau)$ is power delay profile.

### 2.4.2 RMS delay spread

The Root Mean Square (RMS) delay spread provides an even more reliable metric for delay spread measurement than the average delay spread. It represents the RMS of the time delays of the multipath components relative to the earliest arriving path, weighted by their respective power levels. Essentially, it provides a statistical measure of the extent to which the multipath components of a transmitted signal are spread out in time. It is defined as,

$$\sigma_{rms} = \sqrt{\frac{\int_0^{\infty} (\tau - \mu T_m)^2 A_c(\tau) d\tau}{\int_0^{\infty} A_c(\tau) d\tau}} \tag{2.19}$$

## 2.5 COHERENCE BANDWIDTH

In this section, we introduce another important parameter of a wireless communication channel, namely, the coherence bandwidth $B_c$. The frequency response of the channel $h(t)$, is $H(f)$ computed as

$$H(f) = \int_0^{\infty} h(\tau) e^{-j2\pi f t} d\tau \tag{2.20}$$

The coherence bandwidth $B_c$ is defined as the bandwidth of the response $H(f)$ i.e., the frequency band over which the response $H(f)$ is flat as shown in Fig. 2.8

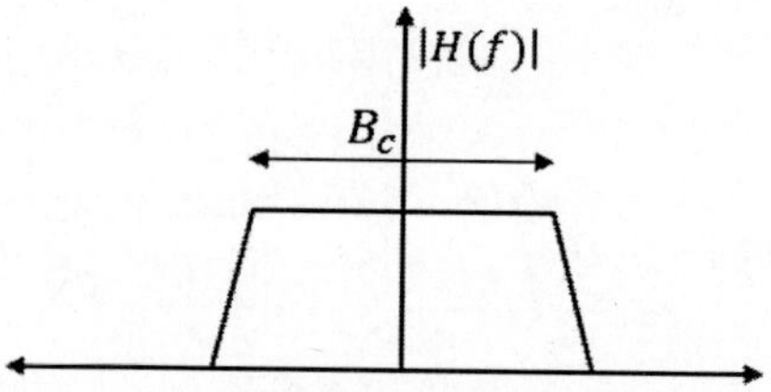


Fig.2.8 Flat channel response

The impact of the frequency spectrum $H(f)$ of the wireless channel on the input signal $x(t)$ and received signal $y(t)$ can be realized with the help of coherence bandwidth as:

$$B_s \leq B_c \Rightarrow No\ distortion\ in\ received\ signal\ (flat\ fading)$$

$$B_s \geq B_c \Rightarrow Distortion\ in\ received\ signal\ (frequency\ selective\ fading)$$

In the subsequent sections, we will learn about flat fading and frequency selective fading in more detail. The distortion caused due to frequency selective nature of channel is termed as inter-symbol-interference (ISI). The coherence bandwidth $B_c$ can be related to the delay spread $\sigma_\tau$ as:

$$B_c = \frac{1}{\sigma_\tau} \tag{2.21}$$

From the above relation it can be inferred that coherence bandwidth $B_c$ decreases as the delay spread $\sigma_\tau$ increases. In the time domain, if the delay spread is much larger compared to the symbol time, it results in ISI. Correspondingly, in the frequency domain, this implies that the bandwidth of the signal is much larger than the coherence bandwidth of the channel. This implies that the transmitter is trying to push a signal of much higher bandwidth through a channel filter, with the channel having a much smaller bandwidth. This results in frequency-selective distortion. To mitigate the effect of ISI, equalization is done at the receiver in which the received signal is multiplied by the inverse of the channel response filter, i.e., $\frac{1}{H(f)}$, to convert the frequency selective channel into a system with a flat-fading response.

## 2.6 COHERENCE TIME

Time duration in which the channel changes significantly due to the mobility of the user is termed the coherence time, $T_c$. In other words, coherence time $T_c$ is the approximate duration of time for which the wireless channel can be assumed to be constant. This can also be expressed as

$$T_c = \frac{1}{2B_d} \tag{2.22}$$

where $B_d = 2f_d$ is the Doppler spread of the wireless channel, and $f_d$ is the Doppler shift. For example, the value of $T_c$ in practical wireless systems, at vehicular velocities around 60 mph and carrier frequencies in the 2 GHz range is of the order of milliseconds (ms). From eq. 2.23 it can also be inferred that a larger Doppler spread $B_d$ corresponds to a smaller coherence time $T_c$ leading to a faster rate of channel variation.

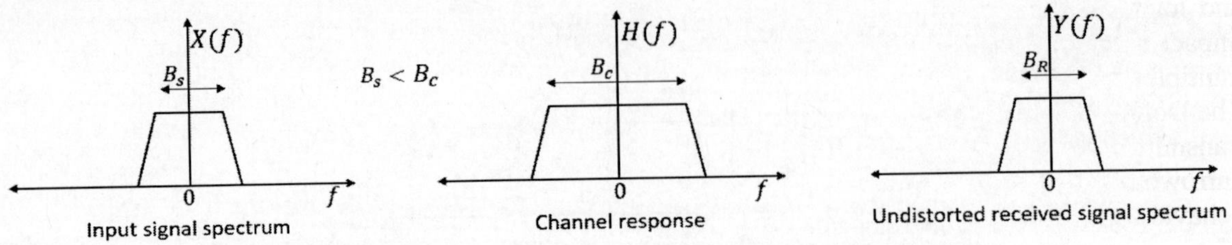


Fig.2.9 Frequency response of X(f), H(f) and Y(f) $B_s < B_c$

## 2.7 FLAT FADING

From Fig. 2.9, when the bandwidth $B_s$ of the input signal $x(t)$, is less than $B_c$, then $X(f)$ spans the flat part of the channel response $H(f)$. Hence, the output $Y(f) = H(f)X(f)$ is simply a scaled version of $X(f)$ corresponding to the magnitude of the flat part. Thus, the input signal spectrum $X(f)$ is undistorted at the output. Such a wireless channel is termed a flat-fading channel.

## 2.8 FREQUENCY SELECTIVE FADING

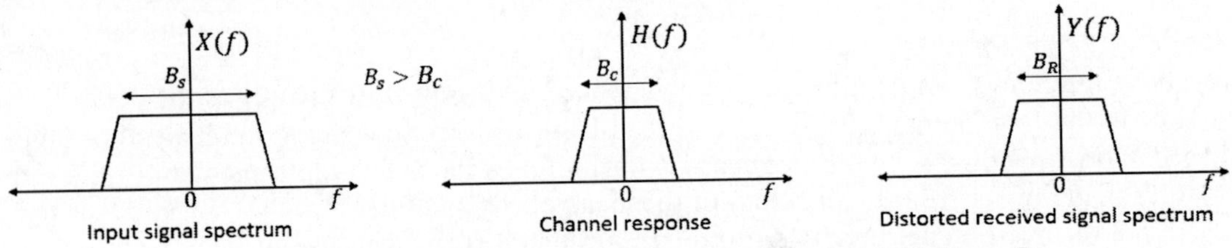


Fig.2.10 Frequency response of X(f), H(f) and Y(f) $B_s > B_c$

From Fig. 2.10, when the signal bandwidth $B_s$ is greater than the coherence bandwidth $B_c$. In this scenario, different parts of the signal spectrum $X(f)$ experience different attenuations, i.e., the attenuation is frequency-selective. Thus, the output spectrum $Y(f)$ is a distorted version of the input spectrum $X(f)$. Such a wireless channel is termed a frequency-selective channel due to the frequency-dependent nature of the attenuation of the signal.

## 2.9 LEVEL CROSSING RATE AND AVERAGE FADE DURATION

Level Crossing Rate (LCR) and Average Fade Duration (AFD) of the signal envelope are two important second-order channel statistics, which convey useful information about the dynamic temporal behaviour of multipath fading channels. The LCR is a measure of the average number of times a radio signal drops below a given threshold level, while the ADF provides the average time interval during which the signal remains below the threshold.

## UNIT SUMMARY

This chapter delves into the intricate aspects of wireless communication and signal propagation. It begins by exploring the fundamental concepts of reflection, refraction, diffraction, and scattering, which describe how signals interact with obstacles in their path. The unit covers large-scale signal propagation and lognormal shadowing to explain how signals attenuate over long distances and how obstacles impact signal strength. It also examines the phenomena of multipath and small-scale fading, where multiple signal paths and rapid changes in signal amplitude and phase affect communication quality. The Doppler shift is discussed in the context of frequency changes due to relative motion between the transmitter and receiver. Various statistical multipath channel models are introduced, including narrowband and wideband fading models, which provide a framework for understanding signal behavior in multipath environments.

The unit further analyzes the power delay profile, average and RMS delay spread, coherence bandwidth, and coherence time to quantify and describe the time and frequency intervals over which the channel can be considered constant. It categorizes fading into flat and frequency selective, as well as slow and fast fading, based on the signal bandwidth relative to coherence bandwidth and the rate of change of the channel. Additionally, it introduces metrics like average fade duration and level crossing rate to describe the duration and frequency of signal fades. Practical applications of these concepts are included to stimulate curiosity and enhance problem-solving skills, supplemented by multiple-choice questions, short and long answer questions, numerical problems, and further reading references.

## EXERCISE

### Multiple Choice Questions (MCQs)

1. Which phenomenon occurs when a signal changes direction due to hitting an obstacle that is larger than the signal's wavelength?
   a) Refraction
   b) Reflection
   c) Diffraction
   d) Scattering
2. What is the term for the bending of a wave as it passes around an obstacle or through a narrow opening?
   a) Reflection
   b) Refraction
   c) Diffraction
   d) Scattering
3. Which effect describes the change in direction of a wave passing from one medium to another, caused by its change in speed?
   a) Reflection
   b) Refraction
   c) Diffraction
   d) Scattering
4. What is the phenomenon where electromagnetic waves are dispersed in different directions due to irregularities in the medium?
   a) Reflection
   b) Refraction
   c) Diffraction

d) Scattering

5. Which model is commonly used to describe signal attenuation in large-scale propagation environments?
   a) Free-space path loss model
   b) Lognormal shadowing model
   c) Rayleigh fading model
   d) Rician fading model
6. In the context of large-scale propagation, what does the term "shadowing" refer to?
   a) Variation in signal strength due to obstacles obstructing the signal path
   b) Rapid changes in signal strength due to multipath
   c) Doppler shift effects on the signal
   d) Signal diffraction around obstacles
7. Which type of fading is caused by the relative motion between a transmitter and a receiver, leading to frequency shifts in the signal?
   a) Multipath fading
   b) Small scale fading
   c) Doppler shift
   d) Lognormal shadowing
8. What is the characteristic of a narrowband fading model?
   a) It assumes the signal bandwidth is larger than the coherence bandwidth.
   b) It models frequency selective fading.
   c) It assumes the signal bandwidth is much smaller than the coherence bandwidth.
   d) It models time-variant channels.
9. What does the power delay profile represent in a multipath channel?
   a) The distribution of signal power over different frequencies
   b) The distribution of signal power over different time delays
   c) The Doppler shift distribution
   d) The amplitude distribution of the received signal
10. What does RMS delay spread measure in a wireless channel?
    a) The average power of the signal
    b) The standard deviation of the power delay profile
    c) The average time delay of the multipath components
    d) The coherence time of the channel
11. What is coherence bandwidth?
    a) The range of frequencies over which the channel can be considered flat
    b) The range of time over which the channel can be considered constant
    c) The maximum frequency shift due to Doppler effect
    d) The bandwidth of the transmitted signal
12. Coherence time is defined as the time duration over which:
    a) The channel impulse response is considered constant

b) The signal strength varies rapidly
c) The signal frequency remains constant
d) The phase of the signal is stable

13. In flat fading, how does the signal bandwidth compare to the coherence bandwidth?
    a) Signal bandwidth is larger than the coherence bandwidth
    b) Signal bandwidth is smaller than the coherence bandwidth
    c) Signal bandwidth is equal to the coherence bandwidth
    d) Signal bandwidth is not related to the coherence bandwidth
14. Frequency selective fading occurs when:
    a) The signal bandwidth is larger than the coherence bandwidth
    b) The signal bandwidth is smaller than the coherence bandwidth
    c) The signal bandwidth is equal to the coherence bandwidth
    d) There is no multipath propagation
15. What distinguishes slow fading from fast fading?
    a) The Doppler shift magnitude
    b) The rate at which the signal amplitude changes
    c) The frequency range of the signal
    d) The power delay profile
16. What does the average fade duration measure in a fading channel?
    a) The average time interval during which the signal strength stays below a certain level
    b) The average time interval during which the signal strength exceeds a certain level
    c) The frequency of signal level crossings
    d) The average time interval between signal level crossings
17. Level crossing rate is defined as:
    a) The rate at which the signal crosses a specified level in a positive direction
    b) The rate at which the signal crosses a specified level in both positive and negative directions
    c) The rate at which the signal changes its frequency
    d) The rate at which the signal power decays

**Answers**

1. b) Reflection
2. c) Diffraction
3. b) Refraction
4. d) Scattering
5. a) Free-space path loss model
6. a) Variation in signal strength due to obstacles obstructing the signal path
7. c) Doppler shift
8. c) It assumes the signal bandwidth is much smaller than the coherence bandwidth
9. b) The distribution of signal power over different time delays

10. b) The standard deviation of the power delay profile
11. a) The range of frequencies over which the channel can be considered flat
12. a) The channel impulse response is considered constant
13. b) Signal bandwidth is smaller than the coherence bandwidth
14. a) The signal bandwidth is larger than the coherence bandwidth
15. b) The rate at which the signal amplitude changes
16. a) The average time interval during which the signal strength stays below a certain level
17. b) The rate at which the signal crosses a specified level in both positive and negative directions

**KNOW MORE**

***For more information related to this topic scan the QR code.***

**OR**

***Type this link in your browser***

**https://archive.nptel.ac.in/courses/117/102/117102062/**

## REFERENCES


1. T. S. Rappaport, "Wireless Communications Prentice Hall PTR." New York, 1996.
2. J. H. Schiller, "Wireless and Mobile Communications." Handbook of Research on Ubiquitous Computing Technology for Real Time Enterprises. IGI Global, 2008.
4. Agrawal, Dharma P., and Qing-An Zeng, "Introduction to wireless and mobile systems." Cengage learning, 2015.
5. Halonen, Timo, Javier Romero, and Juan Melero, eds, "GSM, GPRS and EDGE performance: evolution towards 3G/UMTS." John Wiley & Sons, 2004
6. Richardson, Andrew, "WCDMA design handbook. Vol. 13." Cambridge: Cambridge University Press, 2005

# 3 CAPACITY OF FLAT AND FREQUENCY SELECTIVE CHANNELS

## UNIT SPECIFICS

*In this Unit we will be discussing following aspects:*

- *Describe capacity of flat fading;*
- *Explain frequency selective fading;*
- *Discuss capacity of flat fading;*
- *Discuss different antennas;*
- *Base station antennas and arrays;*

*The practical applications of the topics are discussed for generating further curiosity and creativity as well as improving problem solving capacity.*

*Besides giving a large number of multiple choice questions as well as questions of short and long answer types marked in two categories following lower and higher order of Bloom's taxonomy, assignments through a number of numerical problems, a list of references and suggested readings are given in the unit so that one can go through them for practice. It is important to note that for getting more information on various topics of interest some QR codes have been provided in different sections which can be scanned for relevant supportive knowledge.*

*After the related practical, based on the content, there is a "Know More" section. This section has been carefully designed so that the supplementary information provided in this part becomes beneficial for the users of the book. This section mainly highlights the initial activity, examples of some interesting facts, analogy, history of the development of the subject focusing the salient observations and finding, timelines starting from the development of the concerned topics up to the recent time, applications of the subject matter for our day-to-day real life or/and industrial applications on variety of aspects, case study related to environmental, sustainability, social and ethical issues whichever applicable, and finally inquisitiveness and curiosity topics of the unit.*

## RATIONALE

*Flat fading is a fundamental concept in wireless communication, affecting how signals are transmitted and received. This chapter begins by defining flat fading and its implications on the communication channel. It delves into the capacity of flat fading channels, explaining how signal degradation due to fading impacts the overall performance. The discussion covers the mathematical modeling of flat fading and the methods used to estimate and optimize the capacity in such environments. By understanding these principles, students will gain insights into designing more robust communication systems. Frequency selective fading is another crucial aspect of wireless communication, characterized by the variation in signal fading across different frequencies. This section explains the causes and effects of frequency selective fading, including multipath propagation and its impact on signal quality. Detailed explanations of the time and frequency domain characteristics are provided, alongside methods to mitigate its adverse effects. Techniques such as equalization and diversity reception are discussed to illustrate how to manage frequency selective fading in practical scenarios.*

*Revisiting the concept of flat fading, this section focuses on a deeper analysis of its capacity. It covers theoretical and practical considerations, including the Shannon capacity limit and the factors influencing it in flat fading environments. Various models and simulations are presented to demonstrate the capacity calculations and the strategies to maximize it. This comprehensive discussion aims to equip students with the knowledge to evaluate and improve the performance of communication systems under flat fading conditions. Antennas play a pivotal role in wireless communication, and this section explores the various types used in different applications. The chapter starts with basic antenna theory, including the principles of radiation, gain, and impedance. It then categorizes antennas into different types such as dipole, monopole, patch, and array antennas, discussing their specific characteristics and applications. Practical examples and design considerations are provided to help students understand how to choose and implement the right antenna for different scenarios. Base station antennas are critical components in cellular networks, and this section focuses on their design and functionality. It covers the architecture of base station antennas and the role of antenna arrays in enhancing signal coverage and capacity. Discussions include beamforming techniques, MIMO (Multiple Input Multiple Output) technology, and the benefits of using antenna arrays for spatial diversity. Real-world examples and case studies illustrate the practical aspects of deploying base station antennas and arrays in modern communication networks.*

*This chapter provides a comprehensive understanding of key wireless communication phenomena, equipping students with the necessary knowledge to tackle challenges in the field. Through detailed explanations and practical examples, it lays a solid foundation for advanced studies and applications in wireless communication.*

## PRE-REQUISITES

*Fundamental knowledge of Mathematics: Calculus (Class XII) & Physics: Basic of Communication (Class XII)*

## UNIT OUTCOMES

*After completion of this Unit students will be able to:*

*U3-O1: Describe Capacity*

*U3-O2: Describe flat fading*

*U3-O3: Explain frequency selective fading*

*U3-O4: Explain different antennas*

*U3-O5: Explain different antenna arrays*

| Unit-3 Outcomes | EXPECTED MAPPING WITH COURSE OUTCOMES (1- Weak Correlation; 2- Medium correlation; 3- Strong Correlation) | | | | | |
|---|---|---|---|---|---|---|
| | CO-1 | CO-2 | CO-3 | CO-4 | CO-5 | CO-6 |
| U3-O1 | 3 | 2 | 1 | - | 3 | 1 |
| U3-O2 | 3 | 1 | 3 | - | 1 | - |
| U3-O3 | 3 | 1 | 3 | - | 2 | 1 |
| U3-O4 | 1 | 2 | 1 | - | 2 | 2 |
| U3-O5 | 1 | 2 | 1 | - | 2 | 2 |

## 3.1 CHANNEL CAPACITY

In fading channels, the capacity refers to the maximum rate at which information can be reliably transmitted over the channel. Fading channels are characterized by variations in the channel conditions over time, caused by phenomena such as multipath propagation, shadowing, and scattering.

The capacity of a fading channel depends on several factors

1. **Channel State**: The instantaneous state of the channel, which can vary over time due to fading effects. This includes variations in signal strength, phase shifts, and multipath delays.
2. **Signal-to-Noise Ratio (SNR):** The ratio of the signal power to the noise power in the channel. In fading channels, the SNR can vary rapidly due to fading effects, impacting the achievable data rate.
3. **Bandwidth:** The available bandwidth for transmission. A wider bandwidth allows for higher data rates but may also be more susceptible to frequency-selective fading effects.
4. **Coding and Modulation Scheme:** The choice of coding and modulation techniques used to encode and transmit the information over the channel. More robust coding and modulation schemes can mitigate the effects of fading and improve the achievable data rate.

The capacity of fading channels is often studied using information theory, particularly the Shannon-Hartley theorem, which provides a theoretical limit on the channel capacity. The Shannon-Hartley theorem states that the maximum achievable data rate (in bits per second) over a communication channel is proportional to the bandwidth and the logarithm of the SNR. In fading channels, achieving the theoretical capacity may not always be feasible due to the varying channel conditions and practical constraints. However, various techniques can be employed to approach the channel capacity, including diversity techniques (such as frequency diversity, time diversity, and space diversity), adaptive modulation and coding, and channel estimation and equalization.

### 3.1.1 Shannon's Theorem for Channel Capacity

Shannon's theorem provides the maximum data rate CCC (capacity) that can be achieved with an arbitrarily low error probability over a communication channel. For an AWGN channel, the theorem can be derived as follows:

**1. Channel Model**

The AWGN channel can be modulated as:

$$Y = X + N \tag{3.1}$$

where Y represents the received signal, X represents the transmitted signal and the noise is given by N which is normally distributed with mean 0 and variance $N_0/2$ (i.e., N ~ N (0, $N_0$).

**2. Signal-to-Noise Ratio (SNR)**

Define the SNR as

$$\text{SNR} = \frac{P}{N_0 B} \tag{3.2}$$

where the average power of the transmitted signal X is P, and the noise power spectral density is $N_0$, and the bandwidth of the channel is B.

**3. Mutual Information**

The mutual information I (X; Y) between the transmitted and received signals represents the amount of information that can be reliably transmitted over the channel. For a given power constraint P, the mutual information is maximized when X is normally distributed, N ~ N (0, P). The mutual information for Gaussian signals over an AWGN channel is given by

$$I(X; Y) = \frac{1}{2} \log_2\left(1 + \frac{P}{N_o B}\right) \tag{3.3}$$

**4. Channel Capacity**

The channel capacity C is the maximum mutual information per unit time I (X; Y), which occurs when the signal is bandlimited to the bandwidth B, and it is given as

$$C = B \cdot I(X; Y) \tag{3.4}$$

Substituting the mutual information into the capacity formula, we get

$$C = B \frac{1}{2} \log_2\left(1 + \frac{P}{N_o B}\right) \tag{3.5}$$

Since the AWGN channel has two dimensions (in-phase and quadrature), we need to multiply by 2.

$$C = B.\, log_2(1+\frac{P}{N_o B}) \tag{3.6}$$

This is the Shannon-Hartley theorem for the capacity of an AWGN channel.

## 3.2. CAPACITY OF FLAT FADING CHANNELS

The capacity of a flat fading channel can be derived using the Shannon-Hartley theorem, considering the effects of fading. Here, we will derive the expression for the capacity of a flat fading channel with the assumption of perfect Channel State Information (CSI) at the receiver.

1. **Channel Model** - The received signal $y(t)$ in a flat fading channel can be expressed as

$$y(t) = h(t)\, x(t) + n(t) \tag{3.7}$$

where h(t) is the complex channel gain, x(t) is a transmitted signal and the Additive White Gaussian Noise (AWGN) n(t) with power spectral density $N_o$.

2. **Instantaneous Signal-to-Noise Ratio (SNR)** - The instantaneous SNR at the receiver is given by

$$\text{SNR}\,(t) = \frac{|h(t)|^2}{P_{N_0}} \tag{3.8}$$

where $|\, h(t)\, |^2$ is the instantaneous power gain of the channel, P is the transmitted power, and the noise power spectral density is $N_0$ .

3. **Instantaneous Capacity** - The instantaneous capacity $C(t)$of the flat fading channel with perfect CSI at the receiver is given by the Shannon-Hartley theorem

$$C(t)=Blog_2(1+\frac{|h|^2 P}{N_o B}) \tag{3.9}$$

4. **Average Capacity** - To find the average capacity over time, we need to average the instantaneous capacity over the distribution of the channel gain $|\, \boldsymbol{h}\, |^2$. Assuming that the fading is ergodic, the average capacity $C$ is given by

$$C = E[B\boldsymbol{log_2}(1+\frac{|\boldsymbol{h}|^2 \boldsymbol{P}}{\boldsymbol{N_o B}})] \tag{3.10}$$

where E(.) is the average capacity.

5. **Distribution of** $|\, \boldsymbol{h}\, |^2$- For simplicity, let's consider the case where the fading follows a Rayleigh distribution. The power gain $|\, \boldsymbol{h}\, |^2$ then follows an exponential distribution with mean $\lambda$. The Probability Density Function (PDF) of $|\, \boldsymbol{h}\, |^2$ is

$$f_{|h|^2}(x) = \frac{1}{\lambda} e^{\frac{-x}{\lambda}} \qquad (3.11)$$

6. **Average Capacity Calculation** - The average capacity can be computed by integrating over the distribution of $|\, \boldsymbol{h} \,|^2$ is given as

$$C = B\int_0^{\infty}(1 + \frac{xP}{N_0B})\ \frac{1}{\lambda} e^{\frac{-x}{\lambda}}\ dx \qquad (3.12)$$

Let's introduce a new variable $\gamma = \frac{P}{N_0B}$ (average SNR), then

$$C = B\ (1+\gamma\ x)\frac{1}{\lambda} e^{\frac{-x}{\lambda}}\ dx \qquad (3.13)$$

Now separate the integration into two-part

$$C = B\ (\int_0^{\infty} \frac{1}{\lambda} e^{\frac{-x(t)}{\lambda}} dx + \gamma \int_0^{\infty} x(t)\ \frac{1}{\lambda} e^{\frac{-x(t)}{\lambda}}\ dx) \qquad (3.14)$$

Where the first integral is the integral of the probability density function of an exponential distribution, which equals 1

$$\int_0^{\infty} \frac{1}{\lambda} e^{\frac{-x(t)}{\lambda}} dx = 1 \qquad (3.15)$$

The second integral is the mean of the exponential distribution multiplied by λ –

$$\int_0^{\infty} x(t)\ \frac{1}{\lambda} e^{\frac{-x(t)}{\lambda}}\ dx\ =\ \lambda \qquad (3.16)$$

Combine the results of the two integrals is

$$C = B(1 + \gamma\ \lambda) \qquad (3.17)$$

This integral is known to have a closed-form solution

$$C = B\cdot\frac{1}{ln(2)}\cdot e^{\frac{1}{\gamma\lambda}}\cdot E_1(\frac{1}{\gamma\lambda}) \qquad (3.18)$$

where $E_1$ (·) is the exponential integral function defined as

$$E_1\ (x) = \int_x^{\infty} \frac{1}{t} e^{-t}\, dt. \qquad (3.19)$$

7. **Simplified Average Capacity (High SNR Approximation)**

For high SNR (large $\gamma$), the average capacity can be approximated more simply as

$$C \approx \boldsymbol{Blog_2}(1+\gamma\lambda) \qquad (3.15)$$

## Channel Inversion

Channel inversion is a technique used to counteract the effects of channel fading. In a flat fading channel, the channel gain can vary significantly over time, leading to fluctuations in the received signal power. Channel inversion attempts to mitigate this by adjusting the transmitted power to maintain a constant received power level. However, this technique has implications for the channel capacity.

### Flat Fading Channel Model

In a flat fading channel, the received signal Y can be modeled as

$$Y = hX + N \tag{3.16}$$

where the channel gain h is a complex number that varies with time, the transmitted signal is X, and the AWGN N has a variance of $N_0$ .

Channel inversion adjusts the transmitted power to counteract the variations in the channel gain h. Specifically, if the instantaneous channel gain is h, the transmitter adjusts its power such that the received power remains constant. This can be mathematically expressed as

$$P_t = \frac{P_r}{|h|^2} \tag{3.17}$$

where the transmitted power is $P_t$ , the desired constant received power is $P_r$ , and $|h|^2$ represents the magnitude squared of the channel gain.

### Impact on Channel Capacity

While channel inversion helps maintain a constant received signal power, it can affect the capacity of the channel. The capacity C of a flat fading channel with channel inversion can be derived considering the variations in the channel gain.

1. **Channel Gain Distribution** - Assume the channel gain, h(t), is a random variable with a known probability density function (pdf). For simplicity, let's consider Rayleigh fading where the magnitude of h,(|h|), follows a Rayleigh distribution, and $|h|^2$ follows an exponential distribution.
2. **Average Power Constraint** - The average transmitted power should satisfy the power constraint P.

$$E[P_t] = P \tag{3.18}$$

Given the channel inversion scheme $P_t = \frac{P_r}{|h|^2}$ we have the eq.(3.19).

$$P = E[\frac{P_r}{|h|^2}] \tag{3.19}$$

3. **Received Power**: The received power $P_r$ is constant by design. Therefore, the SNR at the receiver is constant and given by

$$SNR = \frac{P_r}{N_0} \tag{3.20}$$

4. **Capacity Calculation**: The capacity of the channel with constant SNR can be expressed

$$C = B.\ log_2(1+SNR) \tag{3.21}$$

Substituting the constant SNR, we get:

$$C = B.\ log_2(1+\frac{P_r}{N_o}) \tag{3.22}$$

However, to satisfy the average power constraint, the value of $P_r$ must be such that $E[\frac{P_r}{|h|^2}] = P$.

**Effect of Channel Inversion on Capacity**

1. **Power Efficiency** - Channel inversion can be power-inefficient, especially when the channel gain |h| is small. This is because the required transmitted power $P_r$ can become very large, leading to excessive power consumption.
2. **Outage Probability** - If the channel gain |h| drops below a certain threshold, the required transmitted power may exceed practical limits, causing an outage. In practice, a transmitter may not always be able to invert the channel for very low |h| values.
3. **Capacity under Average Power Constraint** - In reality, due to the average power constraint, the achievable capacity can be lower than the theoretical capacity calculated with constant $P_r$. This is because the actual power used will vary depending on the channel conditions.

## 3.3 CAPACITY IN FREQUENCY-SELECTIVE CHANNELS

The capacity of a frequency-selective fading channel can be derived using the principles of information theory, considering the variations in the channel's frequency response. Here, perfect Channel State Information (CSI) at the receiver is assumed.

**Key Parameters**

**B:** Total bandwidth of the channel

**N:** Number of sub-channels or frequency bins (assuming we divide the total bandwidth into N narrow sub-channels where each sub-channel experiences flat fading)

**P:** Totals transmit power

$\boldsymbol{P_k}$**:** Power allocated to the $k^{th}$ sub-channel

$\boldsymbol{H_k}$**:** Channel gain for the $k^{th}$ sub-channel

$\boldsymbol{N_0}$**:** Noise power spectral density

1. **Channel Model**

For a frequency-selective channel, the total bandwidth B is divided into N sub-channels, each with bandwidth $\Delta f = \frac{B}{N}$. The channel gain for the $k^{th}$ sub-channel is $\boldsymbol{H_k}$.

2. **Instantaneous Capacity of Each Sub-Channel**

The capacity of the $k^{th}$ sub-channel with gain $\boldsymbol{H_k}$ and power allocation $\boldsymbol{P_k}$ is given by

$$C_k = \Delta f \, log_2(1+\frac{|H_k|^2 P_k}{N_0 \Delta f}) \tag{3.23}$$

**3.Total Capacity**

The total capacity of the frequency-selective channel is the sum of the capacities of the individual sub-channels can represented as

$$C_{total} = \sum_{k=1}^{N} \Delta f \, log_2(1+\frac{|H_k|^2 P_k}{N_0 \Delta f}) \tag{3.24}$$

**4. Power Allocation (Water-Filling Algorithm):**

To maximize the total capacity, the power $P_k$ should be allocated across the sub-channels according to the water-filling principle. The optimal power allocation is given by

$$P_k = (\mu - \frac{N_0 \Delta f}{|H_k|^2})^+ \tag{3.25}$$

where μ is the water level, determined by the total power constraint and $(x)^+$ = max (x,0).

5. **Average Capacity**

For many sub-channels, the total capacity can be approximated as an integral over the frequency range in equation 3.26.

$$C_{total} = \int_0^B log_2(1+\frac{|H_k|^2 \mathrm{P(f)}}{N_0}) \, \mathrm{df} \tag{3.26}$$

where H(f) is the channel gain as a function of frequency, and P(f) is the power spectral density allocated to frequency f.

### 3.3.1 Some Factors Influencing Capacity in Frequency Selective Channels Include

1. **Bandwidth** - The total bandwidth available for the channel plays a significant role in determining its capacity. Higher bandwidth allows for more sub-channels, increasing the potential capacity. Efficient use of the available bandwidth, including proper allocation and avoidance of interference, further impacts capacity.
2. **Power Allocation** - The total transmit power available for communication directly influences capacity. Higher power generally increases capacity but is constrained by regulatory and hardware limits. Optimal power allocation strategies, such as the water-filling algorithm, maximize capacity by allocating more power to sub-channels with better conditions.

3. **Fading Characteristics** -The nature of multipath fading, which causes frequency-selective fading, affects capacity. The statistical properties of the fading, such as Rayleigh, Rician, or Nakagami distributions, influence the average capacity by affecting the variability and predictability of the channel gain.
4. **Noise and Interference** - The noise power spectral density (N0) and interference from other users or systems are crucial factors. Higher noise levels reduce the Signal-to-Noise Ratio (SNR), decreasing capacity. Interference adds to the noise, further degrading SNR and capacity.
5. **Channel Correlation** - Frequency correlation refers to the correlation between the fading of different sub-channels. Highly correlated sub-channels provide less diversity gain compared to uncorrelated channels. Time correlation, or the variation of the channel over time, also impacts capacity. Rapidly changing channels may require more frequent adaptation and can affect the achievable capacity.
6. **Propagation Environment** - The physical environment, such as urban, rural, indoor, or outdoor settings, affects multipath propagation differently, influencing capacity. Mobility, such as the movement of the transmitter, receiver, or objects in the environment, dynamically changes the fading characteristics, impacting capacity etc.

### 3.3.2 Some Adaptive Techniques for Capacity Optimization

Adaptive techniques play a crucial role in optimizing the capacity of communication systems, especially in challenging environments such as frequency-selective fading channels. These techniques dynamically adjust system parameters based on the prevailing channel conditions to maximize throughput, spectral efficiency, and reliability. Here are some adaptive techniques commonly used for capacity optimization -

1. **Adaptive Modulation and Coding (AMC):** AMC adjusts the modulation scheme and coding rate based on the channel conditions to optimize data rate and error performance. In frequency-selective fading channels, AMC selects the most appropriate modulation constellation and coding rate for each transmission, balancing the trade-offs between spectral efficiency and error resilience.
2. **Adaptive Power Control:** Adaptive power control adjusts the transmit power levels based on the channel conditions to maintain a target Signal-to-Noise Ratio (SNR) or Bit Error Rate (BER). By dynamically adapting the transmit power, adaptive power control optimizes the use of available resources, mitigates interference, and maximizes the coverage area while minimizing power consumption.
3. **Adaptive Equalization:** Adaptive equalization techniques adaptively compensate for the frequency-selective fading effects to mitigate ISI and improve signal quality. These techniques include linear equalizers such as zero-forcing equalizers and decision-feedback equalizers, as well as more advanced algorithms like maximum likelihood sequence estimation (MLSE) and adaptive filter-based equalizers.

4. **Adaptive Channel Estimation and Tracking:** Adaptive channel estimation and tracking algorithms continuously monitor the channel conditions and update CSI to adaptively adjust system parameters. By accurately estimating and tracking the channel response, adaptive techniques enable efficient modulation and coding adaptation, power control, and equalization, leading to improved capacity and reliability.
5. **Adaptive Antenna Techniques:** Adaptive antenna techniques, such as beamforming and spatial multiplexing, adaptively adjust the antenna radiation patterns and spatial processing algorithms based on the channel conditions. By focusing transmit energy towards the desired directions and exploiting spatial diversity, adaptive antenna techniques enhance the channel capacity and reliability, particularly in multipath-rich environments.
6. **Adaptive Packet Scheduling:** Adaptive packet scheduling algorithms dynamically allocate transmission resources, such as time slots or frequency subcarriers, based on channel conditions and traffic demands. By prioritizing users with better channel conditions and adjusting transmission parameters in real-time, adaptive packet scheduling improves system throughput, fairness, and Quality of Service (QoS).

By leveraging these adaptive techniques, communication systems can effectively optimize the capacity and performance in challenging environments characterized by frequency-selective fading, interference, and dynamic channel conditions. Adaptive optimization enables efficient resource allocation, robust error control, and adaptive modulation schemes, leading to enhanced spectral efficiency, throughput, and reliability in wireless communications systems.

## 3.4 ANTENNAS

The inception of mobile communication dates back to 1885, when Thomas Edison pioneered wireless telegraph systems between trains and stations. Telegraph signals were transmitted through trolley wires connected to a metal plate on the train ceiling. Edison also experimented with vehicle communication 1901, employing a cylindrical antenna on the vehicle roof. Wireless telegraph services on ships were initiated by Guglielmo Marconi in 1898, utilizing long vertical wire antennas in configurations like T, inverted L, and umbrella shapes. Portable communication equipment emerged around 1910.

Both World Wars I and II drove advancements in antenna design and technology. Wire antennas became established in the 1920s, while microwave antenna design, as seen today, became prevalent in the 1950s. The 1960s marked a new era for antennas due to the rapid progress in semiconductor integrated circuits, initially driven by the cold war defense industry but later influencing commercial equipment. This era led to redesigning and transforming existing antenna types into smaller, lighter, and more cost-effective structures compatible with integrated electronic packages. Printed antenna technology emerged, enabling multifunction antenna devices. Planar antennas, derived from printed antennas, were found to be used in various mobile systems for both base stations and mobile terminals, where compact, lightweight antennas were necessary. Communication advancements, especially in mobile systems, have been significant drivers of antenna technology. The deployment of new wireless mobile systems and their integration with the IP network has also influenced the development of novel antenna systems. Other emerging information-relaying systems, including control, sensing, and identification systems, are aligning closely with mobile systems, expanding the scope of mobile technology beyond traditional mobile phone systems to include wireless access and radio identification systems.

This historical overview highlights the rapid evolution of antennas in response to global demands driven by the growth and deployment of new wireless mobile systems. The impact of mobile communications and related systems on antennas worldwide over the past decade has been significant in various aspects.

(a) Integrating mobile communications into all parts of the global community has led to social changes and a greater public consciousness of antennas in their daily surroundings. This increased awareness of electromagnetic radiation has already impacted the design specifications for base station and handset antennas.

(b) Concurrently, very short-range wireless systems have become prevalent in public spaces, primarily utilized for control, sensing, and identification rather than communication. These systems require small antennas, the size of which depends on the specific installation requirements. Very compact Electrically Small Antennas (ESA) are employed in particular systems.

(c) The expansion of mobile wireless systems has hastened the increase in data transmission rates, particularly during movement, necessitating antennas capable of handling high-speed data transmission.

(d) The origin is primarily from commercial sources.

(e) The current phase of intense antenna design work has lasted longer than ever, with no indication of slowing down. It is linked to significant and growing investment from the public.

This past decade has witnessed a remarkable surge in the sales of mobile communication devices, surpassing earlier predictions. Cellular phones have become essential for social interactions, daily activities, and entertainment. However, the market for new subscribers is nearly saturated in regions where mobile services were introduced in the 1980s and 1990s. Growth continues primarily in developing nations like China, India, and parts of Africa. Fig. 3.1 illustrates the trend in global cellular system subscribers up to 2005, with an extended line projecting future growth.

Fig. 3.2 outlines critical milestones in the evolution of global mobile systems, both past and future. The initial analog systems of the 1980s, now categorized as 'first generation (1G),' established the subscriber market by demonstrating the benefits of mobile communication. These early systems, though relatively simple compared to modern equipment, were extensive and tailored to local needs. The advent of second-generation (2G) digital systems in the early 1990s demonstrated the advantages of digital over analog processing, leading to increased capacity and service offerings and paving the way for global standardization.

Discussions centered around a Global communication Village, which involves large-scale terrestrial mega cells further divided into nested geometrical regions, including macro, micro, pico, and femtocells, which are particularly relevant for in-building communication. These discussions sparked the idea of comprehensive network configurations for integrated mobile communication systems. The highly successful Global System for Mobile Communications (GSM) played a crucial role in this evolution and laid the foundation for the third-generation (3G) European Universal Mobile Telecommunication Systems (UMTS), which operate in frequency bands up to 2.2 GHz. The International Telecommunication Union Radiocommunication Sector (ITU-R) ultimately settled on specifying five systems, two of which, CDMA2000 and wideband code division multiple access (WCDMA), known as 3G systems, have been implemented and operated worldwide.

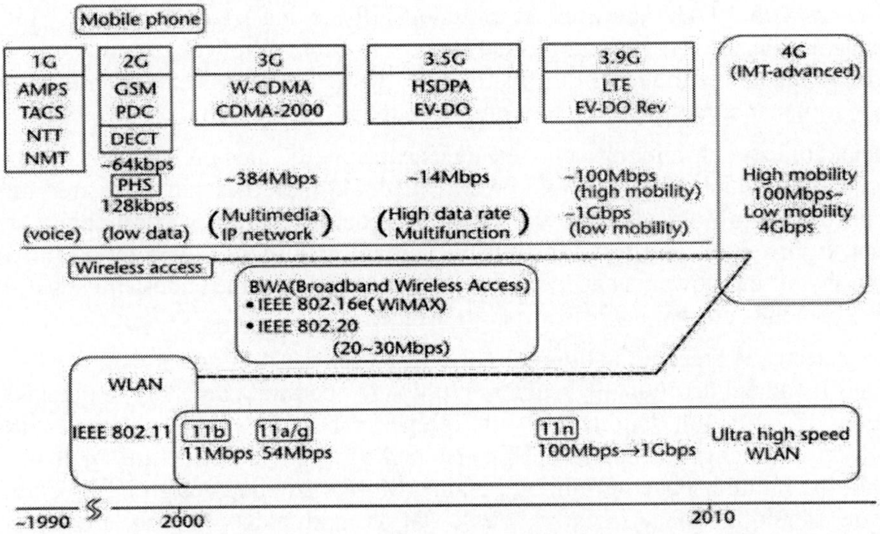


Fig. 3.1 The progression of mobile communication systems, highlighting various prevalent systems and future concepts [1].

It is also essential to consider the importance of wireless mobile systems, encompassing systems operating over short ranges and serving purposes beyond voice communication. For instance, Wireless Local Area Networks (WLANs) replace wired LANs with radio-linked connections. Through access points, computers can communicate wirelessly with each other; in some cases, even voice communication is supported. These wireless systems are categorized based on their communication range:

(i) Wireless Personal Area Network (WPAN) operates within a concise range of less than 10 meters.

(ii) WLAN covers up to a 100-meter range.

(iii) Wireless Metropolitan Area Network (WMAN) spans long or wide ranges, such as in city areas, reaching around 10 kilometers;

(iv) Wireless Wide Area Network (WWAN) extends to suburban areas, with a range of up to 50 kilometers.

Antennas for these systems vary based on their specific requirements. WPAN systems typically use simple, small-sized antennas. Long-range systems use standard antennas similar to those in traditional communication systems. More complex antennas, such as innovative arrays and Multi-Input Multi-Output (MIMO) systems, are used for systems requiring high-quality, high-data-rate transmission.

Another crucial mobile system is the Intelligent Transport System (ITS), designed to enhance safety, efficiency, and economy in vehicular traffic while preserving environmental ecology and improving traffic management. ITS relies on communications and computer systems. The communication system within ITS is known as Dedicated Short-Range Communication (DSRC), which serves two primary purposes: Communication between Vehicles and Roadside infrastructure (CVR) and Vehicle-to-Vehicle Communication (CVV). DSRC is used in Electronic Toll Collection (ETC) systems, where vehicles are automatically charged as they pass through toll gates, eliminating the need to stop. The DSRC system operates at 5.8 GHz and uses Amplitude Shift Keying (ASK) or Phase Shift Keying (PSK) for data transmission. At toll gates, a phased array creates an elliptical communication area on the road for vehicles to interact with the ETC infrastructure. Vehicle antennas are typically simple, such as small microstrip or planar antennas, often mounted on the car's dashboard.

A battery is a crucial component in mobile phones, as its capacity dictates the transmission power and the time between charges, which ideally should be extended. Higher efficiency is desired to maintain high transmitting power and prolonged phone use without frequent recharging. Additionally, the battery should be compact, lightweight, and trim. Increasing antenna gain can reduce the required battery capacity, as lower transmitting power is needed. Like other components, the battery must be considered in antenna design, as antenna current may flow on its surface.

The mobile antenna designer faces an additional challenge because it is now recognized that clever antenna design can offer added functionality, such as multiband operation, diversity in transmission and reception, reduction of multipath fading and interference, or adaptive control to environmental conditions. The primary challenge in antenna design is to make the antenna structure small and compact enough to fit within the limited space of a mobile phone. Mobile antenna design has evolved beyond simple, lightweight, omnidirectional radiators on a flat ground plane; it now involves creating sophisticated electromagnetic configurations that play a significant role in signal processing while operating in a complex and changing environment. It is important to consider the antenna as an integral part of the overall system, as depicted in Fig. 3.2.

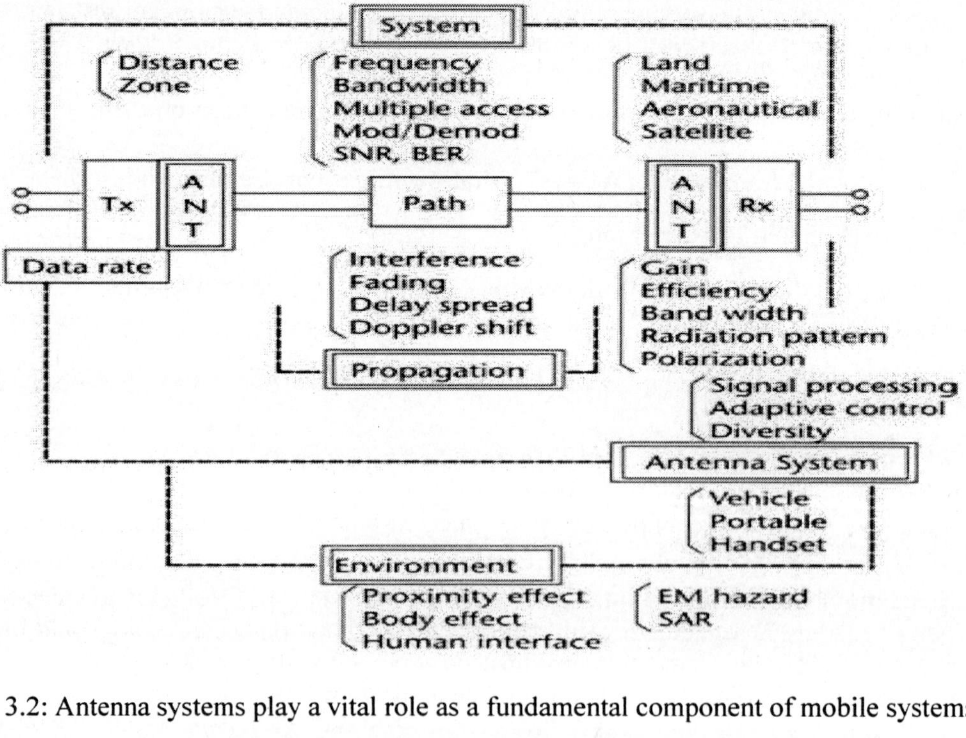


Fig. 3.2: Antenna systems play a vital role as a fundamental component of mobile systems [1].

The design of mobile antennas is significantly influenced by the nature of the mobile system, which can vary between land-based, maritime, aeronautical, and satellite systems, as well as the type of mobile platforms like vehicles, ships, aircraft, and portable devices. Antenna designers must consider factors such as frequency utilization techniques, the kind of information being transmitted, modulation/demodulation schemes, data transmission rates, and the functions of mobile terminals. Another important consideration is the impact of handset operation and potential human exposure to radiation from the handset transmitter, which presents a severe concern for antenna designers. The specific absorption rate (SAR) value is used to assess human exposure and should be minimized, especially near the human brain. Various methods have been explored to reduce SAR values, including using balanced antenna structures fed with balanced lines to minimize current flow on the ground plane inside the handset unit. Additionally, placing antenna elements as far as possible from the human head and within the limited volume of the handset unit is a common approach.

## 3.5 Antennas for Mobile-Terminal

### 3.5.1. Introduction

As mobile communication systems have advanced significantly in recent years, so have antenna systems. Mobile phone systems have evolved from analog (1G) to digital (2G) and multimedia-capable 3G systems. Now, there is a transition to 4G systems via 3.5G systems, bridging the gap between 3G and 4G. Apart from mobile phone systems, various Wireless Mobile Systems (WMS) have been deployed, offering services over different ranges. Depending on their performance needs, WMS operates across multiple frequencies, from kilohertz to gigahertz. These systems provide communication services and handle control, data transmission, identification, and sensing. Examples of short-range systems include Bluetooth, Near Field Communication (NFC), and Ultra-Wideband (UWB). Medium to long-range systems include Wireless Local Area Networks (WLAN), Wireless Metropolitan Area Networks (WMAN), and Worldwide Interoperability for Microwave Access (WiMAX), offering high data rates even at high speeds. The deployment of these systems has driven advancements in antenna technology to cater to their specific needs. Currently, there are two significant trends in antenna design. One trend focuses on antennas for mobile phone systems, which require small, integrated designs capable of operating across multiple frequency bands. The other trend pertains to antennas for Wireless Mobile Systems (WMS), which require diverse antenna capabilities depending on system function, complexity, service area, and data transmission requirements. Many WMS operate over short distances, often indoors. Some have simple structures and operate over very short distances, from a few centimeters to a few meters. In contrast, other WMS have more complex structures and operate over longer distances, ranging from a few meters to several kilometers. The types of antennas used in these systems vary from very small to conventional sizes. For short-range systems, the design of small antennas is often essential to meet specific system requirements.

However, a common trend in mobile phones and WMS is personalization, accelerated by the widespread use of small mobile devices that provide easy access to personal information, media, and data. Antennas required for WMS terminals are typically small, compact, lightweight, yet still functional. Modern mobile phones are equipped with built-in multiband antennas capable of covering various frequency bands used by systems like GSM (800-, 900-, 1,800-, and 1,900-MHz bands), UMTS (1.8-, 1.9-, 2.1-, and 2.5-GHz bands), and GPS (1.5-GHz band). These phones also offer functions beyond telephony, including entertainment features like games, television reception, and music playback, as well as business, industrial, and lifestyle functions like electronic keying, banking, sensing, and identifying, along with data transmission. A growing trend is integrating functions such as Bluetooth, NFC systems (including RFID), and UWB systems into mobile terminals. Consequently, there is a push for developing tiny yet efficient and lightweight multiband antennas. Many mobile terminals now incorporate functions beyond telephony, necessitating small antennas. Additionally, the increased demand for multimedia services and large data quantities has accelerated the deployment of high-speed, high-data-rate transmission systems, leading to the adoption of advanced antenna systems like adaptive arrays and MIMO systems. The propagation challenge should encompass factors beyond just path loss. It should also consider signal transmission rate, bandwidth, delay spread, and Doppler shift in a Rayleigh fading environment. These factors are especially crucial in digital modulation systems used for high-speed data transmission.

Antenna design is tailored to meet the system's specific requirements for the antennas utilized. This includes considerations for rejecting interference and mitigating any negative impacts from multipath fading. Environmental conditions also play a crucial role in antenna design. The presence of materials near the antenna element, such as circuit components, ground planes, and even the user's hand or head, can affect antenna performance. While these materials can sometimes enhance radiation by acting as parasitic elements, they can also degrade performance. This is particularly relevant in mobile terminals with built-in antennas. Modern antenna design approaches address this proximity effect through integration, where nearby materials are considered integral parts of the antenna system, either enhancing or detracting from its performance.

The propagation path can be viewed as a transmission circuit, and understanding it can help optimize communication links for optimal signal transmission. This is crucial in designing communication links, particularly in environments with Rayleigh fading and diversity antenna systems and those using MIMO systems. Reducing specific absorption rate (SAR) values is another crucial consideration in designing antennas for mobile terminals, aiming to minimize exposure, especially to the human brain. There is a widespread acknowledgment that an antenna is not a standalone component but a system influenced by propagation characteristics, system requirements, and environmental conditions.

One notable trend in the mobile communications industry is the substantial reduction in the size of mobile terminals. Simultaneously, there has been a steady increase in radio systems, leading to a greater demand for mobile terminals to operate across multiple frequency bands. This progression has created an urgent requirement for internal antenna structures that are compact and efficient across various frequency bands. However, miniaturizing an already small antenna is a complex endeavor. It has been understood for many years that reducing the electrical size of a small antenna without compromising its bandwidth and efficiency is a challenging task.

Today's mobile terminals typically feature PCBs (Printed Circuit Boards) with continuous ground layers on both sides. Moreover, planar metal surfaces are commonly integrated inside these terminals as EMC (Electromagnetic Compatibility) shields. The quantity, size, and position of these EMC shields can vary between phone models. These components create a solid metal chassis a few millimeters thick, with dimensions roughly corresponding to the PCBs. It has long been understood that the metal chassis of a portable device significantly influences the performance of an antenna element mounted near it. The antenna element induces currents in the chassis, part of the antenna structure. Consequently, understanding the interaction between a small resonant antenna element and the chassis of a mobile terminal has become a crucial consideration for antenna designers.

### 3.5.2 Overview

Antenna technology has advanced alongside the progress of mobile phones and various Wireless Mobile Systems (WMS).

In recent years, there have been significant developments in antenna design for mobile phones. Changes have been observed in the selection of antenna types, how the antenna element is mounted within the mobile terminal, and the overall design process. Initially, monopole antennas were predominantly used in portable devices during the early stages of mobile communication. This practice continued for some time, with a common misconception that the device's case could serve as a ground plane, effectively making the monopole antenna function as a half-wave dipole with its image. However, in 1968, further analysis revealed that the unit case should be treated as part of the radiator, making the monopole antenna and unit case form an asymmetrical dipole.

Subsequent analysis of antenna systems with a monopole antenna mounted on a unit case provided a clearer understanding of antenna performance concerning the dimensions of both the antenna element and the unit case. This analysis laid the groundwork for the design of antennas used in present-day Mobile Terminals (MT) of Japanese PDC systems.

Essential considerations in antenna design include:

(i) Lightweight construction
(ii) Compact design
(iii) Low profile
(iv) Sturdy construction
(v) Size reduction
(vi) Multiband capability
(vii) Flexibility
(viii) Integration with adjacent materials
(ix) Built-in.

Two of the latest additions, multiband operation and built-in antennas, have been incorporated in line with current trends.

In the mid-1980s, planar antennas emerged, and their use has become prevalent in portable devices alongside monopoles. Modern handheld terminals often feature planar antennas, particularly the Planar Inverted-F Antenna (PIFA). The PIFA evolved from a half-wave slot on a rectangular conducting box. In Japanese PDC systems, MTs employ a built-in PIFA as a sub-antenna for diversity systems. Mobile phones in GSM systems have utilized a built-in PIFA for over a decade. These PIFAs have undergone significant modifications from the basic structure, with the antennas no longer rectangular. Instead, they feature slots on the planar element, creating different current paths along the slots and enabling resonance at multiple frequencies. Adopting built-in antennas has become a global trend in mobile phone design.

### 3.5.3 Modern Antenna Technology

The antennas used in modern mobile terminals for 3G systems include modified PIFAs, planar meander lines, folded loops, and modified dipoles. These antennas are designed based on the principles of small antenna technology, where compact size is crucial, but they must also exhibit high gain and wide bandwidth for practical use. To achieve small dimensions, one approach is to employ a slow wave structure in the antenna element. This involves using a traveling wave structure, like helices, meander-lines, or zigzags, to extend the current path on the antenna, allowing resonance at lower frequencies despite the small physical size. Another method involves integrating devices or circuits into the antenna structure, altering the current phase to effectively increase the electric length and enable resonance at lower frequencies without changing the antenna's physical dimensions.

Another crucial consideration in utilizing built-in antennas is the proximity effect, which significantly impacts antenna performance due to the current flow of nearby materials. These materials, including the ground plane, housing, electronic components, and accessories like cameras and speakers, must be treated as part of the radiator and integrated into the antenna design. The proximity materials can either degrade antenna performance due to their lossy nature or enhance it by acting as part of the radiator. This integration technology is of utmost importance and should be implemented as a critical concept in modern antenna design.

The ground plane is the most impactful among the materials that significantly influence antenna performance. It can either enhance radiation or degrade performance due to the body effect from the user's hands, which can alter current distributions on the ground plane and absorb radiation power. One method to mitigate the body effect is to reduce current distribution variation on the ground plane, which can be achieved by implementing a balanced structure in the antenna system. This concept is also crucial in antenna design. Small antenna technology is essential for designing mobile wireless systems, which utilize adaptive and MIMO systems with multiple antenna elements. An advanced integration concept involves using a nonperfect electric conductor (PEC) as the ground plane, such as applying an Electromagnetic Bandgap (EBG) surface.

The proximity effect on antenna performance introduced it. In handset antenna evaluations, a Voltage-Controlled Oscillator (VCO) is often utilized inside the handset instead of connecting a signal generator directly to the test antenna. This approach helps mitigate errors caused by the proximity effect, particularly those stemming from the influence of cables. However, using a VCO introduces potential drawbacks, as the VCO body itself may affect the measurement precision by acting as part of the radiator. Additionally, using a VCO eliminates the availability of a reference signal to the receiver, making it impossible to obtain phase information in radiation patterns, for instance. Moreover, this method limits the measurement to a single VCO frequency at a time, which can be a significant disadvantage in designing diversity systems and multiband antennae.

A new method has been adopted for practical antenna measurements involving an optical fiber cable to overcome the limitations of using a VCO. In this approach, the cable connecting the test antenna and the signal generator is replaced with an optical fiber to eliminate interference and provide a reference signal containing both phase and amplitude information. A small Electrical-to-Optical (E/O) signal converter and an Optical-to-Electrical (O/E) signal converter are employed to convert the RF signal to an optical signal and vice versa. The RF signal (output of the O/E converter) excites the test antenna and is transmitted to the receiver. This system enables measurements at multiple frequencies and significantly reduces the time required.

Another advanced measurement system is the reverberation chamber, which allows the simulation of a random field environment to evaluate antenna performance under Rayleigh fading conditions. This method offers several notable advantages, including evaluating small antenna gain, diversity gain, maximum capacity of multi-input multi-output (MIMO) systems, active terminals gain, active diversity systems, receiver sensitivity, and more.

Electromagnetic simulators have also progressed significantly, enabling the analysis of antenna systems used in mobile terminals with sufficient accuracy to validate experimental results. Standard simulators include the Finite Difference Time Domain (FDTD) method, Method of Moments (MoM), and Finite Element Method (FEM). These tools are valuable for designing antennas for mobile terminals, even when the antennas have a complex structure with materials and the human body nearby.

Future advanced antenna systems are expected to include the ability to adaptively control antenna performance based on environmental conditions to minimize performance degradation. Another significant development is reconfigurable antenna systems, which can adjust their performance to match specific systems by reconfiguring the antenna structure. For example, an antenna structure in a mobile phone operating in a PDC system area can be reconfigured to match a CDMA system when it enters and operates in a CDMA system's location. This reconfiguration can be achieved through switching, potentially using Radio Frequency (RF) Microelectromechanical Systems (MEMS). Further advancements in novel antenna systems are anticipated and will likely be implemented in small mobile terminals shortly.

## 3.5.4 Some Fundamental Terms

### 3.5.4.1 Quality Factor

One crucial parameter that defines an antenna's frequency selectivity is its quality factor, abbreviated as

$$Q = \omega_r.\frac{W}{P_l} = 2\pi.f_r\frac{W}{P_l} \tag{3.26}$$

where $\omega_r$ is the angular resonant frequency, fr is the resonant frequency, W is the total time-average energy stored in the system, and $P_l$ is power loss per second.

### 3.5.4.2 Efficiency

Its radiation and total efficiencies can describe the efficiency of an antenna's losses. Radiation efficiency ($\eta_r$) is the ratio of the power radiated ($P_r$) by an antenna to the input power accepted ($P_{in}$) by the antenna. It can also be represented by the antenna's unloaded and radiation quality factors.

Therefore, the Efficiency factor is defined as

$$\eta_r = \frac{P_r}{P_{in}} = \frac{Q_0}{Q_r}. \tag{3.27}$$

The antenna structure of a mobile terminal is often simplified as a combination of an antenna element and a metal chassis. In ideal conditions, the radiation efficiency of such a fully metallic prototype can exceed 95% across various frequency bands. However, in actual mobile terminals, factors such as the battery, display, loudspeaker, plastic covers, and other components absorb some of the antenna's input power, leading to lower radiation efficiencies. Additionally, a portion of the antenna input power can be lost to the user's head, hand, and other body parts near the terminal. Measurements of the radiation efficiencies of five commercial dual-band phones showed varying results. In free space, the phones had radiation efficiencies averaging 54-80% and 32-72% over the E-GSM900 and GSM1800 bands, respectively. In the talk position, the average radiation efficiencies were lower, ranging from 6-9% for the E-GSM900 band and 6-13% for the GSM1800 band.

Radiation efficiency focuses solely on the power radiated by an antenna relative to the power it accepts, omitting reflection losses at the antenna's input. On the other hand, total efficiency includes these losses, indicating the portion of available power at the antenna's feed that is converted into radiated power. For instance, a return loss of $L_{retn} = 6$ dB at the antenna input signifies a 25% reduction in accepted power ($P_{in}$) compared to a perfectly matched antenna.

### 3.5.4.3 Impedance Bandwidth

In the context of mobile terminal antennas, bandwidth typically refers to impedance bandwidth. This bandwidth is the frequency range where the antenna input's reflection coefficient (S11) remains below a specific predefined level. Recently, $S_{11} \leq -6$ dB (or return loss $L_{retn} \geq 6$ dB) has become a common matching criterion for compact internal antennas in mobile terminals. The specific criterion is determined based on the requirements of the wireless communication system. It can be demonstrated that the relative impedance bandwidth ($B_r$) of a resonant circuit, which describes an antenna, is inversely proportional to its unloaded quality factor ($Q_0$).

### 3.5.4.4 Specific Absorption Rate (SAR)

Specific Absorption Rate (SAR) is a metric used to measure the amount of Radio Frequency (RF) energy absorbed by human tissue, typically expressed in watts per kilogram (W/kg) and given by the eq.

$$SAR = \sigma . mod(E_{rms})^2 / \rho. \tag{3.5}$$

Several regulatory organizations have established mandatory safety limits for Specific Absorption Rate (SAR) values due to mobile devices, where $E_{rms}$ represents the Root Mean Square (RMS) value of the electric field strength (V/m) in the tissue, σ is the effective conductivity of the tissue (S/m). P is the density (kg/m3) of the tissue.

Specific Absorption Rate (SAR) is a significant concern for antenna designers for two reasons. Firstly, designers must ensure that mobile terminals adhere to SAR standards. Secondly, SAR provides valuable insights into the power absorbed by users. Reducing SAR and, consequently, user exposure enhances radiation efficiency and the overall performance of a mobile terminal in its operational position. Currently, two competing theories exist regarding the interaction mechanism between biological tissue and the near fields of an antenna. The first theory suggests that surface currents induced by the magnetic near fields of an antenna in human tissue are the primary power dissipation mechanism, with less importance placed on coupling from electric near fields. Based on simulations with dipole antennas operating above 300 MHz, it concluded that SAR in human tissue is roughly proportional to the square of the antenna's current magnitude. However, these findings are only partially supported by a related study. In SAR generated by a dipole antenna placed beside a homogeneous muscle phantom with and without a covering fat layer was studied at 915 MHz. Without the fat layer, the SAR maximum was located on the muscle surface near the antenna feed point, corresponding to the magnetic field maximum. With the fat layer, however, SAR maxima were observed from the fat layer surface under the dipole's open ends.

### 3.5.4.5 Fundamental Limitations on Antenna Size Reduction

The bandwidth and radiation quality factor ($Q_r$) of an antenna are known to be fundamentally limited by the electrical size of the antenna. A theory has been developed to determine the minimum achievable radiation quality factor of an ideal linearly polarized antenna, constrained to fit within a sphere of radius r and having no reactive energy stored inside.

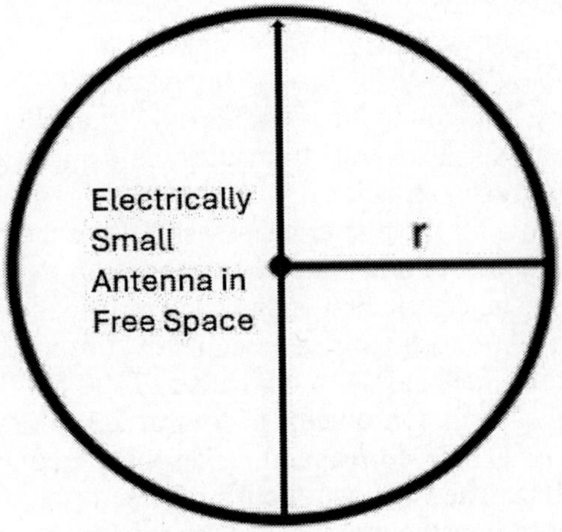


Fig. 3.3 Sphere enclosing an electrically small radiating element.

This theory has been extended to include circularly polarized antennas as well. The lowest possible $Q_r$ for a linearly polarized antenna is achieved when only the lowest order $TM_{01}$ [2] or $TE_{01}$ [2] mode is excited by the ideal antenna. The theoretical fundamental minimum $Q_r$ for this type of antenna structure can be expressed as:

$$Q_r = 1/(k.r)3 + 1/(k.r) \tag{3.6}$$

In the equation, k represents the wave number ($k = 2\pi/\lambda_0$, where $\lambda_0$ is the free space wavelength), and r is the radius of the smallest sphere that encloses the antenna. This equation suggests that the radiation quality factor ($Q_r$) of an ideal electrically small linearly polarized antenna is roughly inversely proportional to the volume V of the antenna in wavelengths ($V/\lambda_0^3$). As the electrical size of the antenna decreases, its bandwidth decreases rapidly.

In the derivative Eq. (3.6), it is assumed that the antenna structure doesn't store any reactive energy inside the sphere. However, antennas do not fill the spherical volume enclosing them and often excite higher-order wave modes. This results in non-propagating energy being stored inside the sphere, which increases the radiation quality factor ($Q_r$) and decreases the antenna's bandwidth.

### 3.5.5 Combining the Antenna and Chassis in Mobile Terminals

Self-resonant IFAs (Inverted-F Antennas), PIFAs (Planar Inverted-F Antennas), and their variations are the predominant internal antenna technologies in present-day mobile terminals. However, the limited dimensions allowed for internal antenna elements often need to be improved to meet the bandwidth requirements of modern mobile devices using only the antenna's resonant modes. To address this limitation, the chassis of a mobile terminal is utilized, which significantly enhances the radiation resistance and efficiency of a small antenna by using the antenna to excite currents on the larger metallic chassis with lower $Q_r$. The impedance bandwidth of a PIFA was found to peak when the chassis' electrical length approximately equals $0.4\lambda_0$, indicating its half-wave resonance. The performance metrics of this antenna-chassis combination, including impedance bandwidth, talk position efficiency, Specific Absorption Rate (SAR), and radiation pattern shape, depend not only on the electrical properties of the antenna element but also firmly on the chassis dimensions and the antenna element's relative position to it. Analyzing this combined performance requires an understanding of the radiation and resonance characteristics of the chassis, which can be achieved using the characteristic mode theory and resonator-based analysis as valuable tools.

### 3.5.5.1 Characteristic Mode Theory

The characteristic mode theory for conducting bodies is a valuable field-theoretic approach for analyzing the wave modes of chassis structures. It enables the expansion of currents on a conducting surface into characteristic modes, each associated with specific eigenvalues that indicate its radiating efficiency. These eigenvalues allow for the numerical assessment of the radiation quality factors linked to each mode. The resonant frequency of a characteristic mode can be determined from the frequency response of its eigenvalues. For instance, the first eight characteristic modes were identified and studied in a rectangular plate measuring 40 mm x 60 mm. Subsequently, this method was applied to analyze the radiation properties of mobile terminal chassis of typical size (100 mm x 40 mm). When excited by a plane wave, the analysis revealed radiation quality factors of 2.3, 3.0, 2.5, and 2.3 for the first four characteristic modes of the chassis. The corresponding resonant frequencies were 1260 MHz, 2679 MHz, 2739 MHz, and 3081 MHz. The first two modes represent the major axis half- and full-wave dipole modes, the third mode represents the minor axis half-wave mode, and the fourth mode represents the magnetic dipole mode. In practice, the currents on the chassis at a given frequency are a superposition of these modes, with the half-wave dipole-type mode being dominant at lower frequencies. The excitation of these modes is highly dependent on the type and location of the exciting element. For example, a patch-type antenna element positioned on the shorter end of a chassis can efficiently excite only the major axis dipole modes.

### 3.5.5.2 Resonator-Based Analysis

In the resonator-based analysis, the waves in the combination of the antenna and chassis are considered to consist of two relatively independent resonant wave modes: the quasi-TEM wave mode of a typical self-resonant antenna element and the thick-dipole type wave mode of a chassis. These resonant wave modes can be represented as two coupled lumped element resonant circuits characterized by their resonant frequencies and unloaded quality factors. An ideal transformer placed between the resonators determines the coupling strength between the wave modes. At 900 MHz, it is estimated that a small self-resonant antenna element like a PIFA typically radiates only about 10% of the total power emitted by a mobile terminal, with the remaining power being radiated by the half-wave dipole-type current distribution of the chassis. At 1800 MHz, the contribution of the antenna element wave mode is significantly more significant, accounting for roughly 50% of the total radiation. Additionally, research has shown that increasing the unloaded quality factor of the antenna element from $Q_0 = 20$ to $Q_0 = 500$ has almost no effect on the maximum achievable bandwidth when combined with the chassis. However, as the antenna element becomes more narrowband, stronger coupling to the chassis wave mode is required to achieve the maximum relative bandwidth, achieved with an optimally coupled dual-resonant response. These findings were based on the assumption that the resonant frequencies of the antenna element and chassis are equal. In practice, achieving equal resonant frequencies may be challenging. For example, a chassis's first-order ($\lambda/2$) resonance with typical dimensions of 100 mm x 40 mm (length x width) is approximately 1.1 GHz, which falls outside the operating bands of current communication systems. Furthermore, it has been demonstrated that even at operating frequencies below the first chassis resonance, such as in the E-GSM900 band (880 MHz – 960 MHz), the maximum achievable relative bandwidth is not limited by the unloaded quality factor of the antenna element.

## 3.5.6 Mobile Terminal Antennas Based on Coupling Elements.

The findings reported in [3] suggest that particularly below 1 GHz, such as in the E-GSM900 band, the antenna element of a mobile terminal primarily serves as a matching element, stimulating the low-Q wave modes of the chassis. To achieve the maximum relative bandwidth available with a certain-sized antenna element, it is crucial for the antenna element to couple as effectively as possible to the dominant wave mode of the chassis [3]. Short-circuited patch-type antennas, like PIFAs, are commonly employed in modern mobile terminals. These self-resonant antenna elements incorporate impedance transformation and resonance tuning within their metallic structures, enabling low production costs and easily attained matching advantages. However, achieving optimal coupling to the dominant wave mode of the chassis can be challenging, as typically, only a portion of the volume occupied by a shorted self-resonant antenna element effectively contributes to coupling. In [3], [4], [5], a new concept was proposed to tackle this challenge. It was suggested that the size of an internal antenna could be significantly reduced by replacing a self-resonant antenna element with an essentially non-resonant coupling element, the primary purpose of which is to excite the wave modes of the chassis efficiently. Separate matching circuitry is used to tune the combination of the coupling element and chassis into resonance at the desired operating frequency. Since the coupling element is separate from the impedance matching functionality, its shape, size, and location can be individually optimized to achieve the most robust possible coupling to the dominant wave mode of the chassis.

### 3.5.6.1 The Ideal form and Positioning of a Coupling Component

The modes of a chassis can be activated through its magnetic or electric fields or, alternatively, with direct electrical contact to isolated parts of the chassis. Patch-type antennas, or coupling elements, primarily couple capacitively, meaning they use electric fields. Maximum coupling is achieved when the electric fields of the chassis and the coupling element are aligned parallel to each other, and their electric field peaks coincide. Patch-type coupling elements have been investigated in studies like [3], [5], and others. Coupling through magnetic fields is feasible, for instance, with an inductive loop positioned to align its magnetic field with the chassis mode. The activation of chassis modes through direct electrical contact, such as with a feed placed over an impedance change on the chassis like a slot. To achieve the maximum bandwidth with an antenna or coupling element of a specific unloaded quality factor, it's crucial to shape and position the element to maximize coupling with the nearest resonant mode of the chassis. A coupling element's optimal shape and position were systematically investigated using IE3D simulations. A small capacitive probe (height = 3mm, diameter = 2mm) was moved over a chassis measuring 100mm x 40mm x 3mm (height x width x thickness). Unloaded quality factors were calculated for each probe location at 920 MHz and 1800 MHz using the IE3D simulation data.

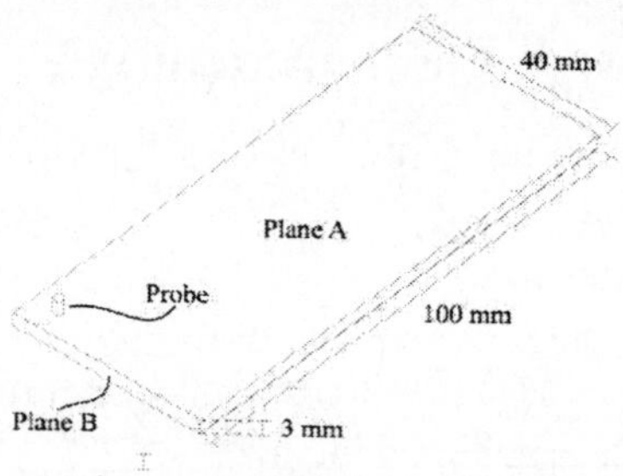


Fig. 3.4 illustrates the simulation setup and the normalized quality factors obtained at 920 MHz with a probe moved over plane A of the chassis [6].

Before interpreting the results depicted in Fig. 3.4, it's helpful to understand how the electric near fields of chassis wave modes behave. The chassis of a mobile terminal supports dipole-type wave modes, which resonate when the electrical length of the chassis is a multiple of λ/2 at the operating frequency. For instance, at the λ/2 resonance of a chassis, current distribution minima and, thus, electric field maxima are situated at the ends of the chassis. Conversely, current distribution maxima and, thus, electric field minima are located at the center of the chassis, similar to a half-wave dipole. The electric near fields of the half-wave dipole mode of a chassis were further examined using the characteristic mode theory. The results showed that the intensity of electric near fields, calculated at a distance of 5 mm above the surface of a chassis, peaks on top of the corners of the chassis. These findings fully explain the results illustrated in Fig. 3.4. When the probe is positioned on top of plane A of the chassis, the most robust coupling and, thus, the lowest quality factors are achieved on top of the shorter ends of the chassis. Conversely, the weakest coupling is observed on top of the center of the chassis. The quality factor reaches its minimum on top of the corners of the chassis, as anticipated.

### 3.5.6.2 Limitations in Achieving Broadband Impedance Matching Theory

In current cellular systems, the input impedance of a coupling element is typically predominantly capacitive, with a relatively low real part. Ideally, the matching network would convert the complex input impedance of the coupling element to purely resistive, such as 50 Ω, across all desired frequency bands. However, achieving this ideal scenario is not possible due to fundamental limitations on broadband impedance matching. While a perfect match can be achieved at specific frequencies, attempting to minimize the reflection coefficient at all points within the passband reduces the theoretical maximum bandwidth. Therefore, it is often more practical to accept less-than-perfect but still effective matching across the entire passband. The acceptable level of deviation can be defined, for example, in terms of the minimum allowable return loss ($L_{retn}$).

Let's consider a scenario where the non-resonant coupling element has been adjusted to a single resonance with an appropriate reactive component. An effective method for enhancing the impedance bandwidth of a resonator involves introducing additional resonances into its frequency response. This can be accomplished using a matching network comprising one or more high-Q matching resonators. However, the improvement in bandwidth diminishes rapidly as the number of matching resonators increases. For instance, with just one matching resonator (n = 2), approximately 60% of the maximum bandwidth is achieved. On the other hand, using five matching resonators leads to roughly 90% of the maximum bandwidth, but it also results in higher ohmic losses and increased complexity in the design of the matching network.

### 3.3.6.3 Single-resonant impedance matching

To achieve a perfect match at the resonant frequency for the combination of the coupling element and chassis, two main tasks are required:

(i) eliminating the input reactance of the antenna structure at $f_r$.

(ii) converting the input resistance of the antenna structure to 50 Ω at $f_r$.

These objectives can be effectively achieved using a straightforward L-section matching network comprising two suitable lumped or distributed elements.

The theoretical maximum relative bandwidth of an optimally over-coupled single-resonant antenna with a specific $Q_0$ can be represented as

$$B_{sr,opt} = S^2 - 1/2SQ_0 \tag{3.7}$$

where S denotes the maximum permissible voltage standing wave ratio.

### 3.5.6.4 Dual-resonant impedance matching

**Tuning of a non-resonant load optimally into dual-resonance:**

Fig. 3.4 illustrates the schematic of the matching network employed to precisely tune a non-resonant antenna structure, such as the coupling element and chassis, into dual-resonance. Resonator 2 in Fig. 3.4 symbolizes the coupling element and chassis combination, fine-tuned into resonance using two appropriate lumped elements (inductor $L_T$ and reactance $X_m$). The input impedance of a typical non-resonant coupling element can be effectively represented as a series-resonant circuit. Hence, Resonator 2 can be viewed as a series-type resonator. Dual-resonance in a series-resonant circuit can be achieved by adding a shunt parallel-type matching resonator into its feed. Alternatively, a series-type matching resonator connected via an impedance inverter can be depicted in Fig. 3.4. Since the input resistance of a coupling element is generally very low at cellular frequencies, typically less than 10 Ω, impedance transformation is also required. In [4], impedance transformation (an inversion) is executed immediately after Resonator 2. This approach allows for the nearly complete integration of the discrete-component realization of the transformer within the matching circuitry.

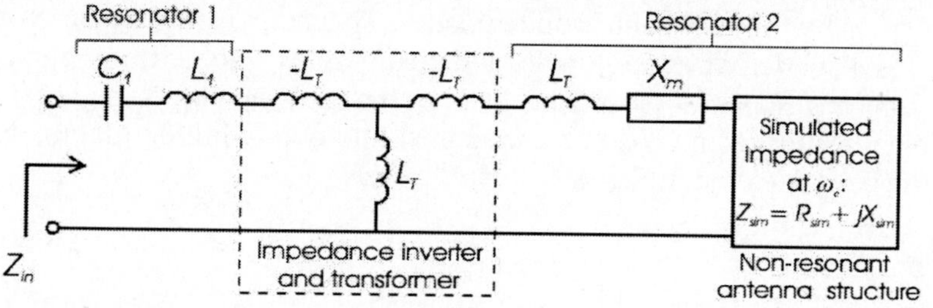


Fig. 3.5: Diagram of the matching network utilized for fine-tuning a non-resonant antenna structure to achieve dual resonance. The block on the right indicates the simulated input impedance ($Z_{sim}$) of the non-resonant antenna structure at the angular matching center frequency ($\omega_c$) [7]

The inverter-transformer can be implemented conveniently as a lumped element T-circuit comprising positive and negative inductors [7], as depicted in Fig. 3.5. Another approach involves replacing the inductors with capacitors [7]. Ideally, the negative components of the inverter-transformer can be merged into adjacent positive series components of the same type, resulting in a circuit with all positive elements and minimal complexity. The negative component on the right-hand side of the inverter-transformer can be absorbed by adding a positive component of equal value (LT) to Resonator 2. Subsequently, Resonator 2 can be tuned into resonance with a reactance $X_m$, which can be realized as an inductor or a capacitor depending on the input impedance ($Z_{sim}$) of the non-resonant antenna structure. The negative inductor on the left-hand side can be absorbed into $L_1$. Consequently, the final matching network will comprise a total of four components.

When the equivalent circuit is utilized as a load, the size of the dual-resonant circle on the Smith chart matches that of the circle representing the minimum allowed return loss ($L_{retn} \geq 6$ dB). This condition for optimum dual-resonant response has also been derived in [8] and [9]. When the simulated antenna structure is employed as a load, the dual-resonance circle is slightly shifted clockwise along the 50 Ω constant-resistance circle. This can be adjusted, for example, by slightly reducing the value of C1. However, the frequency response remains very close to optimal. Additionally, nearly perfect agreement between the two curves was achieved with a 1.8 GHz matching center frequency. Thus, the design equations outlined appear to be practical for application with realistic coupling element-based antenna structures. The theoretical relative bandwidth of a single-resonant antenna optimally tuned into dual-resonance with one lossless matching resonator can be expressed as [10]-[13].

$$B_{dr,opt} = \frac{\sqrt{s^2-1}}{Q_0} \tag{3.8}$$

### 3.5.7 Various Multiband Antenna Concepts

Multiband antenna technology is a compelling area for antenna engineers, particularly in the realm of multiband wireless applications. Since the mid-1990s, driven by the needs of multiband and multistandard requirements in mobile applications, multiband antenna technology has emerged as a crucial technology in modern mobile handsets. This section will outline several types of multiband techniques that have been developed and extensively utilized in the mobile industry since the mid-1990s, showcasing the evolution and trends of this antenna technology in the mobile sector.

#### 3.5.7.1 The External Antenna

In 1996, Z. Ying introduced the concept of a dual-band nonuniform helical antenna, which subsequently gained popularity globally for dual-band mobile phones. This helix features quarter wavelengths at the low band, serving as a quarter-wave monopole, and incorporates a nonuniform pitch angle or diameter to regulate the second resonance frequency band. The antenna boasts high efficiency and cost-effectiveness in manufacturing and has been integrated into over a billion mobile devices worldwide. The antenna prototype is depicted in Fig. 3.6.

**Fig. 3.6:** A nonuniform dual band stubby antenna [14]

Around the same period, P. Haapala introduced a dual-band mono-helix antenna. This design incorporates a helix with a straight wire along its central axis. The helix operates at the low band, while the center wire operates at the high band, with both elements nearly a quarter wavelength. This antenna is notable for its extensive use in numerous cellular phones throughout the 1990s.

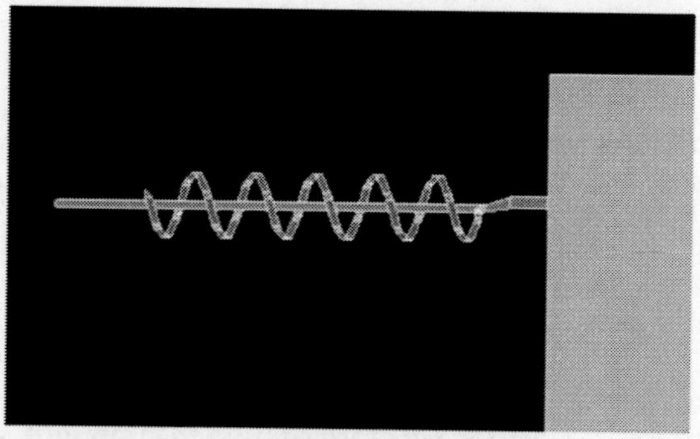

Fig. 3.7 In 1996, P. Haapala invented the mono-helix antenna, a stubby dual-band antenna that became popular [15]

G. Hayes introduced a dual-band performance antenna by combining a meander or helix with a parasitic element. In this design, the antenna's total length functions as a quarter-wave monopole at the low band, while the parasitic element generates the second resonance at the high band. C.G. Blom proposed a spiral broadband impedance transformer to create an effective dual-band stubby antenna, which has since been widely manufactured.

In 1997, Z. Ying introduced a branch multiband antenna featuring a long branch of approximately a quarter wavelength for the low band and a short branch of about a quarter wavelength for the high band. This antenna design, made using the printing technique on meander flex film, is easy to produce and offers good repeatability. The antenna can be rolled to form a stubby antenna or folded into a specific low-profile shape within the chassis to serve as an internal antenna in mobile terminals, as depicted in Fig. 3.7. This antenna type has become a foundational concept.

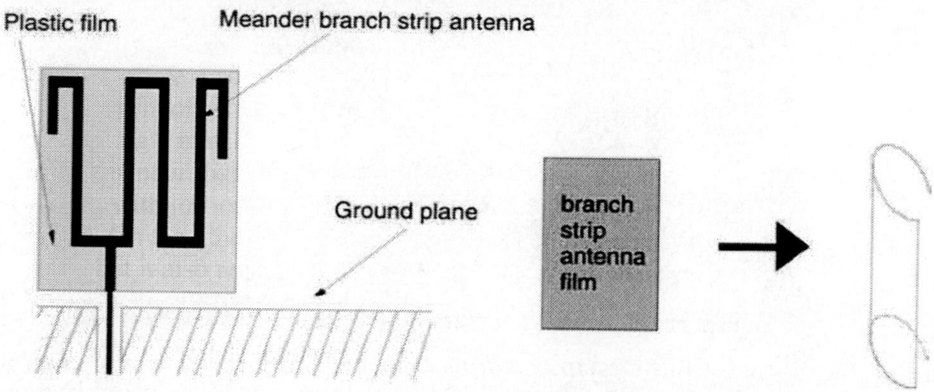


Fig. 3.8 A printed branch meander multiband monopole antenna that can be rolled up to function as a stubby antenna or folded to be used internally [16].

The antenna can be rolled to form a stubby antenna or folded into a specific low-profile shape within the chassis to serve as an internal antenna in mobile terminals, as depicted in Fig. 3.8. This type of antenna became the basic variant of the internal branch meander monopole antenna later on, J. Andersson has proposed several broadband low-profile antennas since 1999, which have become popular choices for implementation as low-profile monopole internal antennas in mobile terminals.

### 3.5.7.2 The Internal Antenna

The use of internal antennas in mobile terminals can enhance their mechanical durability and can also serve as an acoustic cavity, improving audio performance. This aligns with the trend, starting in the late 1990s, of mobile phones evolving into multimedia handsets, contributing to their widespread market acceptance. Presently, external stub antennas are mainly found in low-end models and clamshell phones in the Asian and U.S. markets.

Internal antennas require specific cubic volumes to perform well, limiting their bandwidth due to size constraints. PIFA antennas are more susceptible to detuning when a user's finger is near the antenna element than monopole antennas. Additionally, integration with other components in the terminal makes optimizing internal antennas more complex and time-consuming than optimizing external antennas.

The primary types of internal antennas for stick-type handsets are PIFA antennas and folded monopole antennas. PIFA antennas are typically mounted on a ground plane, possibly with a feeding pin and several ground pins. The ground plane can affect the radiation pattern, especially in the high-frequency range. Fig. 3.8 illustrates a mobile phone equipped with an internal PIFA antenna located at the top of the phone behind the PWB. Folded monopole antennas are often used at the bottom of the handset to minimize head loss, as previously mentioned.

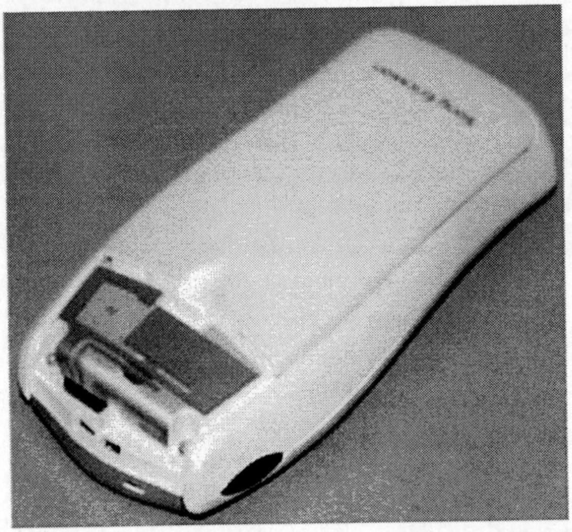

Fig 3.9: A stick mobile phone having an internal multiband PIFA antenna [1].

Foldable phones come in various designs such as clamshell, slide, and swivel styles, making internal antenna design even more complex. The foldable feature leads to variable ground plane sizes, complicating antenna design. Different antenna locations yield varying performance:

## 3.5.8 FREQUENCY-TUNABLE PLANAR MONOPOLE ANTENNA FOR MOBILE TERMINALS

A frequency-tunable planar monopole antenna designed for mobile terminal applications is introduced. The antenna's operating frequency can be electrically switched between the DCS band (1710-1880 MHz) and the WLAN band (2400-2484 MHz). This switching is achieved using an RF pin diode switch positioned in the middle of the antenna. The antenna measures 14 x 15 mm² in size and provides coverage for both bands with a total antenna efficiency margin exceeding 60%. Experimental studies were conducted to analyze the impact of tuning on the antennas' resonant frequency, total antenna efficiency, and radiation pattern. These results were compared with those of reference antennas that lack a tuning circuit.

Planar monopole antennas are extensively used in mobile terminal applications due to their advantages of being low profile, cost-effective, lightweight, and compact. Recent research on planar monopole antennas has focused on developing compact, wide-band, and multiband antenna solutions. However, achieving the desired effective bandwidth can also be accomplished with an antenna that features a tunable operating frequency, especially if it can maintain important radiation characteristics such as total antenna efficiency. The operating frequency of a planar monopole antenna can be tuned electrically, for instance, by switching lengths of resonating strips or by loading the antenna with a variable capacitor.

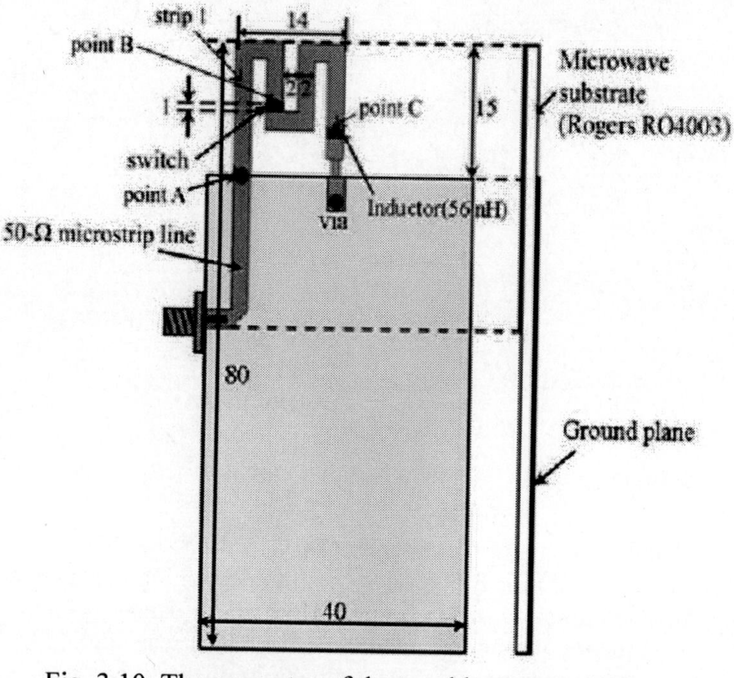


Fig. 3.10 The geometry of the tunable antenna [17].

Fig. 3.10 illustrates the geometry of the tunable antenna. The resonating strip has a meandered shape and is fed with a 50-ohm microstrip line. The antenna is constructed on the top surface of a 65 mm x 40 mm x 0.8 mm reverse-side grounded R4003C printed circuit board (with a dielectric constant of 3.38 and a loss tangent of 0.0027 at 10 GHz). The copper metallization on the board has a thickness of 35 µm. An opening measuring 15 mm x 40 mm in the ground metallization is included to facilitate impedance matching. The frequency tuning is achieved through an RF PIN diode switch integrated into the antenna. By applying either a forward or reverse DC voltage bias to the switch, the electrical length of the resonating strip is altered, allowing the operating frequency to switch between the DCS and WLAN bands. To control the biasing of the diode, the end of the meandered strip is connected to a grounded pad via an inductor (56 nH). This inductor serves as an RF block and a DC short, enabling the supply of DC voltage to the diode alongside the RF signal. The entire length of the resonating strip is responsible for generating the DCS band. The strip's length (from point A to point C in Fig.3.10) is approximately 50 mm, equivalent to 0.3 wavelengths (λ) in free space at 1.8 GHz. Due to the coupling effect between adjacent meandered sections, the physical length of the strip is slightly longer than a quarter wavelength. When the switch is reverse biased (OFF), the physical length of the strip is around 24 mm, equivalent to 0.191 λ at 2.4 GHz.

The antenna was manufactured using a standard photolithography process. An Infineon BAR50-02V RF PIN diode switch and a standard surface-mountable inductor were soldered to the antenna structure. A standard SMA connector was also used to connect the antenna to the measurement cable. The fabricated antenna is depicted in Fig. 3.11.

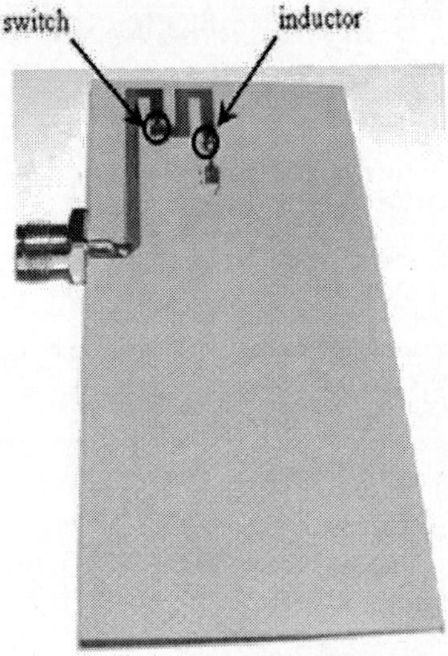


Fig. 3.11. A planar monopole antenna with a switch that can be tuned and fabricated using mender line technology [17].

A small, frequency-tunable planar monopole antenna (14 x 15 mm²) has been proposed and tested in experiments. The antenna includes an RF PIN diode switch for switching between the DCS and WLAN frequency bands. The antenna exhibited high efficiency, with both bands maintaining over 60% total efficiency. The effect of frequency tuning on antenna performance was studied by comparing it with reference antennas lacking a tuning circuit. The tuning circuit resulted in a maximum radiation efficiency reduction of about 20%. However, there was no significant difference in total efficiency between the ON and OFF states of the tunable antenna. It is also noteworthy that the tuning circuit did not significantly alter the shape of the far-field radiation pattern.

## 3.5.9 (a) The Dual Resonance PIFA

In 1997, P. S. Hall introduced a PIFA design comprising two distinct patches of varying sizes to achieve dual-band functionality. This antenna featured separate feedings for the low and high bands [18], with an initial concept of a shared feed for a dual-band PIFA antenna. Subsequent efforts focused on implementing a common feed point for dual-band wireless terminals, which became crucial for many cellular applications in later years.

Between 1997 and 1999, several dual-band PIFA antennas were developed in the mobile phone industry based on a patch with a slot-cutting design, leading to numerous filed patents [19–22]. These antennas were designed to meet the requirements of GSM/DCS dual-band applications within a compact antenna volume. In July 1997, I. A. Korisch proposed a J-shaped dual-band PIFA, while I. Pankinoha suggested a switchable PIFA for multiband applications in the same month. Z. Ying also proposed an internal printed spiral antenna and a dual-band printed antenna in July 1998. Ying's antenna featured two branches of different lengths, operating as a shunt-fed monopole antenna to achieve dual-band performance. Later, in 1998, Ying proposed a slot-cutting version of the antenna. In early 1999, S. Tarvas presented a similar antenna with a single feed and a single shorting pin, utilized in the first commercial dual-band mobile phone featuring an internal antenna. The antenna's current distribution is at the 900-MHz band, with the long arm operating at the low band and the short patch at the high band. The feeding and ground pins form a loop, with the loop size determining the inductance needed to compensate for the patch capacitance and achieve good matching.

The bandwidth of a PIFA antenna has been extensively researched in recent years [23–26]. Several key factors influence the bandwidth:

(i) The size of the antenna element: The bandwidth of a PIFA antenna is influenced by the dimensions of its antenna element, including the patch size and the thickness of the PIFA. Using meander or spiral-shaped loading can help reduce the antenna size but may also decrease the bandwidth. A standard dual-band PIFA antenna element for a cell phone is approximately $20 \times 40$ mm². The thickness of the PIFA is more crucial for enhancing the bandwidth, with typical thicknesses used for cellular bands ranging from 4 to 10 mm. A larger antenna volume allows for a larger bandwidth. Thickness is more critical than the patch area for bandwidth enhancement.

(ii) The location of the feed point: The bandwidth of a PIFA antenna can be influenced by the position of its feed point. The feed point is typically situated at the PCB's edge (Printed Circuit Board). The feed point is often positioned at the end of the handset for cellular antennas.

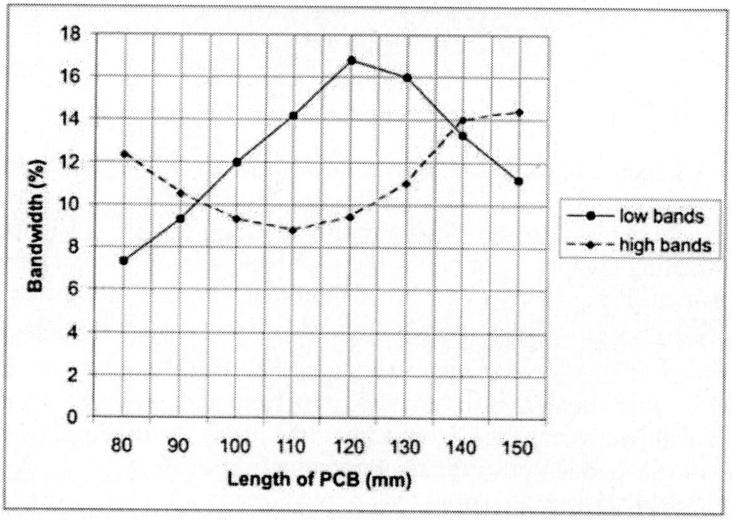


Fig. 3.12 - The bandwidth of a dual-band PIFA antenna is influenced by the length of the PCB (ground plane). For the 900-MHz band, the optimal bandwidth is achieved when the PCB length is approximately 120 mm. In contrast, for the 1,800-MHz band, the optimal bandwidth occurs at PCB lengths of 80 mm and 150 mm.

(iii) The size of the Printed Wiring Board (PWB): As previously discussed, the ground plane of the PWB plays a role in the antenna's performance in a mobile device. It has varying effects on the 900 MHz and 1800 MHz bands. In Fig. 3.12, the bandwidth of a dual-band PIFA antenna (16 × 38 × 8 mm³) is shown with different sizes of the ground plane. It was observed that the bandwidth reaches a maximum when the PWB length is approximately 120 mm for the GSM 900 MHz band. However, for the DCS 1800 MHz band, the bandwidth remains relatively stable, showing good performance with lengths of 80 mm and 140 mm, respectively.

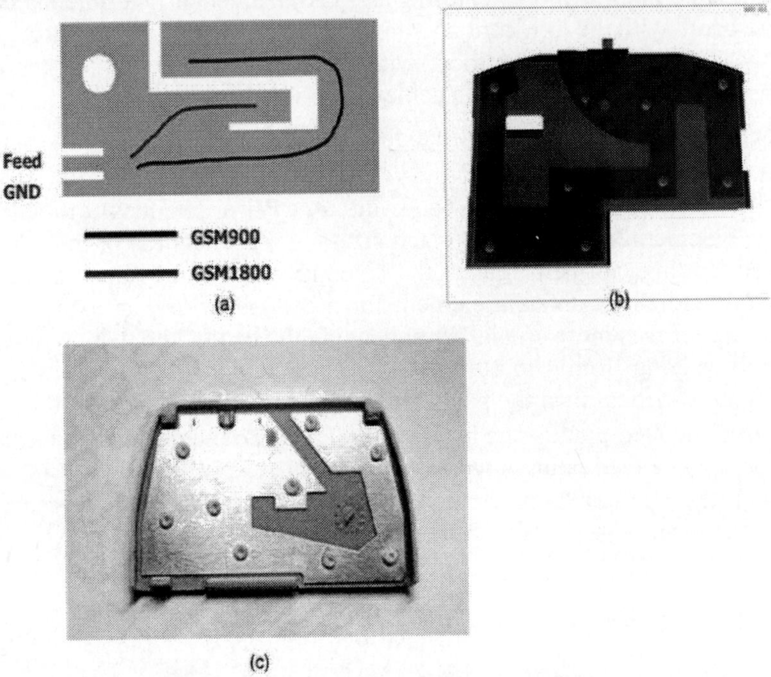


Fig. 3.13 (a) A standard branch Planar Inverted-F Antenna (PIFA) with a long arm for the 900-MHz band and a short arm for the 1,800-MHz band. The additional small part on the left can enhance bandwidth at the high band. (b) The long arm of the branch PIFA is designed to optimize the radiation pattern, providing greater directivity at the high band to reduce signal loss. (c) The widely used center-fed C design enables the low-band branch to resonate at high-band frequencies.

Many branch PIFA antenna designs have been utilized in various products. The figure below shows modified versions of this antenna type with specific characteristics. Fig. 3.13(a) displays a typical branch PIFA featuring a long arm for the 900 MHz band and a short arm for the 1800 MHz band, with an additional small part to enhance bandwidth at the higher band. Fig. 3.13(b) exhibits a branch PIFA with the long arm shaped to optimize radiation pattern, providing more directivity at the high band for reduced head loss. Fig. 3.13(c) illustrates the popular center-fed C design, enabling the low band branch to resonate at higher band frequencies, thereby increasing bandwidth.

## 3.5.9 (b) The Multiresonance PIFA Antenna

To maintain a compact antenna size while meeting the demands of multiband applications, considerable efforts have focused on enhancing the bandwidth of PIFA antennas. One approach involves incorporating additional slots on the patch to create multi-resonant traces, as depicted in Fig. 3.14. By introducing a slot between the feeding and grounding posts, greater bandwidth in the high-frequency range can be achieved. Another method is introducing a parasitic element that couples with the primary antenna, a concept initially proposed by Z. Ying and A. Dalhsto¨rm in 2000. This practical antenna configuration can serve the GSM/DCS/PCS triband application, as illustrated in Fig. 3.15.

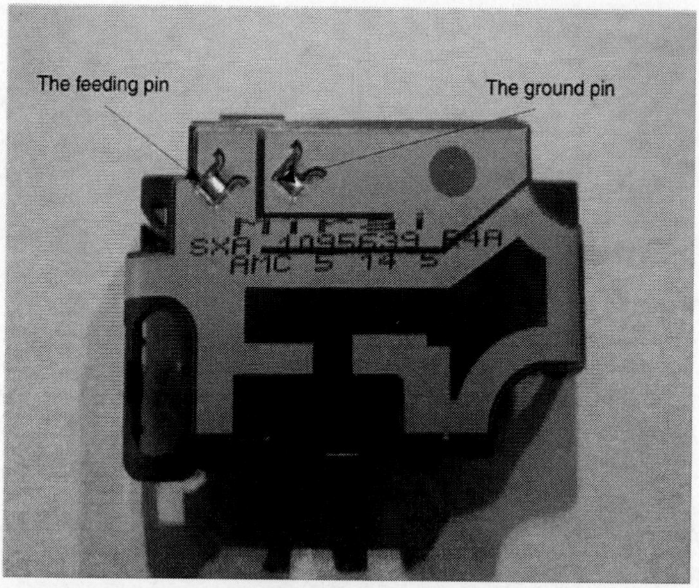


Fig. 3.14 A tri-band PIFA antenna includes a slot positioned between the feeding and ground pins to generate an additional resonance, enhancing the bandwidth in higher frequency bands. (Source: [27]. Courtesy of Laid Technology.)

Efforts to categorize PIFA antenna variants in mobile terminal applications have led to some summarizing work, as depicted in Fig. 3.16. A PIFA antenna with a single slot exhibits dual resonance. A PIFA antenna featuring two slots, one positioned between the feeding and grounding posts, can attain an additional resonance at the high band.

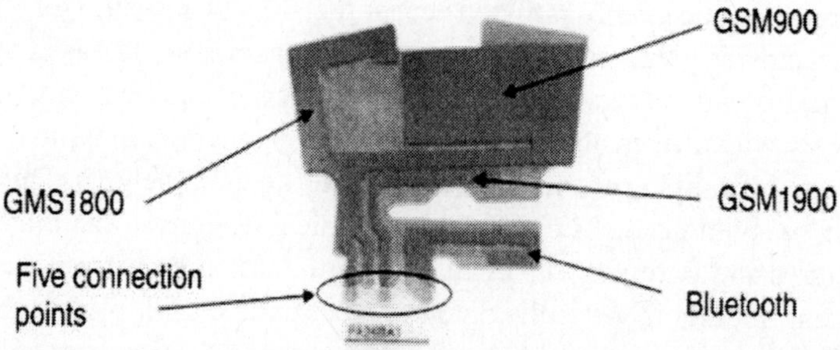


Fig. 3.15 A tri-band PIFA antenna featuring a parasitic element to improve bandwidth in higher frequency bands was proposed by Z. Ying and A. Dalhstorm in 2000. This design has been utilized in numerous high-end mobile devices. Additionally, a 2.4-GHz Bluetooth antenna is incorporated within the same package, achieving an isolation of over 15 dB. (Source: [28]. Courtesy of Sony Ericsson.)

A PIFA antenna incorporating a parasitic element can achieve an extra resonance at the high band. The third design offers a compact solution with three connections and requires strict mechanical tolerances. Conversely, the second design features only two connecting pins, has less stringent mechanical tolerances, and is more straightforward to fabricate.

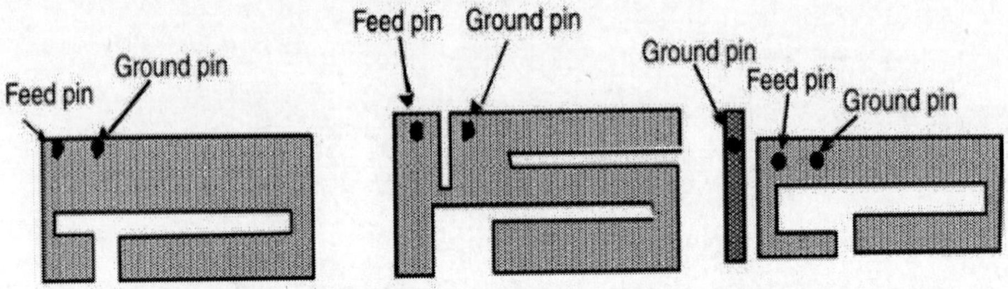


Fig. 3.16: Summary of slot-cutting PIFA antennas: (a) A PIFA antenna with a single slot achieves dual resonance. (b) A PIFA antenna with multiple slots (including one between the feeding and grounding posts) can introduce an additional resonance in the high band. (c) A PIFA antenna incorporating a parasitic element can also add a resonance in the high band (Source: [28]).

## 3.5.10 Base Station Antennas

### 3.5.10.1 System Requirements

The function of antennas in mobile communication systems is to establish a radio link between radio stations, with at least one station typically in motion. Mobile communication systems can be categorized into direct communication between transmitter and receiver and communication via a base station. The latter type has seen significant advancement globally in recent years, encompassing systems like automobile telephone systems, portable telephone systems, and Multichannel Access (MCA) systems for private use. Systems like automobiles and portable telephone systems are structured in a cellular fashion. The relationship between system requirements and necessary antenna technology is depicted in Fig. 3.17. To enable communication between a base station and mobile stations within its service area, radio wave energy must be evenly radiated across the area, necessitating high antenna gain. Since the width of the service area is predetermined, antenna gain cannot be increased by narrowing the beam in the horizontal plane. Instead, narrowing the beam in the vertical plane is essential to enhance gain, a feat achieved effectively with a vertically oriented linear array antenna. In typical cellular systems, base station antennas have gains ranging from 7 to 15 dB, with antenna heights typically between 3m and 5m. Consequently, these antennas require slender mechanical designs to facilitate easy installation and withstand wind pressures and lightning. To enable communication between a base station antenna and multiple mobile stations simultaneously, the antenna must handle multiple channels. This necessitates wide-frequency characteristics and the ability to branch and/or combine channels. For instance, in the Japanese cellular system operating in the 800-MHz band, a single antenna is used for both transmission and reception at the base station. The antenna must have a bandwidth of over 7%, with a specified Voltage Standing Wave Ratio (VSWR) of less than 1.5. Additionally, if the antenna is shared by several systems, a wider frequency bandwidth is required.

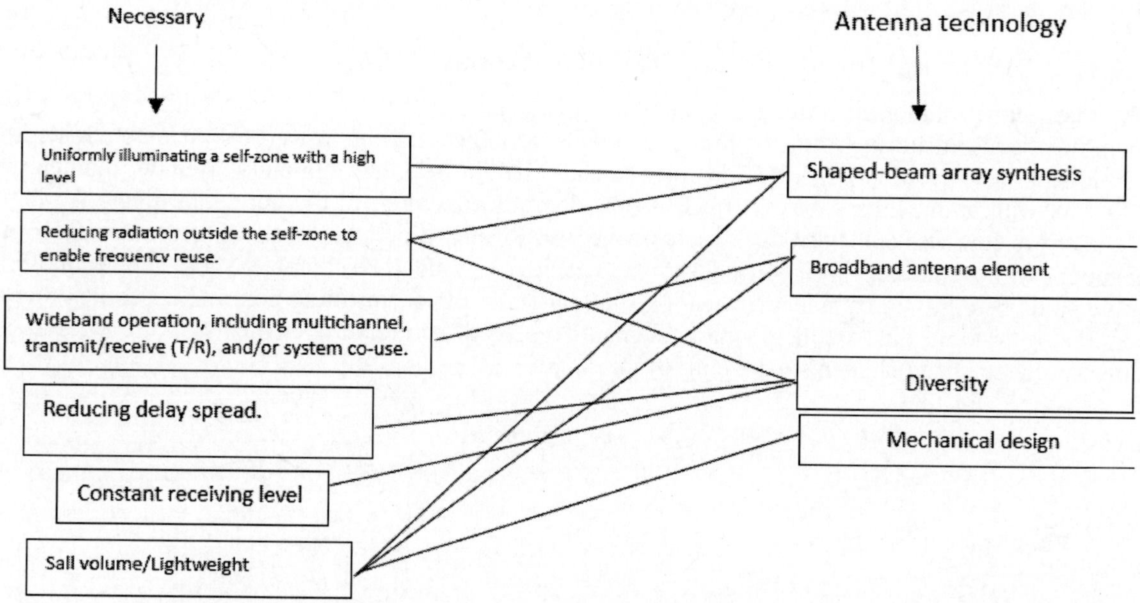


Fig. 3.17: The requirements of the system and the technologies related to antennas.

Table 3.1 illustrates the assigned frequency bands for mobile communication systems in the Japanese Radio Regulation allocations. These bands are grouped into 800, 1,500, and 2,000-MHz bands, highlighting the need for multifrequency band antennas. The evolution of base station antennas and typical multifrequency antenna elements is also outlined.

**Table 3.1** Frequency ranges allocated for mobile communications in Japan.

| Frequency Band (MHz) | Allocated frequency (MHz) |
|---|---|
| 800 | 810-850, 860-901, 915-950 |
| 1500 | 1429-1516 |
| 2000 | 1710-2025, 2110-2200, 2500-2690 |

The rapid increase in demand for communication channels has become a significant issue in metropolitan areas in the United States, Europe, and Japan, necessitating effective technologies for frequency reuse. While cellular systems offer advantages in frequency reuse, their efficiency largely depends on the base station antenna's radiation pattern. Technologies such as main beam tilting and beam shaping have been developed to enhance frequency reuse.

A common challenge in mobile communication is the need for a more direct line of sight between the base station and the mobile station. Additionally, mobile stations operate in complex propagation environments, leading to constant fading and fluctuations in receiving levels, often exceeding 10 dB. Designing systems based on the minimum receiving level leads to excessive device load and high system costs. Diversity reception technology, which has been studied since the 1960s, addresses fading by utilizing multiple antennas to improve signal reliability.

## 3.5.10. 2 Types of Antennas

### 3.5.10.2.1 Historical Trends of Base Station Antennas

The historical evolution of base station antennas in Japan is that the initial base station antenna was omnidirectional, featuring four radiating elements arranged around a vertical axis to create the omnidirectional radiation pattern. This antenna had a height of 5,700 mm and a cylinder diameter of 300 mm, with an antenna gain of 15 dB. A 120-degree beamwidth in the horizontal plane for high-capacity systems was achieved for 3-sector zone use. Printed dipole antennas were used as radiating elements, with excitation coefficients designed to achieve low sidelobe characteristics. The beam tilting angle could be adjusted by selecting beam tilting panels in the beam tilting box. In subsequent digital and analog systems, dual-frequency band elements replaced the radiation elements. In the 3G system, triple-frequency band elements were employed.

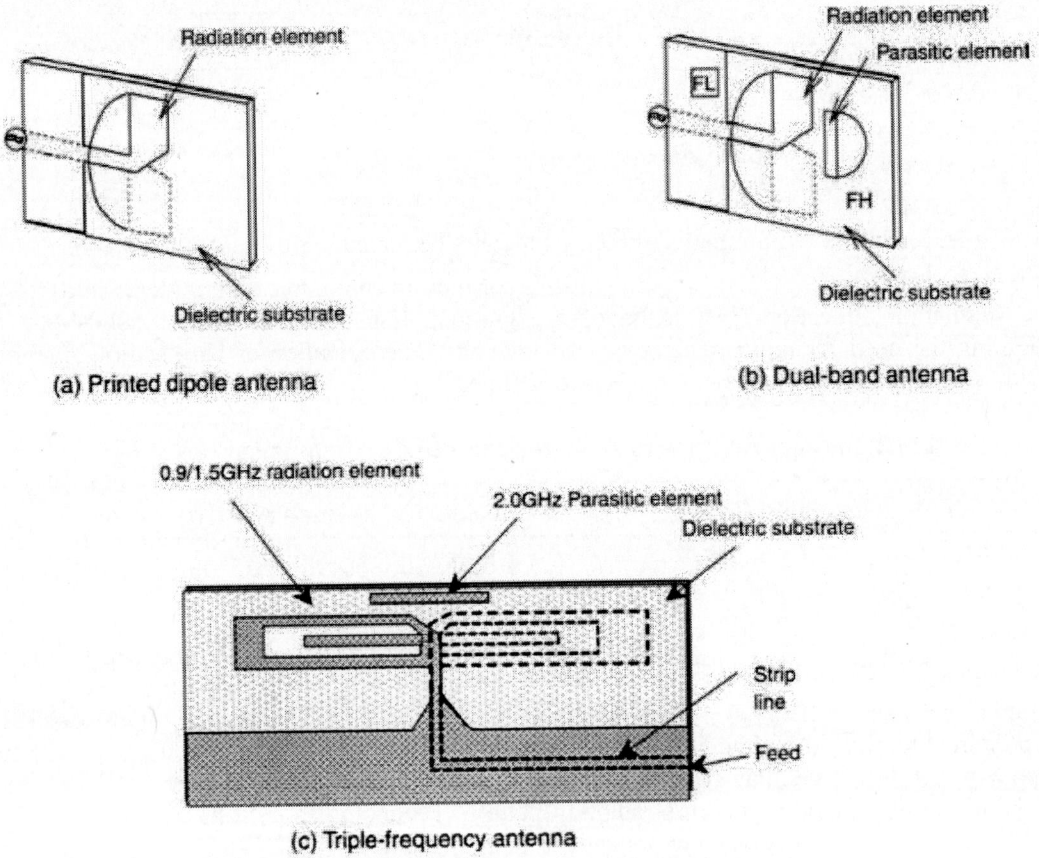


Fig 3.18: Common radiating components found in base station antennas [1].

### 3.5.10.2.2 Types of Radiation Elements

Various types of radiation element antennas commonly used in array antennas for base stations are illustrated in Fig. 3.18(a–c). Fig. 3.18(a) depicts a primary printed dipole antenna with a height of approximately half a wavelength. This antenna exhibits an omnidirectional radiation pattern in the horizontal plane and a figure-eight pattern in the vertical plane. It achieves a relative bandwidth of about 20% for VSWR less than 2. Fig. 3.18(b) shows a dual-frequency band antenna where a parasitic element is coupled to the printed dipole antenna, enabling high-frequency operation. Fig. 3.18(c) demonstrates a triple-frequency band antenna where the printed dipole antenna is designed to operate in multiple frequency bands. When these antennas are element antennas in a base station's array antenna, a small reflector is affixed behind them to create the sector beam.

### 3.5.11 Array Antennas

Driven by the anticipated need for greater capacity and coverage in mobile communication systems, two-dimensional antenna arrays have emerged as a viable solution. These arrays extend horizontally, allowing for the creation of narrow antenna beams in the azimuth plane. This spatial filtering technique reduces interference (improving C/I) and increases network capacity. Additionally, array antennas offer enhanced coverage due to their larger area and higher antenna gain than traditional wide-beam sector antennas. Arrays connected to a base station that can form narrow multibeam or steered beams are often called innovative or adaptive antennas.

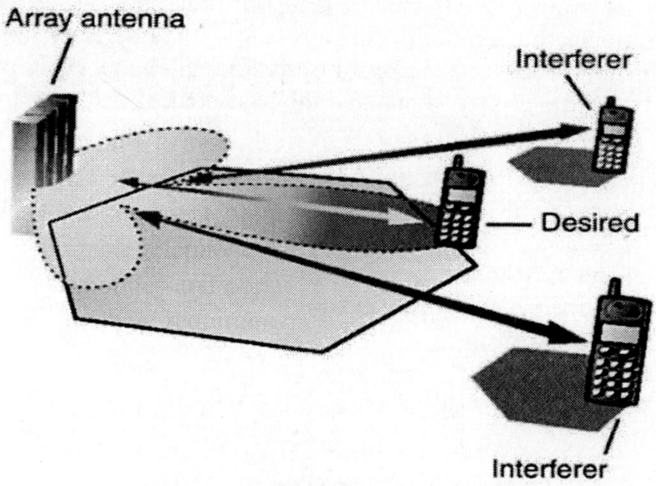


Fig. 3.19: An array antenna used in base stations to suppress interference.

#### 3.5.11.1 Adaptive Antenna

An example of an adaptive antenna is a fixed multibeam array antenna with RF beamforming, depicted in Fig. 3.20. This antenna consists of a dual-polarized five-column array, where four columns are utilized to create narrow interleaved beams in the azimuth direction. In contrast, the fifth column is dedicated to broadcast transmission. The radiating elements are dual-polarized microstrip patches, spaced 0.5 wavelengths apart between columns and 0.9 wavelengths within columns. A triangular grid allows for greater element spacing than a square lattice, avoiding grating lobes in a planar-phased array.

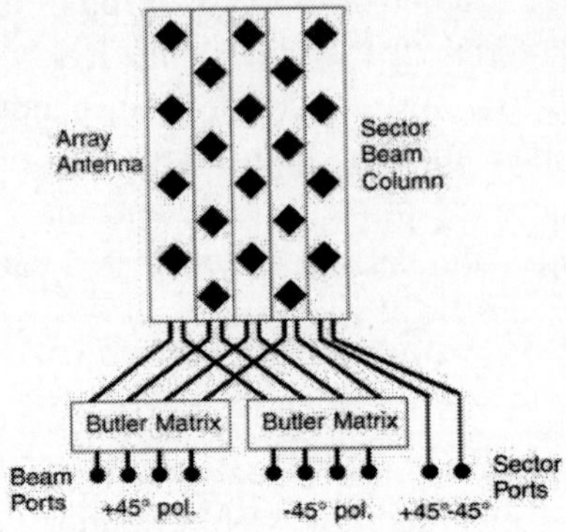


Fig. 3.20: The principle of a fixed dual-polarized multibeam adaptive antenna [29].

These adaptive antennas utilize a fixed multi-beam architecture, where narrow beams are formed within the antenna using RF beamforming networks of the Butler matrix type. The polarization directions employed are slanted ±45° linear orientation. In each polarization, this configuration produces a set of orthogonal beams covering a 120° sector (see Fig. 3.21). In the uplink, the total information from all interleaved beams can be utilized to maximize reception performance and estimate Direction-of-Arrivals (DOA) for communicating terminals. A single beam can be selected for downlink transmission based on the DOA estimate. Choosing a single transmission path helps avoid coherency requirements in the feeder cables between the array antenna and the base station, as the beams are formed at RF in the antenna.

In many communication systems, base stations occasionally need to transmit a control or common channel over the entire sector. This requirement can be met with a separate sector antenna function integrated into the adaptive array antenna system. A practical solution involves using an additional column of radiating elements next to the array antenna columns. It is essential that the sector antenna beam pattern and the array antenna multibeam envelope closely track each other.

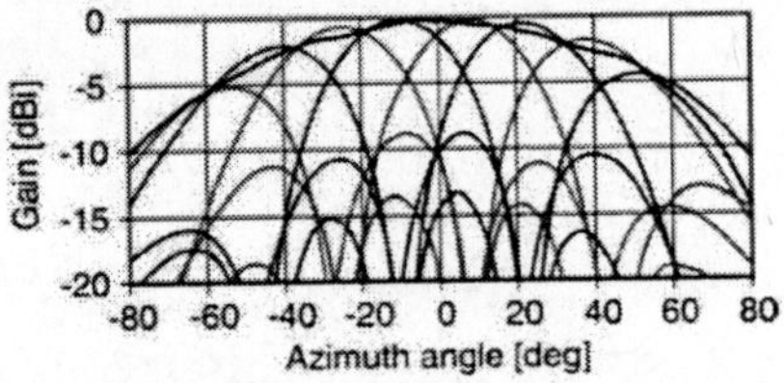


Fig. 3.21 The azimuth radiation patterns of an adaptive array antenna with eight interleaved fixed beams and a sector beam.

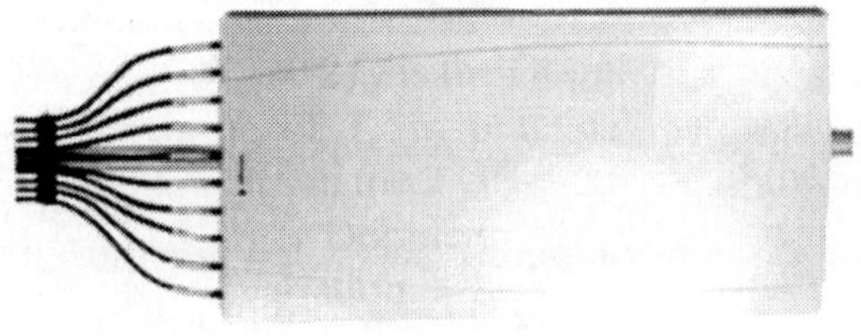

Fig. 3.22: An adaptive array antenna with fixed multiple beams and an integrated sector beam [1].

Thanks to the polarization diversity technique and the integration of sector coverage and narrow beam apertures within the same enclosure, only a single antenna unit is needed in every sector (see Fig. 3.22). This approach reduces aesthetic impact and simplifies the installation procedure, all while significantly improving system performance.

### 3.5.11.2 Cylindrical Antennas

To date, planar antenna arrays have been predominantly used for advanced antenna applications in mobile communication systems. However, there are advantages in many systems to using an antenna that combines high gain and low interference levels with extensive angular coverage. This can be achieved with a cylindrical antenna array as shown in Fig. 3.23, which can direct a narrow beam over a sizeable angular sector. Using such an array prevents pattern degradation over this sector, which would otherwise result in lower gain and broader beams, leading to limitations in capacity and area coverage. In some cases, it may also be beneficial to design the radiating elements of an array antenna in a cylindrical shape. This can be driven by considerations such as wind load or aesthetics, particularly when mounting base station antennas on a pole or cylindrical mast.

Fig. 3.23: Cylindrical array antenna [30].

Before implementing cylindrical antenna arrays, it is essential to fully understand their electromagnetic properties, such as mutual coupling, to facilitate high-quality design. Additionally, the beam-forming properties differ from those of a planar antenna array. A cylindrical array can produce simultaneous narrow and omnidirectional beams with proper feeding.

## UNIT SUMMARY

This unit explores the capacity of flat and frequency-selective fading channels, focusing on their theoretical foundations and practical implications for wireless communication systems. Flat fading, also known as narrowband fading, occurs when the channel's coherence bandwidth exceeds the signal bandwidth, resulting in uniform fading across the signal's spectrum. The capacity of flat fading channels can be analyzed using the Shannon-Hartley theorem, considering the impact of fading. In a flat fading channel, the received signal is affected by the complex channel gain, transmitted signal, and additive white Gaussian noise. The instantaneous Signal-to-Noise Ratio (SNR) at the receiver depends on the channel gain and transmitted power. The instantaneous capacity of a flat fading channel, assuming perfect Channel State Information (CSI) at the receiver, is a function of the SNR. When the fading is ergodic, the average capacity can be computed as the expected value over the distribution of the channel gain, which is often modeled using a Rayleigh distribution in environments with many scatterers. Frequency-selective fading occurs when the coherence bandwidth is smaller than the signal bandwidth, causing different frequency components of the signal to experience varying fading effects. The chapter breaks down the total bandwidth into multiple sub-channels, each with its own channel gain, and examines the instantaneous capacity of each sub-channel. The total capacity of a frequency-selective channel is the sum of the capacities of the individual sub-channels. To maximize this total capacity, the power allocation across sub-channels follows the water-filling algorithm, which distributes power efficiently according to the channel gains. This approach optimizes the overall capacity by balancing the power across sub-channels with varying gains. However, channel inversion, which aims to equalize received power across all channels, can be inefficient and impractical, particularly when the channel gain is low, as it may require excessive power. Understanding these principles is crucial for designing robust communication systems that can handle different fading conditions effectively. The chapter also emphasizes the importance of techniques such as equalization and diversity reception in mitigating the adverse effects of frequency-selective fading. By optimizing power allocation and employing appropriate signal processing methods, communication systems can achieve higher reliability and efficiency. This comprehensive analysis of flat and frequency-selective fading channels provides a foundational understanding for students and practitioners, enabling them to develop more resilient and high-performance wireless communication systems.

## EXERCISE

### Multiple Choice Questions (MCQs)

1. In a flat fading channel, the channel gain:

a) Varies randomly over time and frequency.

b) Remains constant over time and frequency.

c) Increases linearly with time.

d) Decreases exponentially with frequency.

2. The capacity of a flat fading channel depends on:

a) The modulation scheme used.

b) The channel bandwidth.

c) The signal-to-noise ratio.

d) All of the above.

3. Which theorem is used to derive the capacity of fading channels?

a) Shannon-Hartley theorem.

b) Nyquist theorem.

c) Fourier theorem.

d) Bode-Fano theorem.

4. The average capacity of a flat fading channel is calculated by:
a) Integrating the instantaneous capacity over time.
b) Taking the maximum value of the instantaneous capacity.
c) Multiplying the bandwidth by the maximum SNR.
d) Dividing the total transmission power by the noise power.

5. Frequency-selective fading channels exhibit:
a) The same level of fading across all frequencies.
b) Different levels of fading at different frequencies.
c) No fading effects.
d) Constant phase shift across all frequencies.

6. The capacity of a frequency-selective fading channel depends on:
a) The bandwidth.
b) The power spectral density of the transmitted signal.
c) The frequency response of the channel.
d) All of the above.

7. In frequency-selective fading, the water-filling algorithm is used to:
a) Optimize the power allocation across different frequencies.
b) Control the flow of water in the channel.
c) Prevent interference between adjacent frequencies.
d) Filter out noise in the received signal.

8. Which algorithm is used to find the optimal power allocation in frequency-selective fading channels?
a) Maximum likelihood estimation.
b) Least squares algorithm.
c) Water-filling algorithm.
d) Gradient descent algorithm.

9. The capacity of a frequency-selective fading channel is calculated by integrating the instantaneous capacity over:
a) Time.
b) Frequency.

c) Distance.
d) Amplitude.

10. What is the primary advantage of frequency-selective fading over flat fading?
a) Higher capacity.
b) Lower interference.
c) More robustness to noise.
d) Ability to exploit frequency diversity.

11. In frequency-selective fading channels, power allocation is typically higher in frequency regions where:
a) The channel gain is high.
b) The channel gain is low.
c) The noise power is high.
d) The bandwidth is narrow.

12. The water level in the water-filling algorithm represents:
a) The total power transmitted by the sender.
b) The threshold for interference rejection.
c) The optimal power allocation across frequencies.
d) The maximum capacity of the channel.

13. The capacity of a flat fading channel with perfect Channel State Information (CSI) at the receiver is limited by:
a) Interference from adjacent channels.
b) The bandwidth of the channel.
c) The noise power.
d) The fading effects of the channel.

14. Which of the following statements is true about frequency-selective fading channels?

a) They have constant channel gain across all frequencies.
b) They are more susceptible to narrowband interference.
c) They have a flat frequency response.
d) They experience the same level of fading at all frequencies.

15. The capacity of a flat fading channel increases with:

a) Decreasing transmit power.

b) Increasing channel bandwidth.

c) Increasing noise power.

d) Decreasing modulation complexity.

16. Frequency-selective fading channels are commonly found in:

a) Wireless LANs.

b) Fiber optic communication.

c) Satellite communication.

d) Audio

**Answers**

1. b) Remains constant over time and frequency.
2. d) All of the above.
3. a) Shannon-Hartley theorem.
4. a) Integrating the instantaneous capacity over time.
5. b) Different levels of fading at different frequencies.
6. d) All of the above.
7. a) Optimize the power allocation across different frequencies.
8. c) Water-filling algorithm.
9. b) Frequency.
10. d) Ability to exploit frequency diversity.
11. a) The channel gain is high.
12. c) The optimal power allocation across frequencies.
13. c) The noise power.
14. b) They are more susceptible to narrowband interference.
15. b) Increasing channel bandwidth.
16. a) Wireless LANs.

**KNOW MORE**

***For more information related to this topic scan the QR code.***

**OR**

***Type this link in your browser***

**https://archive.nptel.ac.in/courses/108/101/108101092/**

## REFERENCE


1 Fujimoto, Kyohei. Mobile Antenna Systems Handbook. Artech House, 2008.

2 Kramer, B. A., et al, " Fundamental limits and design guidelines forminiaturizing ultra-wideband antennas," IEEE Antennas and Propagation Magazine vol. 51, no.4, pp. 57-69, 2009.

3 Vainikainen, Pertti, et al. Resonator-based analysis of the combination of mobile handset antenna and chassis. IEEE transactions on antennas and propagation vol. 50, no.10 pp.1433-1444, 2002.

4 Vainikainen, P., Ollikainen, J., Kivekäs, O. and Kelander, I., 2000. Performance analysis of small antennas mounted on mobile handset. In COST-259 Final Workshop-The Mobile Terminal and Human Interaction, Bergen, Norway, pp. 8, April, 2000.

5 Vainikainen, Pertti, et al. Radiolaitteen modulaarinen kytkentärakenne ja kannettava radiolaite (Modular coupling structure), 2004.

6 Villanen, Juha. Miniaturization and Evaluation Methods of Mobile Terminal Antenna Structures. Helsinki University of Technology, 2007

7 Villanen, Juha, and Pertti Vainikainen. The design of optimum impedance matching networks for coupling element based antenna structures. IEEE Antennas and Propagation Society International Symposium. IEEE, 2007.

8 Ollikainen, J. Design and Implementation Techniques of Wideband Mobile Communications Antennas. Ph.D. dissertation, Helsinki University of Technology, Radio Laboratory, Espoo, pp. 70, November, 2004.

9 Ollikainen, Jani, and Pertti Vainikainen. Design and bandwidth optimization of dual-resonant patch antennas, 2002.

10 Witt FJ. Optimum lossy matching networks for resonant antennas. InDigest on Antennas and Propagation Society International Symposium pp. 1360-1363, Jun 26,1989.

11 Witt, F. J. Optimum lossy broadband matching networks for resonant antennas. RF Design, vol.13, no.4, pp.44-51, 1990.

12 Anguera Pros, Jaume, et al. An optimum method to design probe-fed single-layer single-path wideband microstrip antenna, 2000.

13 Ollikainen, Jani, and Pertti Vainikainen. Design and bandwidth optimization of dual-resonant patch antennas, 2002.

14 Egorov, Igor, and Zhinong Ying. A non-uniform helical antenna for dual-band cellular phones. IEEE Antennas and Propagation Society International Symposium. Transmitting Waves of Progress to the Next Millennium. Digest. Held in conjunction with: USNC/URSI National Radio Science Meeting, Vol. 2, 2000.

15 Haapala, P. Helical Antennas for Multi-Mode Mobile Phones. Patent, EP-747990, June, 1995.

16 Ying, Z. Multi-Band Branch Meander Antenna. International Patent, WO-09922419, WO-09922420, US-6329962 (granted first in USA), October 1997.

17 Palukuru, V. K., et al. Frequency-tunable planar monopole antenna for mobile terminals. The Second European Conference on Antennas and Propagation, EuCAP. IET, 2007.

18 Liu, Zi Dong, Peter S. Hall, and David Wake. Dual-frequency planar inverted-F antenna. IEEE Transactions on Antennas and Propagation vol.45, no.10, pp. 1451-1458, 1997.

19 Korisch, Ilya A. Planar dual frequency band antenna, U.S. Patent No. 5,926,139, 20 Jul, 1999.

20 Geerert, F. Dual Band Antenna for a Hand Portable Telephone and a Corresponding Hand Portable Telephone. European Patent, EP-1018777, December 10, 1999.

21 Pankinaho, I. Double Resonance Antenna Structure for Several Frequency Ranges. U.S. Patent, US-6140966, October 31, 2000.

22 Ying, Z. Printed Twin Spiral Dual Band Antenna. International Patent, (granted first in USA), US-006166694, WO-200003452, July 1998.

23 Salonen, Pekka, Mikko Keskilammi, and Markku Kivikoski. New slot configurations for dual-band planar inverted-F antenna. Microwave and Optical Technology Letters vol.28, no.5, pp. 293-298, 2001.

24 Viratelle, D., and Richard J. Langley. Dual-band printed antenna for mobile telephone applications. IEE Proceedings-Microwaves, Antennas and Propagation vol.147, no.5, pp.381-384, 2000.

25 Martinez-Vazquez, Marta, Matthias Geissler, and Dirk Heberling. Volume considerations in the design of dual-band handset antennas. IEEE Antennas and Propagation Society International Symposium. Digest. Held in conjunction with: USNC/URSI National Radio Science Meeting (Cat. No. 01CH37229). Vol. 2, 2001.

26 Hsiao, Fu-Ren, et al. A dual-band planar inverted-F patch antenna with a branch-line slit. Microwave and Optical Technology Letters vol.32, no.4, pp.310-312, 2002.

27 Ishimiya, Katsunori, Jun-ichi Takada, and Zhinong Ying. Progress of multi-band antenna technology for mobile phone. Antennas and Propagation Society International Symposium. IEEE, 2007.

28 Ying, Z. Some Important Antenna Innovations in the Mobile Terminal Industry in the Last Decade. Proceedings of EuCAP, Nice, France, November, 2006.

29 Liberti, J. C., Jr., and T. S. Rappaport. Smart Antennas for Wireless Communications: IS-95 and Third CDMA Applications. Englewood Cliffs, NJ: Prentice Hall, 1999.

30 Raffaelli, S., M. Johansson, and B. Johannisson. Cylindrical Array Antenna Demonstrator for WCDMA Application. Proc. International Conference on Electromagnetics in Advanced Applications, ICEAA, Torino, Italy, September, 2003.

# 4 Multiple Access Techniques

## UNIT SPECIFICS

*In this Unit we will be discussing following aspects:*

- *Multiple access schemes,*
- *FDMA, TDMA, CDMA, and SDMA,*
- *Modulation schemes- BPSK, QPSK,*
- *Variants, QAM, MSK and GMSK,*
- *multicarrier modulation, OFDM.,*

*The practical applications of the topics are discussed for generating further curiosity and creativity as well as improving problem solving capacity.*

*Besides giving a large number of multiple choice questions as well as questions of short and long answer types marked in two categories following lower and higher order of Bloom's taxonomy, assignments through a number of numerical problems, a list of references and suggested readings are given in the unit so that one can go through them for practice. It is important to note that for getting more information on various topics of interest some QR codes have been provided in different sections which can be scanned for relevant supportive knowledge.*

*After the related practical, based on the content, there is a "Know More" section. This section has been carefully designed so that the supplementary information provided in this part becomes beneficial for the users of the book. This section mainly highlights the initial activity, examples of some interesting facts, analogy, history of the development of the subject focusing the salient observations and finding, timelines starting from the development of the concerned topics up to the recent time, applications of the subject matter for our day-to-day real life or/and industrial applications on variety of aspects, case study related to environmental, sustainability, social and ethical issues whichever applicable, and finally inquisitiveness and curiosity topics of the unit.*

**RATIONALE**

*This unit on baseband receiver helps students to get a primary idea about the optimum detection of signa. We have first started with the elements of estimation detection theory, where we have introduced basic of detection. Then, we have covered probability of error evaluation, baseband pulse transmission and intersymbol interference and Nyquist criterion in a detailed manner.*

*Pulse modulation is a type of analogue modulation technique which is employed on discrete information signals. The continuous signals which are obtained from nature can be converted to discrete signals with the help of sampling as is explained in this chapter.at the end of this chapter we will understand the advantages of pulse modulation, various effects which deteriorate the performance and then later on as we progress, we will learn about the ways to mitigate them.*

**PRE-REQUISITES**

*Basics of Mathematics: Calculus (Class XII) &*

*Physics: Basic of Communication (Class XII)*

**UNIT OUTCOMES**

*After completion of this Unit students will be able to:*

*U4-O1: Study of multiple access techniques and different modulation schemes.*

*U4-O2: Explain different variant modulation schemes.*

*U4-O3: Describe multicarrier modulation.*

*U4-O4: Explain orthogonal frequency modulation (OFDM).*

| Unit-4 Outcomes | EXPECTED MAPPING WITH COURSE OUTCOMES (1- Weak Correlation; 2- Medium correlation; 3- Strong Correlation) | | | | | |
|---|---|---|---|---|---|---|
| | CO-1 | CO-2 | CO-3 | CO-4 | CO-5 | CO-6 |
| U4-O1 | 2 | 3 | 3 | - | 3 | 1 |
| U4-O2 | 1 | 2 | 2 | - | 1 | 1 |
| U4-O3 | 1 | 2 | 3 | - | 2 | 1 |
| U4-O4 | - | 3 | 3 | - | 3 | 1 |

## 4.1 MULTIPLE ACCESS

The term "multiple access" refers to the sharing of a Communication Resource (CR) be its frequency or time or space or code associated with the resource. In order to save each block of time/frequency/space/code resource, it is important to plan out resource allocation among users in an equitable manner.

There are three methods to increase the total data rate of CR. The first method is to provide more channel bandwidth. The second method is either reduce system losses or to increase the transmitter's Effective Isotropic Radiated Power (EIRP) in order to increase the Signal-to-Noise Ratio (SNR) of received signal. The third method is the discipline of multiple access communication. The basic methods of CR distribution are as follows:

1. Frequency division multiple access (FDMA): This technique divides the available bandwidth into sub-frequency bands, each allocated to a different user. It is commonly used in traditional analog cellular systems and satellite communication.
2. Time division multiple access (TDMA): Periodically recurring time slots are identified. Users are provided a fixed assignment in time. This method is widely used in digital cellular systems, such as Global System for Mobile Communications (GSM).
3. Code division multiple access (CDMA): CDMA allows multiple users to occupy the same time and frequency band by assigning unique set of orthogonal or non-orthogonal spread spectrum code codes to each user. This technique is used in 3G cellular networks and Global Positioning System (GPS).
4. Space Division Multiple Access (SDMA) or multiple beam frequency reuse: This technique uses spatial separation to differentiate users, often using multiple beam antennas. It allows the reuse of the same frequency band. SDMA is employed in advanced wireless communication systems, including MIMO (multiple input multiple output) technologies.

The key to all multiple access schemes is ensuring that different signals utilize a shared CR without causing excessive interference that hinders their detection. The allowable limit of such interference is that the signal on one resource should not significantly increase the probability of error in another channel. Orthogonal signals on different channels will prevent interference among users. Signal waveforms $x_i(t)$, where $i = 1, 2, ...,$ are orthogonal in time domain if

$$\int_{-\infty}^{\infty} x_i(t)x_j(t)\,dt = \begin{cases} K & for\, i = j \\ 0 & otherwise \end{cases} \tag{4.1}$$

where $K$ is a nonzero constant. Similarly, the function $X_i(f)$ is the Fourier transform of signal waveforms $x_i(t)$ can be orthogonal in frequency domain if

$$\int_{-\infty}^{\infty} X_i(f)X_j(f)\,df = \begin{cases} K & for\, i = j \\ 0 & otherwise \end{cases} \tag{4.2}$$

The channelization, defined by orthogonal waveforms, as shown in Eq. (4.1) is called TDMA, and the channelization characterized by orthogonal spectra, as shown in Eq. (4.2) is called FDMA.

### 4.1.1 Frequency Division Multiple Access (FDMA)

In the early 1900s, FDMA technology enabled the simultaneous transmission of multiple telephone signals over a single wire, and thereby transformed telephone transmission methods. The first generation, i.e., 1G cellular standards were based on FDMA. The CR is illustrated in Fig. 4.1 as the frequency-time plane. The characterized spectrum shown here is an example of FDMA. The FDMA system divides the signalling dimensions along the frequency axis, and each frequency channel is assigned to each user. For example, if the channel bandwidth is 1MHz and number of users be 10, then each user is given bandwidth of 100kHz, i.e. Each user is assigned one independent frequency band of 100kHz, and the channel bandwidth is divided into 10 sub-frequency bands. Since the exact (Sharpe) cutoff is not possible in practice, the filter being imperfect lead for spectral spreading due to doppler and adjacent channel interference. To circumvent this problem sufficient guard band are proposed as shown in Fig. 4.1. A Guard band is present between each adjacent frequency channel, acting as buffer zones to reduce interference. Each user has its assigned frequency band for the entire duration of the communication session. This ensures real-time transmission without the need for time-sharing mechanisms termed as full time slot.

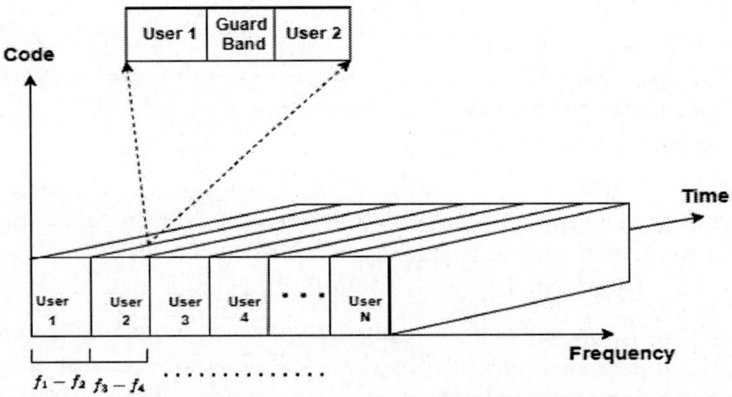


Fig. 4.1: Frequency-division multiple access

We might ask: how does one transform a baseband signal to passband signal? The answer is heterodyning or mixing, also known as modulating, the signal with a fixed frequency from a sine-wave oscillator. If two sinusoidal input signals are mixed with frequencies $f_a$ and $f_b$, the mixing or multiplication will produce new frequencies at $f_{a+b}$ and $f_{a-b}$. The trigonometric identity

$$cosA\ cosB = \frac{1}{2}[\cos(A+B) + \cos(A-B)] \quad (4.3)$$

A simple FDMA example with three translated voice channels is illustrated in Fig. 4.2. In channel 1, the 250 to 2500 Hz voice signal is mixed with a 20 kHz oscillator. In channels 2 and 3, a similar voice signal is mixed with 15 kHz and 10 kHz oscillators, respectively. Only the lower sidebands are retained; the result of mixing and filtering (to remove the upper sidebands) produces the frequency-shifted voice signals ranging from 17.5 kHz to 19.75 kHz, 12.5 kHz to 14.5 kHz and 7.5 kHz to 9.75 kHz as shown in Fig. 4.2. The composite output waveform is the sum of the three lower sideband signals, with a total bandwidth range 7.5 to 19.75 kHz. To tune different channel carrier FDMA requires frequency aligned radios. It is commonly used for analogue communication system in case of continuous transmission and for cellular phone standard serve as basis of AMPS and ETACS. Under FDMA, for a user, it is difficult to assign multiple channels due to the difficulty of demodulating at different frequencies simultaneously. The main advantage of FDMA compared to TDMA is that FDMA channels do not require synchronization or central timing. Each channel operates almost independently of all other channels.

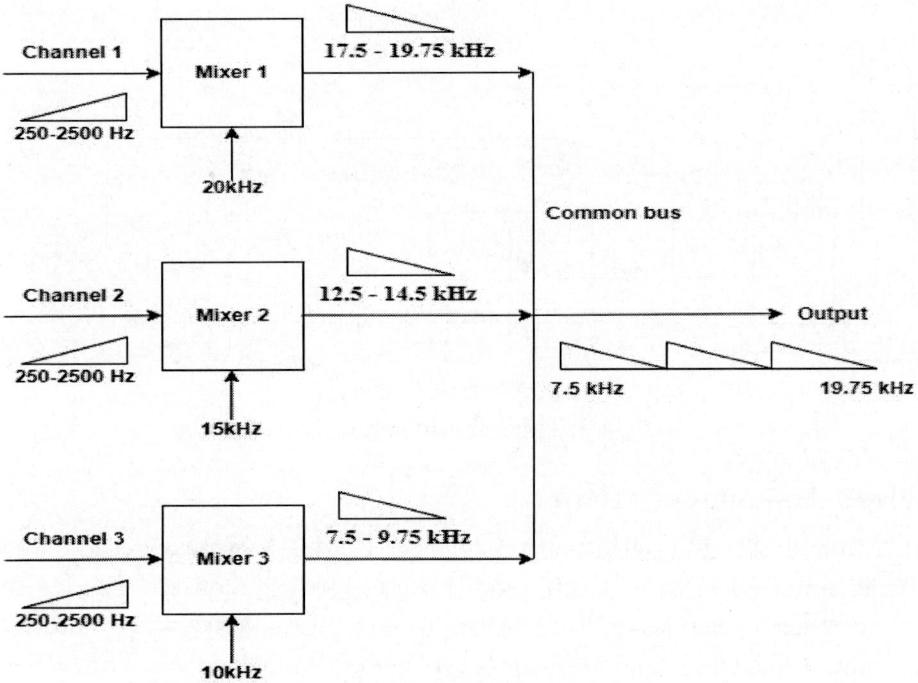


Fig. 4.2: Simple FDMA example. Three frequency-shifted voice channels.

### 4.1.2 Time-Division Multiple Access (TDMA)

In TDMA, information is transmitted over a non-overlapping channel having different time slots. The division of the system dimensions is done along the time axis by occupying the full spectrum of the system as shown in Fig. 4.3. Each user is assigned a different non-overlapping time slot. The unused time regions between slot assignments, known as guard times, provide a buffer for time uncertainty between signals in adjacent time slots, reducing interference. Time is segmented into intervals called frames, which are further divided into user time slots. This frame structure repeats, so a fixed TDMA assignment consists of one or more slots that regularly appear in each frame. This cyclic repetition leads to a non-continuous transmission for any user. The multipath propagation of the signal destroys both uplink and downlink time division orthogonality due to the significant delay in the time slot. To conserve orthogonality, TDMA channels are assigned guard bands for multipath and synchronization error compensation. In each cycle, Changes in channel characteristics with time slots repetition is another challenge of TDMA, which can be corrected by implementing equalization on each cycle to re-estimate the channel to maintain continuous and efficient transmission.

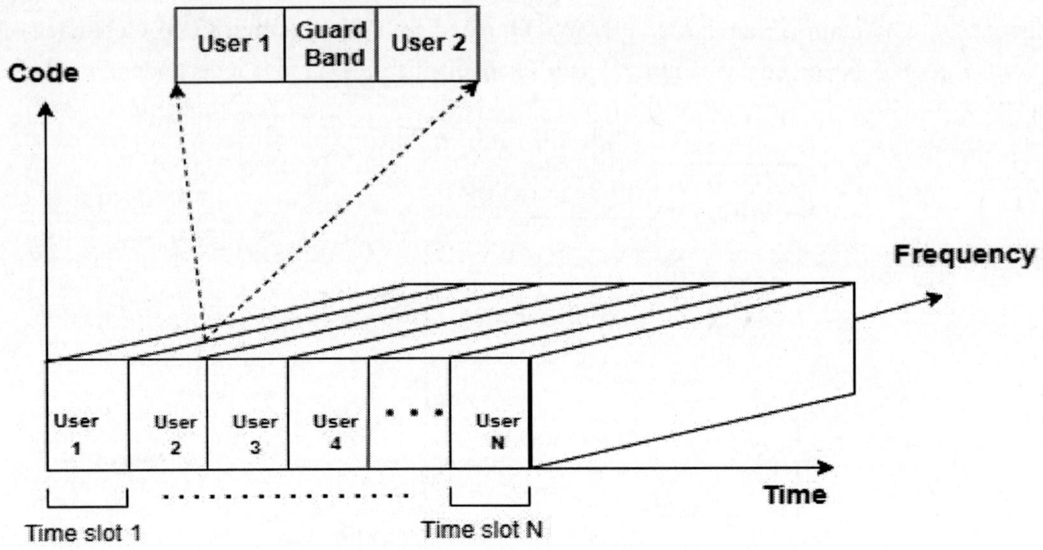


Fig. 4.3: Time-division multiple access

### 4.1.2.1 Fixed-Assignment TDMA

The simplest form of TDMA, called fixed assignment TDMA, named so, because the N time slots within a frame are preallocated to specific signal source for long term use. Fig. 4.4 shows a block diagram of the system operations. In this scheme, the multiplexing process allows each source to use one or more slots, while the demultiplexing process involves deslotting the information and delivering it to the intended destination. The two commutating switches in Fig. 4.4 must be synchronized so that, for instance, the message from source 1 appears at the output of channel 1, and so on. Typically, the message comprises a preamble portion and a data portion, with the preamble portion containing synchronization, addressing, and error control sequences. The fixed assignment TDMA scheme is highly efficient when source requirements are predictable, and traffic is heavy (the time slots are fully occupied). However, this scheme is inefficient for bursty traffic or infrequent patterns of data transmission.

Consider the simple example shown in Fig. 4.5. In this scenario, there are four time slots per frame, allocated to users A, B, C, and D, respectively. Fig. 4(a) shows the typical activity profile of these four users. In the first frame time, user C has no data to transmit; in the second time frame, user B has no data to transmit; and in the third time frame, user A has no data to transmit. In a fixed assignment TDMA scheme, all slots within a frame are preassigned. If the "owner" of a slot has no data to send during a particular frame, that slot goes unused. The data stream in Fig. 4(b) demonstrates these wasted time slots. When source requirements are unpredictable, as illustrated in this example, more efficient schemes can be employed by dynamic assignment of slots instead of using a fixed assignment. These schemes are known as packet-switched systems, statistical multiplexers, or concentrators. As shown in Fig. 4(c), the result is that all slots in a frame are utilized, conserving capacity.

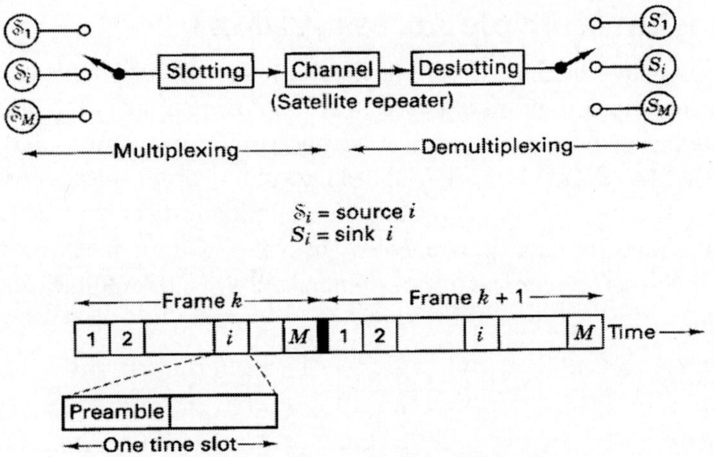


Fig. 4.4 Fixed-assignment TDMA

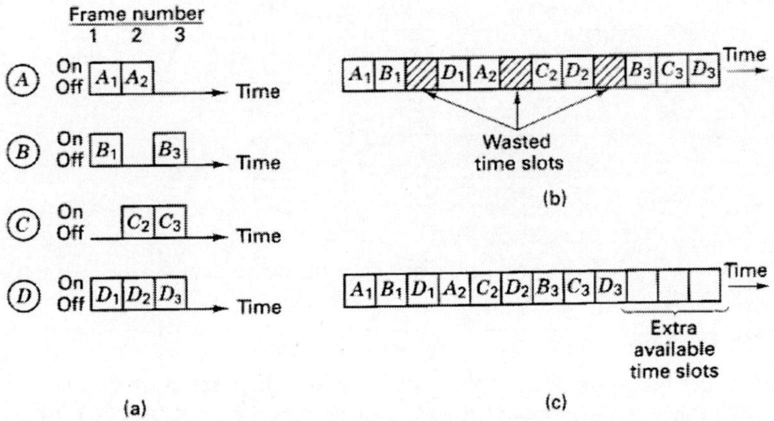


Fig. 4.5 Fixed-assignment TDMA versus packet switching. (a) Data source activity profile. (b) Fixed-assignment TDMA. (c) Time-division packet switching

By assigning multiple time slots to a user, multiple channels can be allocated to that user. Inter-symbol interference (ISI) mitigation is necessary in TDMA. A major challenge of the TDMA technique is the synchronization requirement for different users in the uplink communication due to the fact that the signals are transmitted with different delays over respective channels. However, in the downlink scenario, the signal passes through the same channel from the transmitter to the receiver. For flat fading, the receiver will maintain orthogonality if the signal is transmitted on orthogonal time slots, which can be achieved after synchronized transmission of the signal through the channel coordinated by the axis point or base station. The TDMA channel might be affected by slow narrowband fading, but it also has advantages such as less severe crosstalk problems, full utilization of available channel bandwidth, simple circuitry, and the absence of intermodulation distortion.

### 4.1.3 Code Division Multiple Access (CDMA)

CDMA is considered a path-breaking wireless technology. It was first implemented in the second-generation IS-95 cellular standard, primarily used in North America under the brand name cdmaOne. CDMA also serves as the foundation for several advanced third-generation (3G) cellular standards, including Wideband CDMA (WCDMA), High-Speed Downlink Packet Access (HSDPA), High-Speed Uplink Packet Access (HSUPA), CDMA 2000, and 1x Evolution Data Optimized (1xEV-DO). CDMA allows multiple users to transmit data simultaneously over the same frequency band as shown in Fig. 4.6. This enables multiple users to communicate simultaneously, increasing the efficiency and capacity of the wireless network.

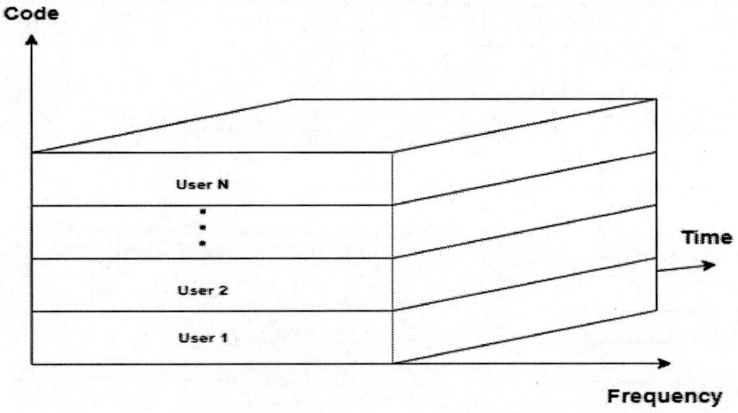


Fig. 4.6: Code-division multiple access

#### Basic CDMA Mechanism

CDMA, as indicated by its name, is a multiple-access technology based on code division. This means that different users are multiplexed using distinct codes. Consider a scenario with two users accessing the radio channel simultaneously. Let $a_0$ represent the symbol of user 0, while $a_1$ represents the transmit symbol of user 1. The code $c_0$ for user 0 is given as $c_0 = = [1,1,1,1]$, This code $c_0$ has a length of $L = 4$ chips, where each element of the code is called a chip. The transmitted signal $x_0$ for user 0 is obtained by multiplying the code $c_0$ with the symbol $i_0$ as:

$$\begin{aligned} x_0 &= a_0 \times [1,1,1,1] \\ &= [a_0, a_0, a_0, a_0] \end{aligned} \tag{4.4}$$

The structure of the transmitted signal $x_0$ can be understood as follows: The symbol $a_0$ of user 0 is multiplied by the code $c_0$ to generate 4 chips $x_0(i), 0 \leq i \leq L - 1$. Similarly, consider the code $c_1$, given as $c_1 = [1,1,-1,-,1]$, which corresponds to the code for user 1. Hence, the sequence of chips for user 1's transmission is given as:

$$\begin{aligned} x_1 &= a_1 \times [1,1,-1,-1] \\ &= [a_1, a_1, -a_1, -a_1] \end{aligned} \tag{4.5}$$

The signals $x_0$and $x_1$, corresponding to users 1 and 2 respectively, are now summed to produce the net signal $x$.

$$x = x_0 + x_1 = [(a_0 + a_1), (-a_0 + a_1), (a_0 - a_1), (a_0 - a_1)] \tag{4.6}$$

This combined, or composite, signal is then transmitted on the downlink channel, from which users 0 and 1 detect their own signals. This process works as follows: User 1 correlates the received signal $x$ with code $c_0$. Specifically, each chip of the received signal $x$ is multiplied by the corresponding chip of the code $c_0$= [1,1,1,1], and the results are summed across the chips as follows.

$$\begin{array}{ccccc} & a_0 + a_1 & a_0 + a_1 & a_0 - a_1 & a_0 - a_1 \\ \times & 1 & 1 & 1 & 1 \\ \hline \end{array} \tag{4.7}$$

$$\boxed{(\boldsymbol{a_0} + \boldsymbol{a_1}) + (\boldsymbol{a_0} + \boldsymbol{a_1}) + (\boldsymbol{a_0} - \boldsymbol{a_1}) + (\boldsymbol{a_0} - \boldsymbol{a_1})} = \mathbf{4}\boldsymbol{a_0}$$

The outcome of the above correlation is $4a_0$, which is directly related to the transmitted symbol $a_0$ . Likewise, at user 1, the received signal $x$ is correlated with the chip sequence $c_1$= $[1,1,-1,-1]$ of user 1

$$\begin{array}{ccccc} & a_0 + a_1 & a_0 + a_1 & a_0 - a_1 & a_0 - a_1 \\ \times & 1 & 1 & -1 & -1 \\ \hline \end{array} \tag{4.8}$$

$$\boxed{(\boldsymbol{a_0} + \boldsymbol{a_1}) + (\boldsymbol{a_0} + \boldsymbol{a_1}) - (\boldsymbol{a_0} - \boldsymbol{a_1}) - (\boldsymbol{a_0} - \boldsymbol{a_1})} = \mathbf{4}\boldsymbol{a_1}$$

results in $4a_1$, which is directly proportional to the transmitted symbol $a_1$ of user 1. Unlike in GSM or FDMA, where signals from different users are transmitted in separate time slots or frequency bands, CDMA integrates all users' signals into a single signal $x$ across time and frequency. However, in CDMA, the symbols of different users are combined using distinct codes. For example, in the above scenario, the symbols $a_0$and $a_1$ of users 0 and 1 are multiplied with codes $c_0$ and $c_1$ before transmission. Consequently, users of different signals are multiplexed over the common wireless channel employing different codes. This approach is termed CDMA, wherein multiple access is based on different codes. The essential operations in CDMA can be summarized as follows.

1. Multiply or modulate the symbols of different users with their corresponding unique codes, similar to the process outlined in Eq. (4.4) and (4.5).
2. Combine or add the code-modulated signals of all users to create the composite signal, as depicted in Eq. (4.6), followed by subsequent transmission of this signal.
3. Finally, correlate the composite received signal $x$ at each user with the corresponding user code to retrieve the transmitted symbol, as detailed in Eq. (4.7) and (4.8).

## Multi-User CDMA

Let us analyse multi-use CDMA performance. Using $a_0$ and $a_1$ to represent the symbols of users 0 and 1 respectively, and denoting the transmit powers of the users be $\mathrm{E}\{|a_0|^2\} = P_0$ and $\mathrm{E}\{|a_1|^2\} = P_1$, the downlink signals $x_0$ and $x_1$ for user 0 and user 1 are obtained by respectively modulating $a_0$ and $a_1$ with their corresponding spreading sequences $c_0$ and $c_1$ as

$$x_0(n) = a_0 c_0(n) \tag{4.9}$$

$$x_1(n) = a_1 c_1(n) \tag{4.10}$$

The net downlink multiplexed signal $x\,(n)$ is formed from these constituent signals as

$$x\,(n) = x_0(n) + x_1(n) \tag{4.11}$$

Considering a simplified Additive White Gaussian Noise (AWGN) channel model, the received signal by User 0 is

$$\begin{aligned} y(n) &= x(n) + w(n) \\ &= a_0 c_0(n) + a_1 c_1(n) + w(n), \end{aligned} \tag{4.12}$$

where the noise $w(n)$ satisfies $\mathrm{E}\{w(n)\} = 0$ and $\mathrm{E}\{|w(n)|^2\} = \sigma_n^2$, and its property implies $\mathrm{E}\{w(n_1)w^*(n_2)\} = 0$ if $n_1 \neq n_2$. As previously discussed in Section 4.3.1, correlation with the spreading code $c_0$ is employed to retrieve the symbol of user 0,

$$d_0 = \frac{1}{L}\sum_{n=0}^{L-1} y(n)c_0(n)$$

$$= \underbrace{\frac{1}{L}\sum_{n=0}^{L-1} a_0 c_0(n)c_0(n)}_{\text{Desired user}} + \underbrace{\frac{1}{L}\sum_{n=0}^{L-1} a_1 c_1(n)c_0(n)}_{\text{Inleferere}} + \underbrace{\frac{1}{L}\sum_{n=0}^{L-1} w(n)c_0(n)}_{\text{Nose}}, \tag{4.13}$$

the component $\frac{1}{L}\sum_{n=0}^{L-1} a_0 c_0(n)c_0(n)$ represents the desired user signal when decoding is performed at user 0. The second component, $\frac{1}{L}\sum_{n=0}^{L-1} a_1 c_1(n)c_0(n)$, which arises due to $a_1$, corresponds the interference and is also known as multi-user interference in the context of CDMA. The last component, $\frac{1}{L}\sum_{n=0}^{L-1} w(n)c_0(n)$, arises due to the noise at the receiver. The analysis and derivation of the statistical properties of each of the components mentioned above are described below. We begin by examining the signal of the desired user as,

$$\frac{1}{L}\sum_{n=0}^{L-1} a_0 c_0(n)c_0(n) = a_0\left(\frac{1}{L}\sum_{n=0}^{L-1} c_0(n)c_0(n)\right)$$

$$= a_0 r_{00}(0) = a_0 \tag{4.14}$$

Where $r_{00}(0)$ corresponds to the autocorrelation of the spreading code $c_0(n)$ of User 0 for a delay $n_o$ = 0. Hence, the desired signal power is represented as $\mathrm{E}\{|a_0|^2\} = P_0$. Subsequently, we determine the power in the multi-user interference component, $I_1$, representing interference from User 1, shown as:

$$I_1 = \frac{1}{L}\sum_{n=0}^{L-1} a_1 c_1(n)c_0(n)$$

$$\begin{aligned} &= a_1\left(\frac{1}{L}\sum_{n=0}^{L-1} c_1(n)c_0(n)\right) \\ &= a_1 r_{01}(0) \end{aligned} \tag{4.15}$$

Hence, the interference power $E\{|I_1|^2\}$ is,

$$\{|I_1|^2\} = E\{|a_1 r_{01}(0)|^2\}$$

$$= E\{|a_1|^2\} E\{|r_{01}(0)|^2\}$$

$$= P_1 \times \frac{1}{N} = \frac{P_1}{N} \tag{4.16}$$

Unlike the previous scenarios outlined in Eq. (4.7) and (4.8), the interference from User 1 is not completely zero due to the approximate orthogonality of the random spreading codes. However, the interference power decreases as $\frac{1}{L}$, which becomes significantly smaller for larger spreading lengths $L$. The noise power $\tilde{w}_0$ can be computed as

$$\tilde{w}_0 = \frac{1}{L}\sum_{n=0}^{L-1} w(n) c_0(n) \tag{4.17}$$

It is evident that $\tilde{w}_0$is a linear combination of Gaussian noise components $w\,(n)$, making it Gaussian. Furthermore, the expected or average value of $\tilde{w}_0$ can be derived as follows:

$$E\{\tilde{w}_0\} = E\left\{\frac{1}{L}\sum_{n=0}^{L-1} w(n) c_0(n)\right\}$$

$$= \frac{1}{L}\sum_{n=0}^{L-1} E\{w(n)\} c_0(n)$$

$$= \frac{1}{L}\sum_{n=0}^{L-1} 0 \times c_0(n) = 0$$

The noise average value is 0. The average power of noise can be obtained as

$$E\{|\tilde{w}_0|^2\} = E\left\{\frac{1}{L^2}\left(\sum_{n=0}^{L-1} w(n) c_0(n)\right)\left(\sum_{m=0}^{L-1} w^*(m) c_0^*(m)\right)\right\}$$

$$= \frac{1}{L^2}\sum_{n=0}^{L-1}\sum_{m=0}^{L-1} E\{w(n) c_0(n) w^\star(m) c_0^\star(m)\}$$

$$= \frac{1}{L^2}\sum_{n=0}^{L-1} E\{|w_0(n)|^2 |c_0(n)|^2\}$$

$$= \frac{1}{L^2}\sum_{n=0}^{L-1} \sigma_n^2 = \frac{1}{L^2} \times L\sigma_n^2$$

$$= \frac{\sigma_n^2}{L}$$

In the above Eq., the effective noise power is $\frac{\sigma_n^2}{L}$, the noise samples are uncorrelated. Therefore, if $n \neq m$,

$$\begin{aligned} \mathrm{E}\{w(n)c_0(n)w^*(m)c_0^*(m)\} &= \mathrm{E}\{w(n)\}\mathrm{E}\{w^*(m)\}c_0(n)c_0^*(m) \\ &= 0 \times 0 \times c_0(n)c_0^*(m) = 0 \end{aligned}$$

The SINR for above CDMA scenario is,

$$\begin{aligned} SINR &= \frac{\text{Signal Power}}{\text{Interference Power } + \text{ Noise Power}} \\ &= \frac{P_0}{\frac{P_1}{N} + \frac{\sigma_2^2}{N}} \\ &= N \times \frac{P_0}{P_1 + \sigma_n^2} \end{aligned} \tag{4.18}$$

From the above expression, it is obvious that the signal power is decreased at the receiver not only due to noise but also due to interference. Consequently, CDMA operates within an interference-limited framework, requiring control over interference power for enhanced performance. Additionally, it is notable that there is a $L$ factor in the numerator, this occurs due to the fact that the interference and noise power are reduced by a factor of $L$. This phenomenon is termed the spreading gain of the CDMA system, which corresponds to the spreading length. The SINR expression in Eq. (4.18) for a CDMA network can be generalized for more than two users. Considering $N + 1$ CDMA users, denoted as 0, 1, ..., $N$ transmitting with powers $P_0, P_1, \ldots, P_N$ respectively on codes $c_0(n),\ c_1(n), \ldots, c_N(L)$, the received signal $y(n)$ is expressed as:

$$\begin{aligned} y(n) &= a_0c_0(n) + a_1c_1(n) + \cdots + a_Nc_N(n) + w(n), \\ &= \sum_{k=0}^{N} a_kc_k(n) + w(n) \end{aligned}$$

The SINR for user 0 after correlation and decoding with its code $c_0(n)$ can be shown as

$$\begin{aligned} SINR &= \frac{P_0}{\frac{P_1}{L} + \frac{P_2}{L} + \cdots + \frac{P_N}{L} + \frac{\sigma_0^2}{L}} \\ &= L \times \frac{P_0}{\sum_{n=1}^{N+1} P_n + \sigma_n^2} \end{aligned} \tag{4.19}$$

## Advantages of CDMA

In this section, we explore the benefits of CDMA-based cellular systems compared to 1G FDMA and 2G TDMA-based cellular systems.

### Jammer Margin

A significant advantage of CDMA over traditional cellular systems is its capability for jammer suppression. Jammers, malicious users in communication networks, transmit at exceptionally high-power levels to cause interference, disrupting communication links. This is illustrated schematically in Fig. 4.7. Jammers present a concern, particularly in highly secure communication systems such as military and defence applications. The impact of jammer suppression in a CDMA system can be understood as follows: Imagine a communication system where the received signal $x(n)$ with power $P$ accompanied by AWGN $w(n)$ with power $\sigma_w^2$. The baseband system model can be represented as

$$y(n) = x(n) + w(n)$$

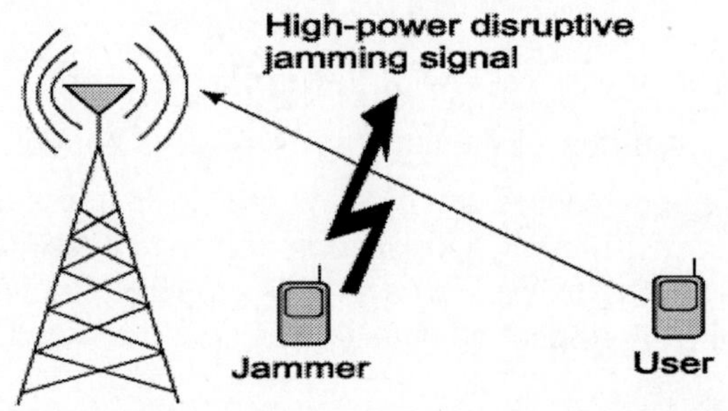


Fig. 4.7 Disruption by jammer in wireless communication

Consequently, the SNR at the receiver is $\frac{P}{\sigma_w^2}$. However, when a jamming signal $x_j(n)$ with power $P_j$ is introduced, the received signal becomes

$$y(n) = x(n) + x_j(n) + w(n).$$

Therefore, the jammer's interference affects signal reception, and the Signal-to-Interference-Noise Ratio (SINR) can be computed as $\frac{P}{P_j+\sigma_w^2}$. The jammer significantly disrupts the communication signal. Now, consider a CDMA system where the transmitted signal $x(n)$ is a spread-spectrum signal. As shown above, the SINR for a CDMA scenario is expressed by,

$$SINR = \frac{P}{\frac{P_j}{L}+\frac{\sigma_w^2}{L}} \tag{4.20}$$

Hence, it becomes apparent that the jamming power $P_j$ is suppressed by a factor of $L$. Additionally, as the spreading factor $L$ increases, jammer suppression enhances, reducing the jammer's impact on the communication system. This phenomenon is termed jammer suppression in CDMA systems. Therefore, CDMA, tolerate to jamming attacks, is highly captivating for defence applications. In fact, CDMA earliest applications were in tactical military secure communications, demonstrating resistance to jammer attacks. It was only later that CDMA benefits were recognized and utilized in civilian cellular networks. Furthermore, it's noteworthy that the gain of $L$ in the context of jammer suppression is also referred to as the jammer margin. Thus, the jammer margin equals $L$, i.e., the spreading length of the CDMA codes.

**Graceful Degradation**

Graceful degradation is another characteristic of CDMA-based wireless networks. It enables much more efficient interference management, ultimately facilitating frequency reuse and higher spectral efficiency. Let us examine the expression for the SINR at user 0 in Eq. (4.19). Now, assume that another user, indexed as N+1, joins the network. Let $P_{N+1}$ denote the corresponding transmission power of this $(N+1)^{th}$user, and $a_{N+1}$, $c_{N+1}(n)$ denote their transmitted symbol and spreading code, respectively. The SINR of user 0 now changes to:

$$SINR = \frac{P_0}{\frac{P_1}{L} + \frac{P_2}{L} + \cdots + \frac{P_N}{L} + \frac{P_{N+1}}{L} + \frac{\sigma_0^2}{L}}$$

$$= L \times \frac{P_0}{\sum_{n=1}^{N+1} P_n + \sigma_n^2} \quad (4.21)$$

Hence, the introduction of a new user N+1 with power $P_{N+1}$ only results in gradual interference of $\frac{P_{N+1}}{L}$ at user 0. Therefore, the addition of the new user N+1 does not adversely affect any single user. Instead, the additional interference caused by this new user is shared among all existing users in the system, leading to interference distribution. This sharing of interference among all existing users results in a graceful degradation of the SINR at each user. This property, known as graceful degradation, is essential for understanding the significant advantage of CDMA networks: universal frequency reuse, which we will discuss next.

**Universal Frequency Reuse**

To understand the concept of universal frequency reuse, we need to start by understanding the frequency allocation in conventional 1G and 2G cellular systems. Consider a cellular network organized into cells, as shown in Fig. 4.8. Let, two adjacent cells, be $C_0$ and $C_1$, as depicted in the Fig. 4.8. Assume that the same frequency $f$ is allocated for transmission to users in both cells $C_0$ and $C_1$. Consider $x_0\,(n)$ with power $P_0$ denote the signal of the user on frequency $f$ in cell $C_0$, while $x_1\,(n)$ with power $P_1$ denotes the signal of the user in cell $C_1$. Since both signals are being transmitted on the same frequency $f$, they will interfere with each other. More specifically, the received signal $y_0\,(n)$ at user 0 is given as follows:

$$\mathbf{y_0\,(n)} = \underbrace{\mathbf{x_0\,(n)}}_{\textit{Signal}} + \underbrace{\mathbf{x_1\,(n)}}_{\textit{Interferer from } C_1} + \underbrace{\mathbf{w(n)}}_{\textit{Noise}}$$

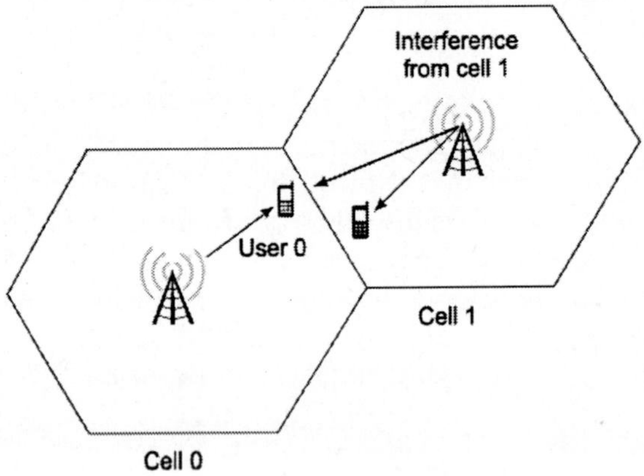


Fig. 4.8 Intercell interference for the user 0 on the cell edge

As a result, the SINR at user 0 is represented by $\frac{P_0}{P_1+\sigma_w^2}$. This scenario is similar to the situation of jamming interference described in Eq. (4.20). Therefore, allocating the same frequency $f$ in adjacent cells leads to significant interference, causing a decline in user SINR due to adjacent cell interference. In typical 1G or 2G cellular networks such as GSM, only a fraction of the total available frequencies is assigned in each cell, ensuring that the same frequency is not allocated in adjacent cells. For instance, in the hexagonal-lattice-based cellular structure illustrated in Fig. 4.9, each hexagonal cell has 6 neighbours. Consequently, to prevent adjacent cell interference, any frequency assigned to $C_0$ cannot be used in its neighbouring cells $C_1, C_2, \ldots, C_6$. This principle applies to all cells in the network. Therefore, only $\frac{1}{7}$ of the total available frequency bands can be allocated to each cell. This fraction, $\frac{1}{7}$, is known as the frequency-reuse factor of the cellular network. Thus, since only a portion of the frequencies are utilized in the cell, the total spectral efficiency is proportional to the frequency-reuse factor, resulting in a rate that is $\frac{1}{7}$ compared to using all available bandwidth, given that capacity is linearly related to bandwidth.

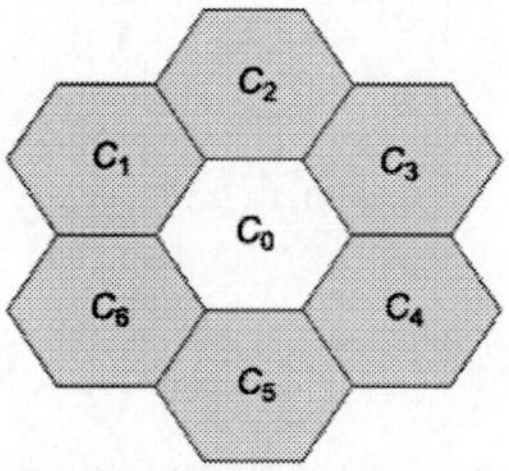


Fig. 4.9 Grid or lattice of hexagonal cells

Now, consider the same scenario in a CDMA network. Assume the same frequency $f$ is assigned for transmission to users in both cells $C_0$ and $C_1$. However, $x_0(n)$ with power $P_0$ is now transmitted using code $C_0(n)$ while $x_1(n)$ with power $P_1$ is transmitted using a different code $C_1(n)$. Consequently, similar to the jamming scenario in a CDMA system, the interference caused by the user on the same frequency $f$ in the adjacent cell is now reduced by a factor of $L$ to $\frac{P_1}{L}$. Therefore, the SINR is:

$$SINR = \frac{P_0}{\frac{P_1}{L} + \frac{\sigma_W^2}{L}} \tag{4.22}$$

This is the result of degradation described in the previous advantage in section 4.3.3.2. As a result, the interference encountered by each user is limited to a fraction $\frac{1}{L}$ of the interfering power. Consequently, the jammer margin, typically employed in defense applications, can also be utilized to suppress adjacent cell interference powers in modern cellular networks! This represents a notable benefit of CDMA, suggesting that the same frequency bands can be employed in all cells throughout the network. Another way to express this is that every cell uses all available bands, denoted as a frequency reuse factor of 1. Thus, unlike GSM, which utilizes only $\frac{1}{7}$ of the frequency bands in each cell, CDMA can utilize all the available frequency bands in each cell. Consequently, this leads to an immediate enhancement in spectral efficiency and resulting capacity by a factor of 7. Therefore, CDMA-based cellular networks boast significantly higher capacities compared to conventional 1G and 2G cellular networks. This has led to widespread adoption and acceptance of CDMA-based technologies for mobile communication.

### 4.1.4 Space Division Multiple Access (SDMA)

SDMA uses multiple antennas for transmitting, receiving, or both. The antennas are spaced in such a way that the fading events they encounter in the channel are independent of each other. SDMA in signal space uses angles as dimensions which are assigned to different uses by using the directional antenna as shown in the Fig. 4.10. The angular distance between the user should be greater than the angular resolution of the antenna to obtain an orthogonal channel for the user. In practice, SDMA uses sectorized antenna arrays to overcome the directionality obtained by antenna arrays, which require high angular resolution. The sectorized antenna array divides the 360-degree angular space into N portions, where interference may arise among sectors with high directional gain. SDMA adapts to changes in user angle for mobile users, utilizing factorized antennas to achieve directionality. When a mobile user moves from its original sector, it must hand off to a new sector in the space division. TDMA or FDMA channel is the mobile user in the same sector.

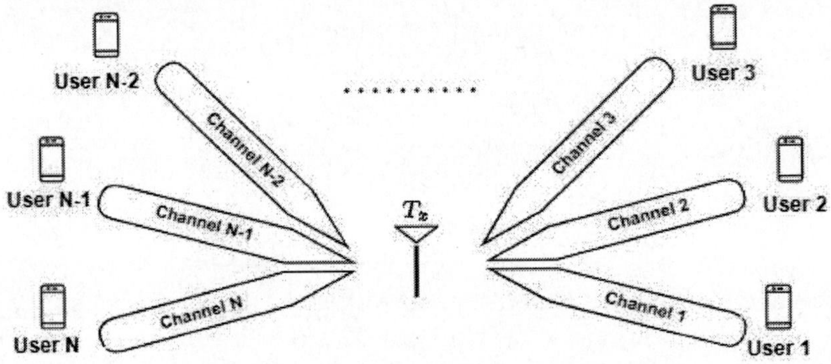


Fig. 4.10: Space-division multiple access

Depending on which side of the wireless link has multiple antennas, SDMA can be categorized into three types:

1. ***Receive diversity*** uses one transmit antenna and several receive antennas.
2. ***Transmit diversity*** employs multiple transmit antennas with a single receive antenna.
3. ***Diversity on both transmit and receive*** combines multiple antennas at both the transmitting and receiving ends.

Receive diversity is the oldest form of these three, while the other two are more recent developments. In the following sections, we will examine these three types of diversity in this sequence.

## Space Diversity-on-Receive Systems

In "space diversity on receive," multiple receiving antennas are employed with a spacing between adjacent antennas selected to ensure their outputs are essentially uncorrelated. This condition can be fulfilled by positioning the adjacent receiving antennas several radio wavelengths apart, typically within a range of 10 to 20 wavelengths or less. A separation of several radio wavelengths is generally considered for effective space diversity on receive. However, larger spacing may be necessary for elevated base stations, particularly when the angle spread of the incoming radio waves is minimal. Note that the spatial coherence distance is inversely proportional to the angle spread. By applying diversity on receiver as outlined above, we generate a corresponding set of fading channels that are essentially independent. Consequently, the challenge lies in combining the outputs of these statistically independent fading channels in a manner that enhances receiver performance. In this section, we illustrate two different diversity-combining systems, all of which share a common characteristic: they employ linear receivers.

## Selection Combining

The diagram illustrates a diversity-combining structure comprising $N_r$ linear receivers and a logic circuit, representing a selection-combining system where the receiver output with the highest SNR is chosen from the $N_r$ produced by a commonly transmitted signal. Conceptually, selection combining represents the most basic form of space-diversity-on-receive systems as shown in Fig. 4.10.

To explain the advantages of selection combining statistically, let us assume a wireless communication channel characterized by a frequency-flat, slowly fading Rayleigh channel. This assumption implies that all frequency components of the transmitted signal experience the similar random attenuation and phase shifts, fading remains relatively constant throughout the transmission of each symbol, and the fading effect characterize by the Rayleigh distribution.

## Representation of Received Signal

The complex envelope of the received signal in the $k^{th}$ diversity branch during the interval $0 \leq t \leq T$ can be defined as:

$$\tilde{x}_k(t) = a_k \exp(j\theta_k)\tilde{s}(t) + \tilde{w}_k(t), \quad 0 \leq t \leq T \quad k = 1,2,\dots,N_r \tag{4.23}$$

Here, $a_k \exp(j\theta_k)$ represents the fading term, and $\tilde{w}_k(t)$, presents the additive channel noise. Since the fading is assumed to be slowly varying relative to the symbol duration T, we can estimate and remove the unknown phase shift $\theta_k$ accurately. This simplifies the expression to:

$$\tilde{x}_k(t) \approx \alpha_k\tilde{s}(t) + \tilde{w}_k(t), \quad 0 \leq t \leq T, \quad k = 1, 2, \dots, N_r \tag{4.24}$$

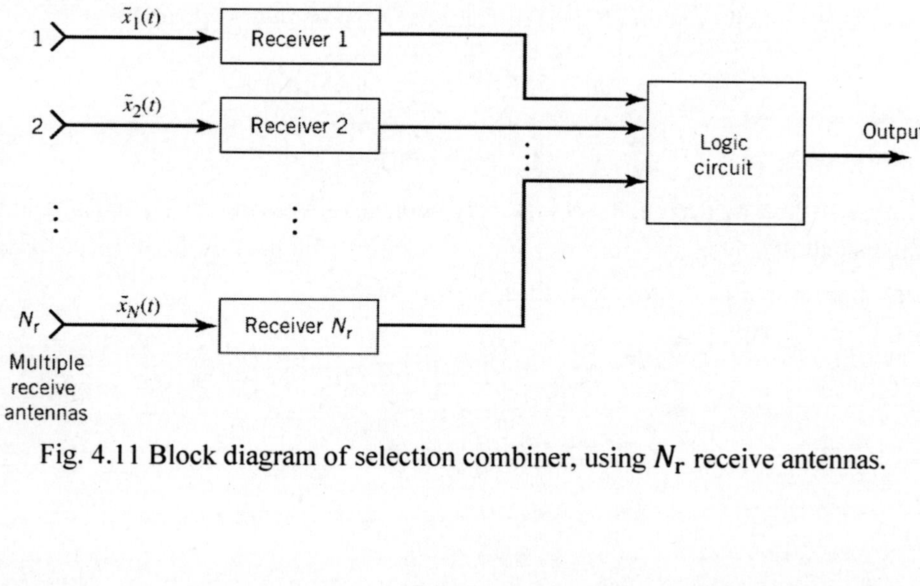


Fig. 4.11 Block diagram of selection combiner, using $N_r$ receive antennas.

### Signal-to-Noise Ratio (SNR):

The average SNR at the output of the $k^{th}$ receiver is given by:

$$(\mathrm{SNR})_k = \frac{\mathbb{E}[(a_k \tilde{s}(t))^2]}{\mathbb{E}[(\tilde{w}_k(t))^2]}$$

$$= \left(\frac{\mathbb{E}[[\tilde{s}(t)]^2]}{\mathbb{E}[\tilde{w}_k(t))^2]}\right) \mathbb{E}[\alpha_k^2],\ k = 1,2,\dots,N_\mathrm{r}$$

Ordinarily, the mean-square value is the same for all $k$. Accordingly, we may express the $(\mathrm{SNR})_k$ as

$$(\mathrm{SNR})_k = \frac{E}{N_0}\mathbb{E}[a_k^2],\ k = 1,2,\dots,N_\mathrm{r} \tag{4.25}$$

where $E$ is the symbol of energy and $N_0/2$ is the noise spectral density. For binary data, E equals the transmitted signal energy per bit $E_b$.

The instantaneous SNR ($\gamma_k$) measured at the output of the $k^{th}$ receiver during the transmission of a given symbol can be represented as:

$$\gamma_k = \frac{E}{N_0} a_k^2,\ k = 1,2,\dots,N_\mathrm{r} \tag{4.26}$$

### Probability Distributions:

Assuming that the random amplitude $a_k$ is Rayleigh distributed, the squared amplitude $a_k^2$ will follow an exponential distribution. If the average SNR over short-term fading is the same ($\gamma_{\mathrm{av}}$) for all diversity branches, then the probability density functions of the individual branches can be expressed as:

$$f_{\Gamma_k}(\gamma_k) = \frac{1}{\gamma_{\mathrm{av}}}\exp\left(-\frac{\gamma_k}{\gamma_{\mathrm{av}}}\right),\quad \begin{matrix}\gamma_k \geq 0, \\ k = 1,2,\dots,N_\mathrm{r}\end{matrix} \tag{4.27}$$

### Cumulative Distribution Function (CDF):

The Cumulative Distribution Function (CDF) of the selection combiner is given by:

$$\mathbb{P}(\gamma_k \leq \gamma) = \int_{-\infty}^{\gamma} f_{\Gamma_k}(\gamma_k)\mathrm{d}\gamma_k$$

$$= 1 - \exp\left(-\frac{\gamma}{\gamma_{\mathrm{av}}}\right),\ \gamma \geq 0 \tag{4.28}$$

for $k = 1, 2,\dots, N_\mathrm{r}$. Since, by design, the $N_\mathrm{r}$ diversity branches are essentially statistically independent, the probability that all the diversity branches have an SNR less than the threshold $\gamma$ is the product of the individual probabilities that $\gamma_k < \gamma$ for all $k$: thus, we write

$$\mathbb{P}(\gamma_k < \gamma) = \prod_{k=1}^{N_r} \mathbb{P}(\gamma_k < \gamma)$$

$$= \prod_{k=1}^{N_r}\left[1 - \exp\left(-\frac{\gamma}{\gamma_{\mathrm{av}}}\right)\right]$$

$$= \left[1 - \exp\left(-\frac{\gamma}{\gamma_{av}}\right)\right]^{N_r}, \gamma \geq 0 \tag{4.29}$$

For $k$ =1, 2, …, $N_r$; it should be noted that as $N_r$ increases, the probability in Eq. (4.29) decreases. The Cumulative Distribution Function (CDF) of Eq. (4.29) is equivalent to the CDF of the random variable described by

$$\gamma_{SC} = \max\{\gamma_1, \gamma_2, \dots, \gamma_N\} \tag{4.30}$$

where the variable is less than the threshold γ if, and only if, all individual SNRs are less than γ. Specifically, the CDF of the selection combiner (i.e., the probability that all $N_r$ diversity branches have an SNR less than γ is given by

$$F_\Gamma(\gamma_{SC}) = \left[1 - \exp\left(-\frac{\gamma_{SC}}{\gamma_{av}}\right)\right]^{N_r}, \gamma_{SC} \geq 0 \tag{4.31}$$

The probability density function $f_\Gamma(\gamma_{SC})$ is the derivative of the cumulative distribution function $F_\Gamma(\gamma_{SC})$ with the argument $\gamma_{SC}$. Therefore, differentiating Eq. (4.31) concerning $\gamma_{SC}$ yields:

$$f_\Gamma(\gamma_{SC}) = \frac{\mathrm{d}}{\mathrm{d}\gamma_{SC}} F_\Gamma(\gamma_{SC})$$

$$= \frac{N_r}{\gamma_{av}} \exp\left(-\frac{\gamma_{SC}}{\gamma_{av}}\right)\left[1 - \exp\left(-\frac{\gamma_{SC}}{\gamma_{av}}\right)\right]^{N_r - 1}, \gamma_{SC} \geq 0 \tag{4.32}$$

For convenience of graphical presentation, we use the scaled probability density function

$$f_X(x) = \gamma_{av} f_{\Gamma_{sin}}(\gamma_{sc})$$

where the sample value $x$ of the normalized variable $X$ is defined by

$$x = \gamma_{sc}/\gamma_{av}$$

Fig. 4.12 plot illustrates the behavior of the probability density function $f_X(x)$ versus $x$ as the number of receive-diversity branches $N_r$ varies, if SNRs for all branches share the same value $\gamma_{av}$. From this Fig., two observations can be made:

1. Increasing the number of diverse branches $N_r$ uses the probability density function $f_X(x)$ of the normalized random variable to shift progressively to the right.
2. The probability density function $f_X(x)$ becomes increasingly symmetrical and Gaussian-like as $N_r$ is increased.

In other words, employing selection combining transforms a frequency-flat, slowly fading Rayleigh channel into a Gaussian channel when the number of diversity channels $N_r$ is sufficiently large. This transition to a Gaussian channel is highly desirable in digital communication theory. The practical benefit of using selection combining lies in the ability to achieve this transformation. However, the implementation of selection combining involves continuous monitoring of receiver outputs to select the receiver with the strongest signal at each instant. To address this challenge, a scanning version of the selection-combining procedure can be adopted:

- Start by selecting the receiver with the strongest output signal.
- Maintain the use of this receiver's output as the combiner's output if its instantaneous SNR remains above a prescribed threshold.
- When the instantaneous SNR falls below the threshold, select a new receiver with the strongest output signal and continue the procedure.

## 4.2. OUTAGE PROBABILITY OF SELECTION COMBINER

The outage probability of a diversity combiner is defined as the percentage of time the instantaneous output SNR of the combiner falls below a specified threshold for a given number of branches. Using the cumulative distribution function from Eq. (4.31), Fig.4.13 depicts the outage curves for the selection combiner with $N_r$ as the variable parameter. The horizontal axis of the figure indicates the instantaneous output SNR of the combiner relative to 0 dB (i.e., the 50th percentile point for $N_r = 1$), while the vertical axis represents the outage probability, expressed as a percentage. From the figure, the fading depth decreases quickly as the number of diversity branches increases when implementing space diversity on receive.

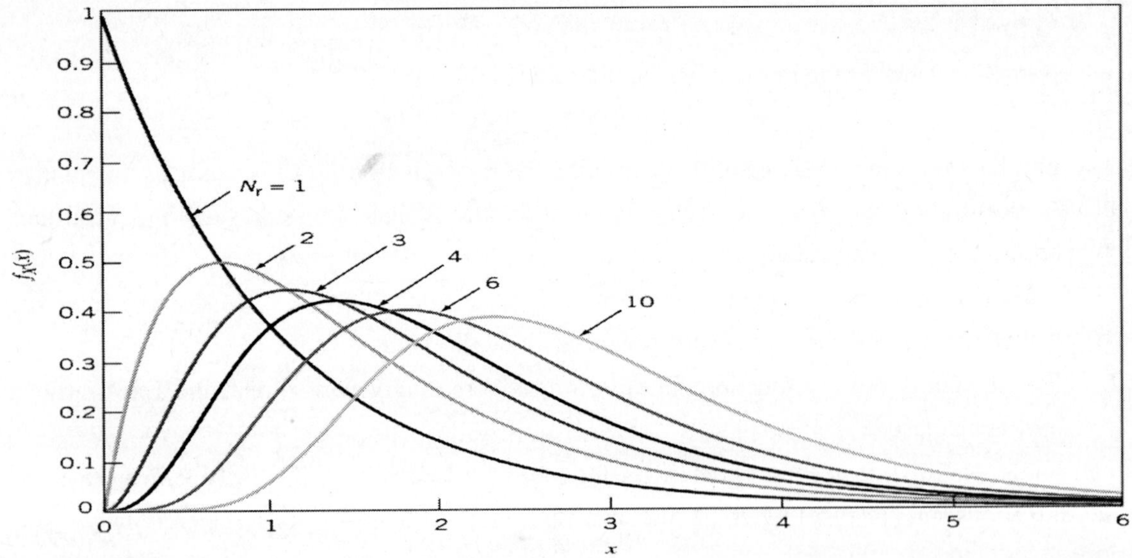


Fig. 4.12 Normalized probability density function for a varying number Nr of receive antennas.

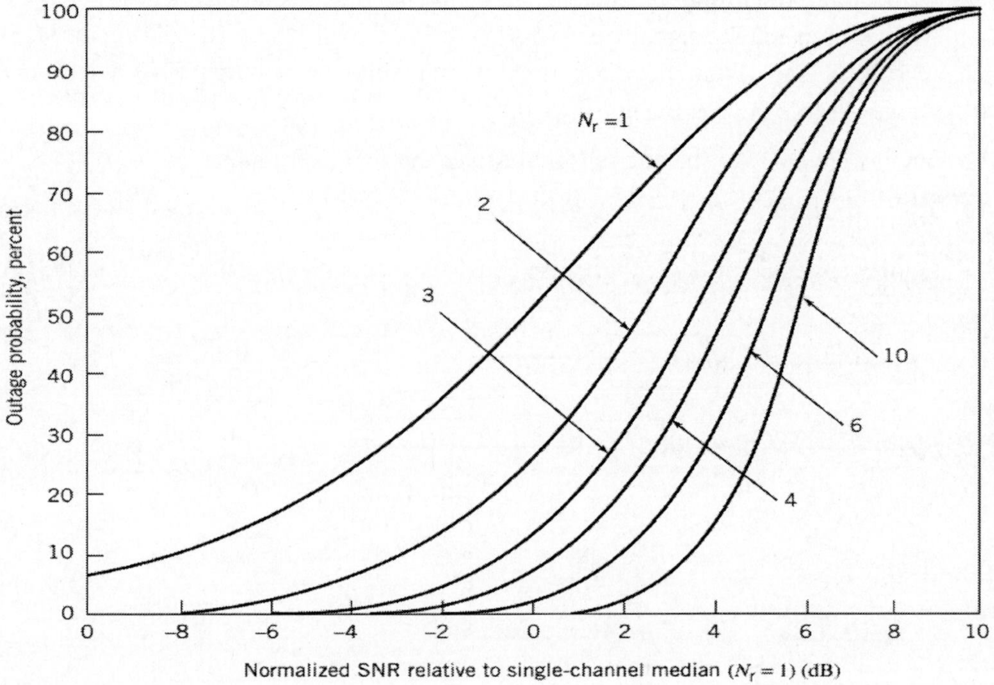


Fig. 4.13 Outage probability for selector combining for a varying number Nr of receive antennas.

### 4.2.1 Maximal-Ratio Combining

The selection-combining technique described is relatively easy to implement. However, it is not optimal from a performance perspective, as it disregards the information available from all diversity branches except for the one that yields the highest instantaneous power of its own demodulated signal. This limitation of the selection combiner is mitigated by the maximal-ratio combiner, which is illustrated by the block diagram in Fig. 4.14. This diagram comprises $N_r$ linear receivers followed by a linear combiner. Using the complex envelope of the received signal at the $k^{th}$ diversity branch as given in Eq. (4.23), determines the complex envelope of the linear combiner output.

$$\tilde{y}(t) = \sum_{k=1}^{N_x} a_k \tilde{x}_k(t)$$

$$= \sum_{k=1}^{N_k} a_k [\alpha_k \exp(j\theta_k) \tilde{s}(t) + \tilde{w}_k(t)] \tag{4.33}$$

$$= \tilde{s}(t) \sum_{k=1}^{N_r} a_k \alpha_k \exp(j\theta_k) + \sum_{k=1}^{N_r} a_k \tilde{w}_k(t)$$

where the $a_k$ are complex weighting parameters that define the linear combiner. These parameters are adjusted continuously to match the signal variations in the $N_r$ diversity branches during the short-term fading process. The goal is to design the linear combiner to maximize the output SNR at each moment. From Eq. (9.70), we observe the following two points:

1. The complex envelope of the output signal equals the first expression: $\tilde{s}(t)\sum_{k=1}^{N_r} a_k \alpha_k \exp(j\theta_k)$
2. The complex envelope of the output noise equals the second expression: $\sum_{k=1}^{N_r} a_k \tilde{w}_k(t)$

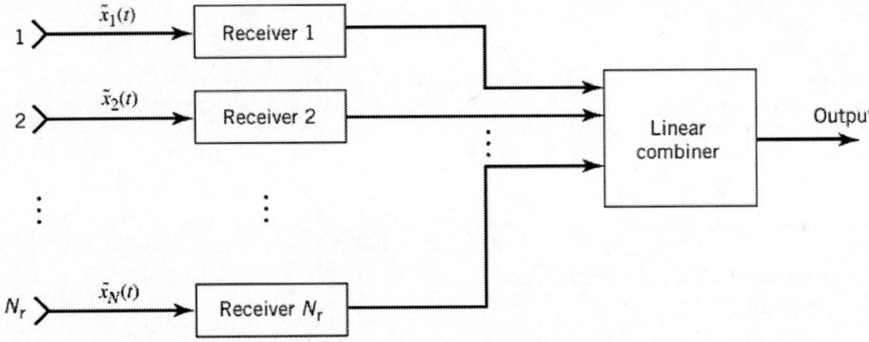


Fig. 4.14 Block diagram of maximal-ratio combiner using Nr receive antennas.

Assuming that $\tilde{w}_k(t)$ are mutually independent for $k$ = 1, 2, …, $N_r$, the output SNR of the linear combiner is therefore given by

$$(\text{SNR})_c = \frac{\mathbb{E}\left[\left|\tilde{s}(x)\sum_{k=1}^{N_r} a_k\alpha_k \exp(j\theta_k)\right|^2\right]}{\mathbb{E}\left[\left|\sum_{k=1}^{N_r} a_k\tilde{w}_k(x)\right|^2\right]}$$

$$= \frac{\mathbb{E}[|\tilde{s}(t)|^2]\mathbb{E}\left[\left|\sum_{k=1}^{N_r} a_k\alpha_k\exp(j\theta_k)\right|^2\right]}{\mathbb{E}[|\tilde{w}_k(t)|^2]\ \mathbb{E}\left[\sum_{k=1}^{N_r}|a_k|^2\right]} \tag{4.34}$$

$$= \frac{E}{N_0}\ \frac{\mathbb{E}\left[\left|\sum_{k=1}^{N_r} a_k\alpha_k\exp(j\theta_k)\right|^2\right]}{\mathbb{E}\left[\sum_{k=1}^{N_r}|a_k|^2\right]}$$

where $\frac{E}{N_0}$ is the symbol energy-to-noise spectral density ratio. Let $\varphi_c$ denote the instantaneous output SNR of the linear combiner. Then, using the two terms

$$\left|\sum_{k=1}^{N_r} a_k\alpha_k\exp(j\theta_k)\right|^2 \text{ and } \sum_{k=1}^{N_r}|a_k|^2$$

as the instantaneous values of the expectations in the numerator and denominator of (4.34), respectively, is

$$\gamma_c = \frac{E}{N_0}\frac{\left|\sum_{k=1}^{N_r} a_k\alpha_k \exp(j\theta_k)\right|^2}{\sum_{k=1}^{N_r} |a_k|^2} \tag{4.35}$$

The objective is to maximize $\varphi_c$ concerning the $a_k$ parameters. This maximization can be achieved by applying the standard differentiation method, considering that the weighting parameters $a_k$ are complex. Let

$a_k$ and $b_k$ represent any two complex numbers for $k = 1, 2, \ldots, N_r$. According to the Schwarz inequality for complex parameters, we have

$$\left|\sum_{k=1}^{N_r} a_k b_k\right|^2 \le \sum_{k=1}^{N_r} |a_k|^2 \sum_{k=1}^{N_r} |b_k|^2 \tag{4.36}$$

This equality holds when $a_k = cb_k^*$ , where $c$ is any arbitrary complex constant, and the asterisk denotes complex conjugation. Thus, by applying the Schwarz inequality to the instantaneous output SNR of Eq. (4.35), with $a_k$ left unchanged and $b_k$ set equal to $\alpha_k \exp(j\theta_k)$, we derive

Top of Form

Bottom of Form

$$\gamma_c \le \frac{E}{N_0}\frac{\sum_{k=1}^{N_r} |a_k|^2 \sum_{k=1}^{N_r} |\alpha_k \exp(j\theta_k)|^2}{\sum_{k=1}^{N_r} |a_k|^2}$$

After Cancelling the common terms, we obtain

$$\gamma_c \le \frac{E}{N_0}\sum_{k=1}^{N_r} \alpha_k^2 \tag{4.37}$$

The equation (4.37) demonstrates that, $\gamma_c$ cannot surpass $\sum_{k=1}^{N_r} \gamma_k$, as in Eq. (4.26). Equality in (4.37) holds for

$$\begin{aligned} a_k &= c[\alpha_k \exp(j\theta_k)]^* \\ &= c\alpha_k^* \exp(-j\theta_k),\ k = 1,2,\ldots,N_r \end{aligned} \tag{4.38}$$

where c is some arbitrary complex constant.

Eq. (4.38) outlines the complex weighting coefficients of the maximal-ratio combiner. According to this equation, we can assert that the optimal weighting coefficient $a_k$ for the $k^{th}$ diversity branch exhibits a magnitude proportional to the signal amplitude $\alpha_k$ and a phase that nullifies the signal phase $\theta_k$ up to a certain uniform value across all $N_r$ diversity branches. This alignment of phases facilitates the complete coherent summation of the $N_r$ receiver outputs by the linear combiner.

Eq. (9.74), equality is achieved, specifies the instantaneous output SNR of the maximal-ratio combiner, formulated as:

$$\gamma_{mrc} = \frac{E}{N_0}\sum_{k=1}^{N_r} \alpha_k^2 \tag{4.39}$$

As per Eq. (4.37), $\frac{E}{N_0}\alpha_k^2$ represents the instantaneous output SNR of the $k^{th}$ diversity branch. Hence, the maximal-ratio combiner yields an instantaneous output SNR equivalent to the summation of the individual branch instantaneous SNRs as shown below

$$\gamma_{\text{mrc}} = \sum_{k=1}^{N_r} \gamma_k \tag{4.40}$$

The term "maximal-ratio combiner" refers to the combiner depicted in Fig. 9.21, which achieves the optimal result outlined in Eq. (4.40). This result indicates that the instantaneous output SNR of the maximal-ratio combiner can be huge even when the SNRs of the individual branches are weak. Comparatively, the performance of selection combiner is notably inferior, as its instantaneous SNR is merely the maximum among the $N_r$ terms of Eq. (4.40). The maximal SNR $\gamma_{\text{mrc}}$ is the sample value of a random variable denoted by $\Gamma$. As per Eq. (4.39), $\gamma_{\text{mrc}}$ is equals to the sum of $N_r$ exponentially distributed random variables for a frequency-flat, slowly fading Rayleigh channel. The probability density function of such a sum follows a chi-square distribution with $2N_r$ degrees of freedom.

$$f_\Gamma(\gamma_{\text{mrc}}) = \frac{1}{(N_r-1)!}\frac{\gamma_{\text{mrc}}^{N_r-1}}{\gamma_{\text{av}}}\exp\left(-\frac{\gamma_{\text{mrc}}}{\gamma_{\text{av}}}\right) \tag{4.41}$$

For Nr = 1, Eq. (4.32) and (4.40) yield identical values, as noted.

### 4.2.2 Outage Probability for Maximal-Ratio Combiner

The CDF for the maximal-ratio combiner is given as

$$\mathbb{P}(\gamma_{\text{mrc}} < x) = \int_0^x f_\Gamma(\gamma_{\text{mrc}})d\gamma_{\text{mrc}}$$

$$= 1 - \int_x^\infty f_\Gamma(\gamma_{\text{mrc}})d\gamma_{\text{mrc}} \tag{4.42}$$

The probability density function is further defined by Eq. (4.41).

### 4.2.3 Space Diversity-on-Transmit Systems:

This terminology is warranted for the following reasons in wireless communications literature, space diversity-on-receive techniques are frequently:

1. The transmitted symbols create an orthogonal set.
2. The transmission of incoming data streams is performed on a block-by-block basis.
3. Space and time serve as the coordinates for each transmitted block of symbols.

In a general sense, Fig. 4.15 depicts the baseband diagram of a space-time block encoder, which comprises two functional units: a mapper and a block encoder. The mapper processes the incoming binary data stream $\{b_k\}$, where $b_k = \pm 1$, and generates a new sequence of blocks, each consisting of multiple complex symbols.

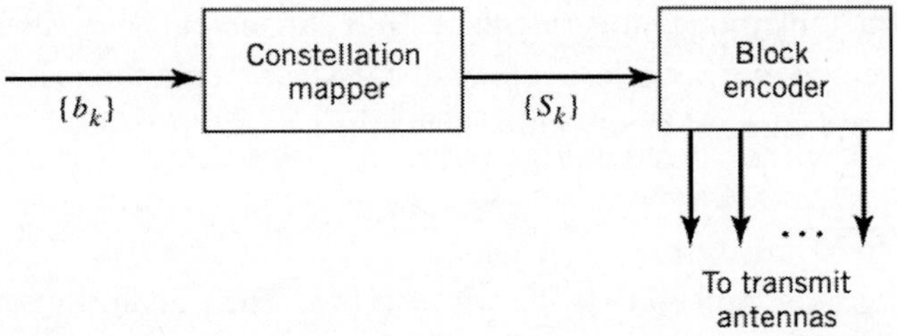


Fig 4.15 Block diagram of orthogonal space–time block encoder.

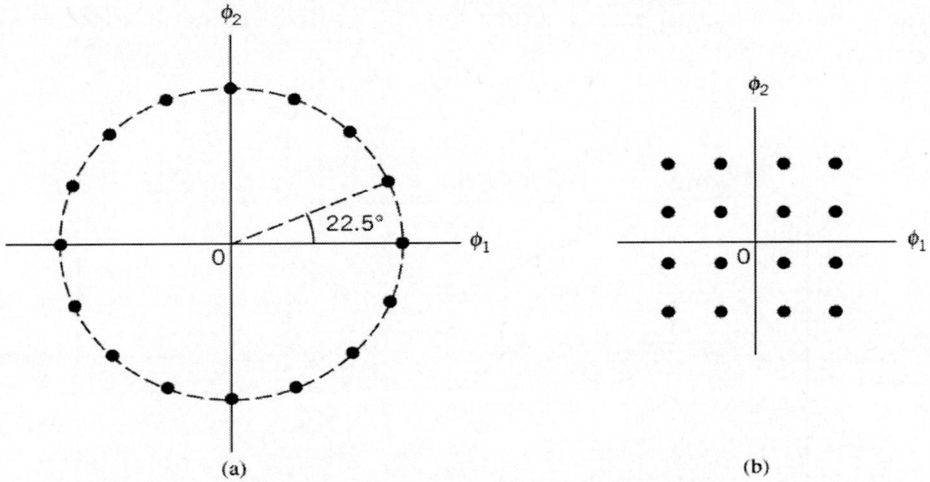


Fig 4.16 (a) Signal constellation of 16-PSK. (b) Signal constellation of 16-QAM.

For instance, the mapper may utilize an *M-ary* PSK or *M -ary* QAM message constellation, illustrated for $M = 16$ in the signal-space diagrams of Fig. 4.16. All symbols in each column of the transmission matrix are pulse-shaped and then modulated for simultaneous transmission over the channel by the transmit antennas. The pulse shaper and modulator are not shown in Fig. 4.15 because the primary focus is on baseband data transmission, specifically the formulation of space-time block codes. The block encoder transforms each block of complex symbols generated by the mapper into an $l$ -by-$N_t$ transmission matrix S, where $l$ and $N_t$ represent the temporal and spatial dimensions of the transmission matrix, respectively. The elements of the transmission matrix S consist of linear combinations of the complex symbols and their complex conjugates.

## 4.2.4 Multiple-Input, Multiple-Output Systems: Basic Considerations

In this section, we examine MIMO wireless communication, which is distinct in the following ways:

1. The fading phenomenon is not seen as a hindrance but rather as a beneficial environmental factor to be utilized.
2. Space diversity at both the transmitting and receiving ends of the wireless communication link can significantly boost channel capacity.

3. Unlike traditional methods, this increase in channel capacity is attained by enhancing computational complexity while keeping the primary communication resources (i.e., total transmit power and channel bandwidth) unchanged.

### Coantenna Interference:

Fig. 4.17 presents the block diagram of a MIMO wireless link. The signals transmitted by the $N_t$ transmit antennas over the wireless channel are all designed to occupy a common frequency band. The transmitted signals are scattered differently by the channel. Additionally, due to multiple signal transmissions, the system experiences a spatial form of signal-dependent interference known as Co-antenna Interference (CAI).

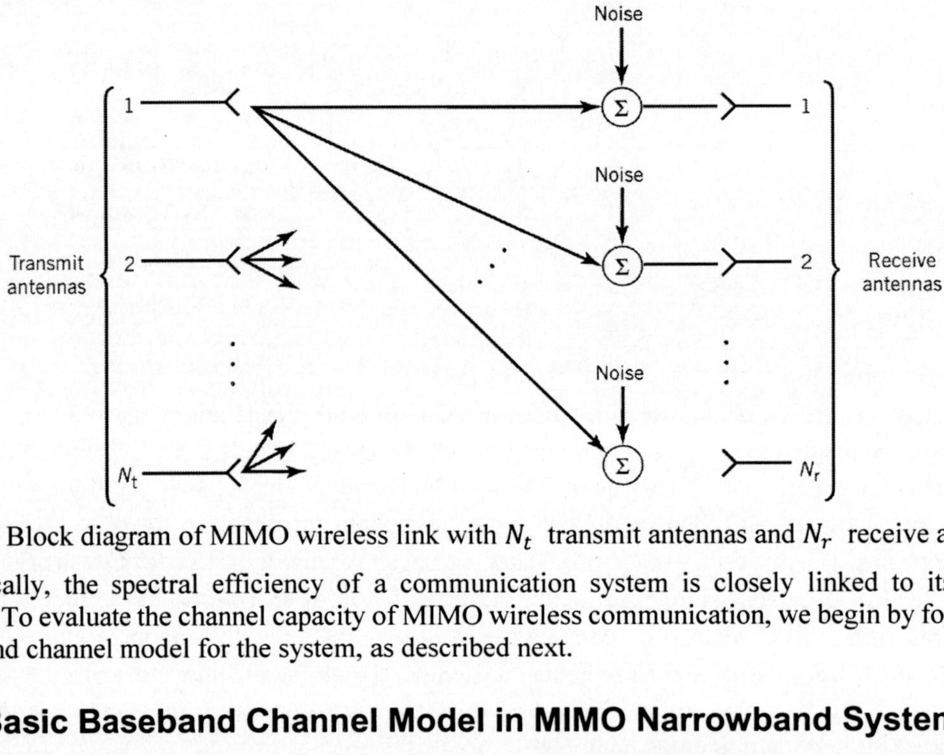


Fig 4.17 Block diagram of MIMO wireless link with $N_t$ transmit antennas and $N_r$ receive antennas.

Theoretically, the spectral efficiency of a communication system is closely linked to its channel capacity. To evaluate the channel capacity of MIMO wireless communication, we begin by formulating a baseband channel model for the system, as described next.

## 4.2.5 Basic Baseband Channel Model in MIMO Narrowband Systems

In MIMO narrowband systems, the baseband channel model characterizes how signals are transmitted and received across multiple antennas. Here's an overview of the basic baseband channel model:

### Transmitted Signal Vector:

- The transmitted signal from $N_t$ antennas are represented by a vector $S(t)$.

$$\tilde{\mathbf{s}}(n) = \left[\tilde{s}_1(n), \tilde{s}_2(n), \dots, \tilde{s}_{N_t}(n)\right]^{\mathrm{T}} \tag{4.43}$$

where $\tilde{s}_i(n)$ is the signal transmitted from the $i^{th}$ antenna.

### Received Signal Vector:

- The received signal at Nr antennas is represented by a vector y(t).

$$\tilde{\mathbf{x}}(n) = [\tilde{x}_1(n), \tilde{x}_2(n), \ldots, \tilde{x}_{N_r}(n)] \quad (4.44)$$

where $\tilde{x}_j(n)$ is the signal received at the $j^{th}$ antenna.

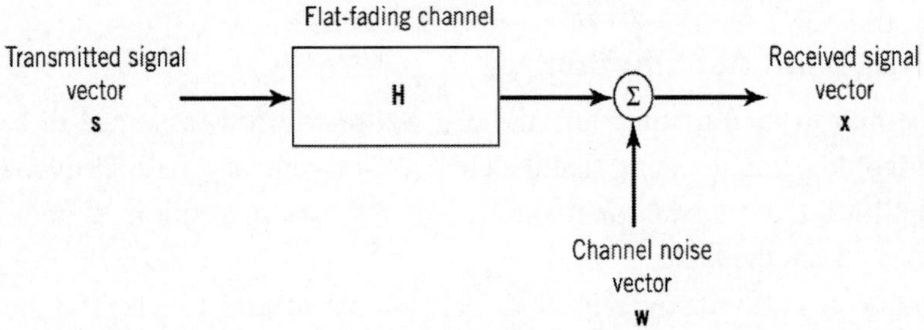


Fig. 4.18 Basic channel model of MIMO.

### Channel Matrix:

- The wireless channel is characterized by an $N_r \times N_t$ channel matrix H.
- Each element $\tilde{h}_{ij}$ of H represents the complex gain (including amplitude and phase shift) of the channel from the $i^{th}$ transmit antenna to the $j^{th}$ receive antenna.

$$\mathbf{H}(n) = \begin{bmatrix} \tilde{h}_{11}(n) & \tilde{h}_{12}(n) & \cdots & \tilde{h}_{1N_t}(n) \\ \tilde{h}_{21}(n) & \tilde{h}_{22}(n) & \cdots & \tilde{h}_{2N_t}(n) \\ \vdots & \vdots & & \vdots \\ \tilde{h}_{N_r1}(n) & \tilde{h}_{N_r2} & \cdots & h_{N_rN_t}(n) \end{bmatrix} \quad (4.45)$$

### Received Signal Model:

- The received signal vector $\tilde{\mathbf{x}}(n)$ is given by:

$$\tilde{\mathbf{x}}(n) = \mathbf{H}(n)\tilde{\mathbf{s}}(n) + \tilde{\mathbf{w}}(n) \quad (4.46)$$

Where, the complex noise vector is,

$$\tilde{\boldsymbol{w}}(n) = [\tilde{w}_1(n), \tilde{w}_2(n), \ldots, \tilde{w}_{N_r}(n)]^{\mathrm{T}} \quad (4.47)$$

Here, $\tilde{\mathbf{w}}(n)$ is the noise vector at the receiver, typically modelled as AWGN with a mean of zero and covariance matrix $\sigma_w^2 I_{N_r}$. The channel noise vector $\boldsymbol{w}$ consists of $N_r$ elements, each of which is an independent and identically distributed (iid) complex Gaussian random variable. These variables have a zero mean and share a common variance $\sigma_w^2$. Consequently, the correlation matrix of the noise vector $\boldsymbol{w}$ can be expressed.

$$\mathbf{R}_w = \mathbb{E}[\mathbf{w}\mathbf{w}^\dagger] = \sigma_w^2 \mathbf{I}_{N_r} \quad (4.48)$$

The transmitted signal vector, denoted by s, comprises $N_t$ symbols, which iid complex Gaussian random variables. These symbols have a zero mean and share a common variance $\sigma_s^2$. Consequently, the correlation matrix of the transmitted signal vector s is determined.

$$\mathbf{R}_s = \mathbb{E}[\mathbf{s}\mathbf{s}^{\dagger}] = \sigma_s^2 \mathbf{I}_{N_t} \tag{4.49}$$

Where $\mathbf{I}_{N_t}$ is the $N_t$-by-$N_t$ identity matrix and $I_{N_r}$ is the $N_r$-by-$N_r$ identity matrix.

### Simplified Narrowband Assumption:

1. Under the narrowband assumption, the channel matrix H is assumed to be constant over the bandwidth of interest, meaning that the channel does not vary with frequency within this band.
2. This simplifies the analysis and allows for the use of a single channel matrix H for all frequencies within the band.
3. The formula provides the average SNR at the input of each receiver in the MIMO channel is mentioned below

$$\rho = \frac{P}{\sigma_w^2} = \frac{N_t \sigma_s^2}{\sigma_w^2} \tag{4.50}$$

4. This means that for a given noise variance, once the total transmit power $P$ is set, the SNR remains constant. Additionally, all $N_t$ transmitted signals share the same channel bandwidth, and the average SNR is not influenced by $N_r$.

### Spectral Efficiency and Capacity:

1. The spectral efficiency and channel capacity of the MIMO system are determined by the properties of the channel matrix **H**.
2. For example, the capacity C of a MIMO channel can be expressed as:

$$C = \log_2 \det\left(\mathbf{I}_{N_r} + \frac{\rho}{N_t}\mathbf{H}\mathbf{H}^H\right) \quad \text{bits/sec} \tag{4.51}$$

Here, ρ is the SNR, and $H^H$ is the Hermitian transpose of H.

## MIMO Capacity for Channel Known at the Receiver

In MIMO systems where the Channel State Information (CSI) is known at the receiver, the capacity analysis can be classified into two main types: **ergodic capacity** and **outage capacity**.

1. **Ergodic capacity:** The ergodic capacity represents the average capacity over all possible channel realizations, if the channel varies rapidly, and the transmitter has no instantaneous knowledge of the channel. It is given by the expected value of the mutual information between the transmitted and received signals.

   For a MIMO system with $N_t$ transmit antennas and $N_r$ receive antennas, the ergodic capacity $C_{erg}$ can be expressed as:

$$C_{\text{erg}} = \mathbb{E}\left[\log_2 \det\left(\mathbf{I}_{N_r} + \frac{\rho}{N_t}\mathbf{H}\mathbf{H}^H\right)\right] \text{ bits/sec for } N_t \geq N_r \quad (4.52)$$

where E denotes the expectation over all channel realizations, ρ represents the SNR, **H** stands for the $N_r \times N_t$ channel matrix, $\mathbf{I}_{N_r}$ represents the $N_r \times N_r$ identity matrix and $\mathbf{H}^H$ denotes the Hermitian transpose of **H**.

2. **Outage Capacity:** The outage capacity defines the capacity for a given probability of an outage. It is particularly useful in scenarios where the channel variations are slow, and the transmitter cannot adapt to instantaneous channel conditions. The outage capacity Cout for a given outage probability $P_{out}$ is defined as the maximum rate R such that the probability that the mutual information $I\ (x;\ y)$ falls below R is less than or equal to $P_{out}$t:

$$C_{\text{out}}\,(P_{\text{out}}) = \max\left\{R; \Pr\left(\log_{g_2}\ \det\left(I_{N_F} + \frac{\rho}{N_t}HH^H\right) < R\right) \text{ for some burst } k \quad (4.53)$$

Where $P_r$ denotes the probability.

### Example:

Let's consider a simplified example with $N_t = N_r = 2$ and ρ = 10 db.

### Ergodic Capacity Example Calculation:

- **Channel Matrix**: Assume a random channel matrix **H**.
- **Eigenvalues**: Compute the eigenvalues of **H**.
- Use the eigenvalues to compute the ergodic capacity.

### Outage Capacity Example Calculation:

1. **Determine the Rate for Given Outage Probability**: For $P_{out}$= 0.1 (10% outage probability), solve for the rate R that satisfies:

$$\Pr\left(\log_2 \det\left(\mathbf{I}_2 + \frac{\rho}{2}\mathbf{H}\mathbf{H}^H\right) < R\right) = 0.1$$

$$C_{\text{out}}\,(P_{\text{out}}) = \max\left\{R: \Pr\left(\log_2 \det\left(I_{N_r} + \rho H^H \mathrm{H}\right) < R\right) \leq P_{\text{out}}\right\}$$

With transmitter CSI, the capacity analysis in MIMO systems considers the transmitter's ability to adapt its transmission strategy based on knowledge of the channel. Both ergodic capacity and outage capacity are fundamental metrics for understanding the performance of MIMO systems in practical communication scenarios.

## 4.3 DIGITAL MODULATION

Digital modulation lies at the core of modern communication systems, providing a means to transmit digital information over analog channels. In digital communications, modulation is the process where some characteristics of a carrier signal is varied in accordance with a modulating signal/wave. Fig. 4.19 shows how modulating signal changes the carrier signal. The modulating wave consists of encoded digital information/binary data in the form of an analog signal and the carrier is a sinusoidal wave. There are several digital modulation schemes, each with their own advantages and disadvantages. From the simplicity of Binary Phase Shift Keying (BPSK) to the complexity of Orthogonal Frequency Division Multiplexing (OFDM), each modulation scheme plays a crucial role in shaping the efficiency, reliability, and data rates of contemporary communication systems.

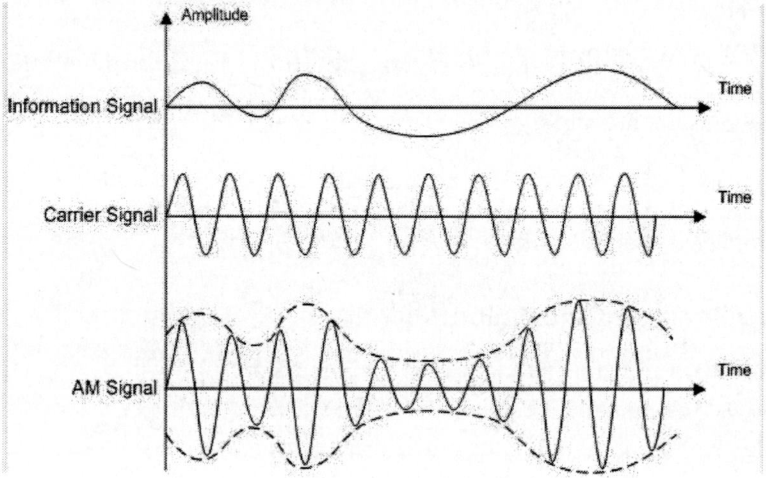


Fig. 4.19 Depiction of information, carrier signal and modulated signal

### 4.3.1 Overview

Before diving into some of the main modulation schemes, we will have some general idea/overview about most fundamental modulation techniques based on keying. These are as follows:

1. **Amplitude Shift Keying (ASK):**

   The simplest digital modulation technique is amplitude-shift keying (ASK) (similar to standard Amplitude Modulation (AM) except there are only two output amplitudes possible), where a binary information signal directly modulates the amplitude of the carrier signal to represent digital data. It is straightforward but susceptible to noise. The modulated ASK signal can be represented as

   $$S_1(t) = \sqrt{\frac{2E_b}{T_b}} \text{Cos } 2\pi f_c t \text{ , for symbol binary '1'}$$

   $$S_0(t) = 0 \text{ , for symbol binary '0'}$$

   Here, $E_b$ is the average energy transmitted per bit, $T_b$ is bit period and $f_c$ is the carrier frequency.

2. **Phase Shift Keying (PSK):**

   Phase Shift Keying (PSK) is a digital modulation technique where the phase of a carrier wave is varied in accordance with the digital signal being transmitted. It is widely used in communication systems for its efficiency and robustness in transmitting data over various types of media. PSK modulates the phase of the carrier signal to represent binary 0 or 1. The modulated PSK signal can be represented (using same notation as before) as

   $$S_1(t) = \sqrt{\frac{2E_b}{T_b}}\,\text{Cos}\,2\pi f_c t \quad \text{, for symbol binary '1'}$$

   $$S_0(t) = \sqrt{\frac{2E_b}{T_b}}\,\text{Cos}\,(2\pi f_c t + \pi) = -\sqrt{\frac{2E_b}{T_b}}\,\text{Cos}\,2\pi f_c t \quad \text{, for symbol binary '0'}$$

3. **Frequency Shift Keying (FSK):**

   Similar to standard Frequency Modulation (FM), FSK is a form of constant-amplitude angle modulation where the modulating signal is a binary signal that varies between two discrete voltage levels rather than a continuously changing analog waveform. FSK modulates the carrier signal's frequency to represent binary data. Common variations include Binary FSK (BFSK) for two-level frequency modulation and M-ary FSK for multiple frequency levels. The modulated FSK signal can be represented as

   $$S_1(t) = \sqrt{\frac{2E_b}{T_b}}\,\text{Cos}\,2\pi f_1 t \quad \text{, for symbol binary '1'}$$

   $$S_0(t) = \sqrt{\frac{2E_b}{T_b}}\,\text{Cos}\,2\pi f_2 t \quad \text{, for symbol binary '0'}$$

   Here, $f_1$ and $f_2$ are the carrier frequencies for symbol '1' and '0' respectively.

4. **Quadrature Amplitude Modulation (QAM):**

   QAM combines both amplitude and phase modulation, where both amplitude and phase are changed. It allows for the transmission of multiple bits per symbol, with higher-order QAM supporting higher data rates.

## 4.3.2 Modulation Schemes

### Binary Phase Shift Keying (BPSK)

Binary phase shift keying is a digital modulation scheme that transmits data by modulating, the phase of a carrier signal or the carrier wave. BPSK uses two phases, 0° and 180°. These two phases are separated by 180°, hence the name Binary phase shift keying. Each of these phases represents a binary digit, either a 0 or a 1. For example, a phase of 0° could represent a binary 1, and a phase of 180° could represent a binary 0 (or vice versa). BPSK is the most robust form of PSK because it can handle the highest levels of noise or distortion before the demodulator makes an incorrect decision. However, BPSK can only modulate at 1 bit per symbol, meaning it can only transmit one bit of data in each symbol (a symbol could be a cycle, pulse, or shift in the carrier wave). This makes BPSK unsuitable for high data-rate applications.

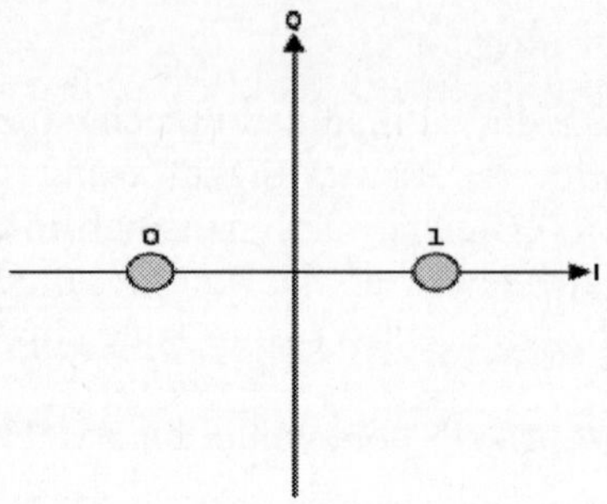


Fig. 4.20 BPSK Constellation diagram : I & Q denote in-phase & quadrature components respectively.

For a particular modulation scheme a set of basis functions, which are generally orthogonal to each other, are chosen. Once the basis functions are chosen, any vector in the signal space can be represented as a linear combination of them. These basis functions can be generated using Gram Schmidt orthogonalization procedure. For BPSK we have only one basis function.

The constellation diagram for BPSK, as shown in Fig. 4.20, will show two constellation points, lying entirely on the x-axis, in-phase. It has no projection on the y axis i.e. no quadrature. This means that the BPSK modulated signal will have an in-phase component but no quadrature component. This is because it has only one basis function. The waveform of BPSK is presented in Fig. 4.21.

The general form for BPSK is given by,

$$S_n(t) = \sqrt{\frac{2E_b}{T_b}}\cos(2\pi f_c t + \pi(1-n)) \;\; ; \;\; n = 0,1 \; ; \; ( 0 \le t \le T_b.) \tag{4.54}$$

Here $E_b$ is average energy transmitted per bit, $T_b$ is bit period, $f_c$ is the carrier frequency.
For binary '0' symbol, n = 0,

$$S_0(t) = \sqrt{\frac{2E_b}{T_b}}\cos(2\pi f_c t + \pi) \, ,$$

$$\text{Or,} \;\; S_0(t) = -\sqrt{\frac{2E_b}{T_b}}\cos(2\pi f_c t) \tag{4.55}$$

For binary '1' symbol, n = 1,

$$S_1(t) = \sqrt{\frac{2E_b}{T_b}}\cos(2\pi f_c t) \tag{4.56}$$

From here it is clear that we need only one basis function, $\phi(t) = \sqrt{\frac{2}{T_b}}\cos(2\pi f_c t)$ to generate the signal space.

**Bit Error Rate (BER) for BPSK modulation:**

We can represent the binary digits 1 and 0 maybe by the analog levels $+\sqrt{E_b}$ and $-\sqrt{E_b}$ respectively in case of BPSK. Here an example of theoretical equation for Bit Error Rate (BER) with BPSK modulation scheme in Additive White Gaussian Noise (AWGN) channel will be given. It is assumed that the transmitted waveform gets corrupted by noise 'n', typically referred to as AWGN.

The received signal with added noise can be written as, y = $S_1 + n$, when bit 1 is transmitted and y = $S_0 + n$, when bit 0 is transmitted.

The conditional probability distribution function of 'y' for the two cases are:

$$p(y \mid S_0) = \frac{1}{\sqrt{\pi N_0}} e^{\frac{-(y+\sqrt{E_b})^2}{N_0}}$$

$$p(y \mid S_1) = \frac{1}{\sqrt{\pi N_0}} e^{\frac{-(y-\sqrt{E_b})^2}{N_0}}$$

The values of the noise 'n' follows the Gaussian probability distribution function,

$$p(x) = \frac{1}{\sqrt{2\pi\sigma^2}} e^{\frac{-(x-\mu)^2}{2\sigma^2}} \text{ with } \mu = 0 \text{ and } \sigma^2 = \frac{N_0}{2}. \quad (4.57)$$

Assuming that $S_1$ and $S_0$ are equally probable i.e. $p(S_1) = p(S_0) = 1/2$, the threshold 0 forms the optimal decision boundary. If the received signal y is greater than 0, then the receiver assumes $S_1$ was transmitted. If the received signal y is less than or equal to 0, then the receiver assumes $S_0$ was transmitted.

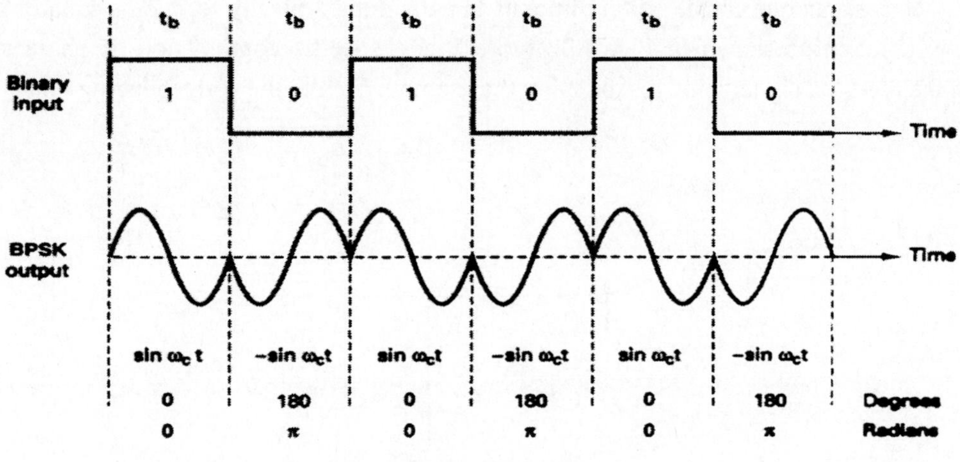


Fig. 4.21 BPSK waveform

With this threshold, the probability of error given $S_1$ is transmitted can be written as

$$p(e \mid S_1) = \frac{1}{\sqrt{\pi N_0}} \int_{-\infty}^{0} e^{\frac{-(y-\sqrt{E_b})^2}{N_0}} dy$$

$$= \frac{1}{\sqrt{\pi}} \int_{\sqrt{\frac{E_b}{N_0}}}^{\infty} e^{-z^2} dz = \frac{1}{2} \operatorname{erfc}\left(\sqrt{\frac{E_b}{N_0}}\right)$$

Similarly, the probability of error given $S_0$ is transmitted can be written as

$$p(e \mid S_0) = \frac{1}{\sqrt{\pi N_0}} \int_0^{\infty} e^{\frac{-(y+\sqrt{E_b})^2}{N_0}} dy$$

$$p(e \mid S_0) = \frac{1}{\sqrt{\pi}} \int_{\sqrt{\frac{E_b}{N_0}}}^{\infty} e^{-z^2} dz = \frac{1}{2} \operatorname{erfc}\left(\sqrt{\frac{E_b}{N_0}}\right) \quad (4.58)$$

Total probability of bit error = $P_b = p(S_1)p(e \mid S_1) + p(S_0)p(e \mid S_0). = \frac{1}{2}\operatorname{erfc}\left(\sqrt{\frac{E_b}{N_0}}\right)$

## Quadrature Phase Shift Keying (QPSK)

Quadrature Phase Shift Keying (QPSK) stands as a pivotal digital modulation scheme, strategically balancing spectral efficiency and implementation complexity. QPSK relies on the manipulation of phase to encode information, utilizing two orthogonal carrier waves to transmit data. This modulation technique allows for the representation of two bits per symbol, enhancing the data throughput compared to BPSK, which transmits one bit per symbol. The four possible phase shifts in QPSK—0°, 90°, 180°, and 270°—create a unique constellation of points in a diagram, typically forming a square. Each point in this constellation as shown in Fig. 4.22 represents a specific combination of phase shifts, and decoding the received signal involves mapping these points back to the corresponding binary values.

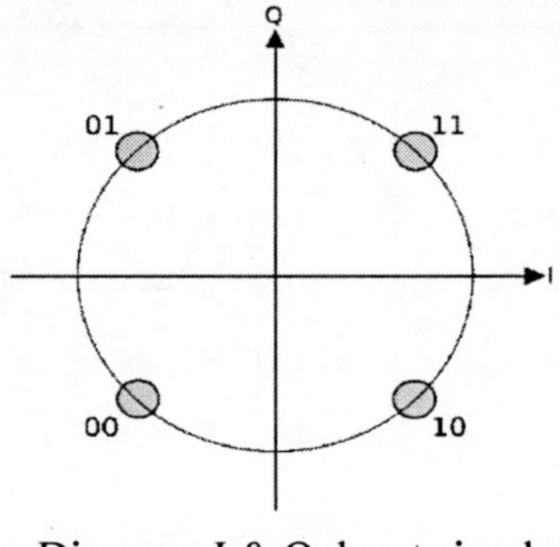


Fig. 4.22 QPSK Constellation Diagram: I & Q denote in-phase & quadrature components respectively.

One of the primary advantages of QPSK lies in its spectral efficiency. By transmitting two bits of information per symbol, QPSK effectively doubles the data rate compared to BPSK while occupying the same bandwidth. This attribute makes QPSK, whose waveform is presented in Fig. 4.23, particularly attractive in applications where maximizing data throughput within a constrained bandwidth is crucial. Common scenarios include satellite communication, digital television broadcasting, wireless LANs (Wi-Fi), and certain Digital Subscriber Line (DSL) systems. In satellite communication, for instance, where bandwidth is often limited and expensive, QPSK's efficiency plays a pivotal role in optimizing the utilization of available resources.

However, this spectral efficiency comes at a trade-off with susceptibility to errors induced by noise and interference. In communication systems, signals traverse various channels and mediums, each introducing its own set of challenges. QPSK, being a phase-based modulation scheme, is sensitive to phase distortions introduced by factors such as channel noise, atmospheric conditions, and electronic interference. Consequently, the error performance of QPSK is not as robust as higher-order modulation schemes like 16-QAM or 64-QAM, which can transmit more bits per symbol but often at the cost of increased complexity.

To address some of these challenges, Differential QPSK (DQPSK) emerges as a variant that alters the approach to encoding information. Rather than relying on absolute phase values, DQPSK encodes data based on the phase differences between consecutive symbols. This differential encoding scheme introduces resilience to variations in absolute phase, offering improved performance in the presence of phase noise. While DQPSK may not match the raw data rates achievable with QPSK, its enhanced robustness makes it a preferred choice in scenarios where maintaining reliable communication is paramount, even in less-than-ideal channel conditions. The complexity of modulation schemes is a critical consideration in practical implementations. QPSK strikes a balance by providing a level of complexity that is manageable for real-world applications. While more straightforward than higher-order modulation schemes, QPSK still demands sophisticated signal processing and modulation/demodulation circuitry. This balance is crucial in scenarios where implementation simplicity is valued alongside the need for moderate data rates.

QPSK signals are defined by –

$$S_i(t) = A\cos(2\pi f_c t + \theta_i), 0 \le t \le T, i = 1,2,3,4 \quad ; \text{where, } \theta_i = \frac{(2i-1)\pi}{4} \tag{4.59}$$

$$= A\cos\theta_i \cos 2\pi f_c t - A\sin\theta_i \sin 2\pi f_c t$$

$$= s_{i1}\phi_1(t) + s_{i2}\phi_2(t)$$

Where, $\phi_1(t) = \sqrt{\frac{2E}{T}}\cos(2\pi f_c t)$ & $\phi_2(t) = -\sqrt{\frac{2E}{T}}\sin(2\pi f_c t)$ are the basis functions, A is the amplitude of the signal wave, E = $\frac{A^2T}{2}$ is the symbol energy.

Here, $s_{i1} = \int_0^T s_i(t)\phi_1(t)dt = \sqrt{E}\cos\theta_i$ and $s_{i2} = \int_0^T s_i(t)\phi_2(t)dt = \sqrt{E}\cos\theta_i$

We observe that this signal is a linear combination of two orthonormal basis functions: I(t) and Q(t). On a coordinate system of I(t) and Q(t) we can represent these four signals by

$$S(t) = AI(t)/\sqrt{2}\cos 2\pi f_c t - AQ(t)/\sqrt{2}\sin 2\pi f_c t \tag{4.60}$$

**where I(t) and Q(t) are pulse trains determined by the odd-numbered bits and even numbered bits, respectively.** The angle of vector $s_i$ with respect to the horizontal axis is the signal initial phase

$\theta_i$. The length of the vectors is $\sqrt{E}$. The modulator of QPSK is based on S(t). This leads to the modulator in Fig. 4.24.

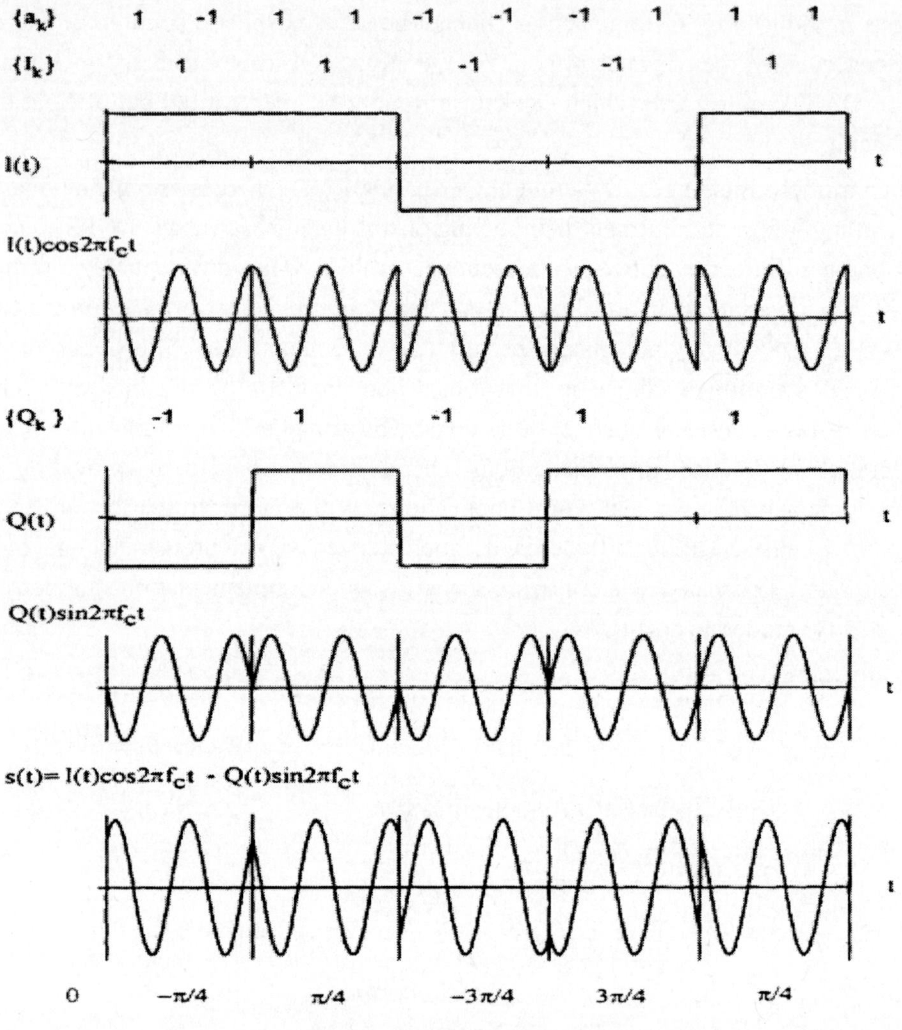


Fig. 4.23 QPSK Waveform

The channel with cosine reference is called in-phase (I) channel and the channel with sine reference is called quadrature (Q) channel. The data sequence is separated by the serial-to-parallel converter (S/P) to form the odd-numbered-bit sequence for I-channel and the even-numbered-bit sequence for Q-channel.

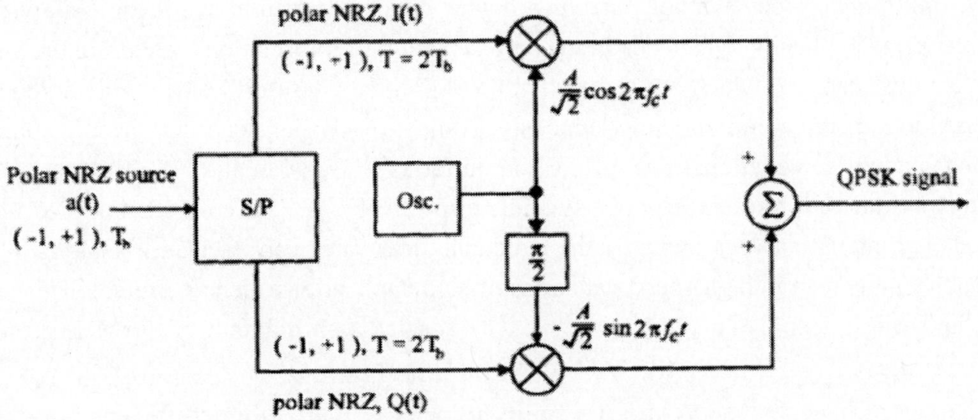


Fig. 4.24 QPSK Modulator

Then logic 1 is converted to a positive pulse and logic 0 is converted to a negative pulse, both have the same amplitude and a duration of T. Next the odd-numbered-bit pulse train is multiplied to cos $2\pi f_c t$ and the even-numbered-bit pulse train is multiplied to sin $2\pi f_c t$. It is clear that the I-channel and Q-channel signals are BPSK signals with a symbol duration of $2T_b$. Finally, a summer adds these two waveforms together to produce the final QPSK signal.

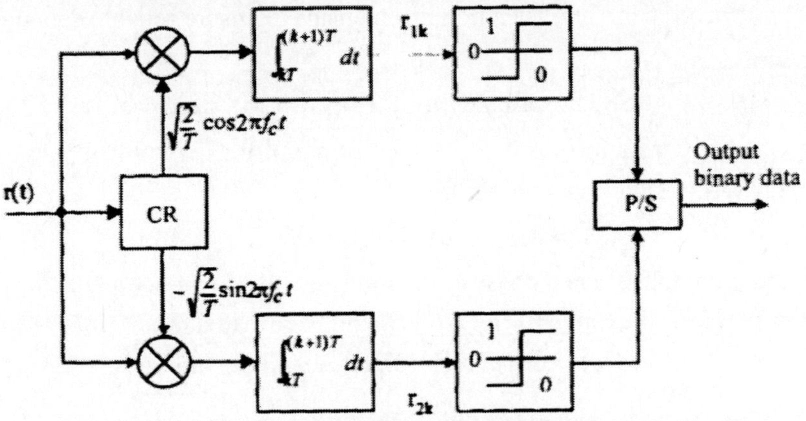


Fig. 4.25 QPSK Demodulator

It is shown in Fig. 4.25, I- and Q-channel signals are demodulated separately as two individual BPSK signals. A Parallel-to-Serial converter (PIS) is used to combine two sequences into a single sequence. This is possible because of the one-to-one correspondence between data bits and I- and Q-channel signals and their orthogonality.

## Quadrature Amplitude Modulation (QAM)

Quadrature Amplitude Modulation (QAM) stands as a sophisticated and widely utilized modulation scheme in modern communication systems, seamlessly combining amplitude and phase modulation to transmit data efficiently. In essence, QAM manipulates both the amplitude and phase of a carrier signal to encode multiple bits per symbol, enabling higher data rates within the same bandwidth. The fundamental principle behind QAM lies in the representation of information by altering the amplitude of two quadrature carriers, which are signals with a 90-degree phase difference. This unique feature allows QAM to transmit a multitude of distinct signal states, each representing a specific combination of amplitude and phase variations. The most common forms of QAM include 16-QAM and 64-QAM, which can transmit four and six bits per symbol, respectively. As the constellation size increases, accommodating more bits per symbol, the potential data rate also escalates, making QAM an indispensable component in high-speed data transmission applications such as digital television, cable modems, and wireless communication systems. The constellation diagram of QAM is presented in Fig. 26.

One of the key advantages of QAM is its ability to achieve high spectral efficiency, enabling the transmission of large amounts of data within limited bandwidth. This efficiency is particularly crucial in scenarios where bandwidth is a scarce resource, such as in wireless communication networks. By packing multiple bits into a single symbol, QAM significantly increases the data rate without requiring additional bandwidth, making it a preferred choice for various communication standards like Wi-Fi, digital television, and 4G/5G cellular networks. However, this heightened spectral efficiency comes at the cost of increased susceptibility to noise and channel impairments, necessitating the implementation of sophisticated error correction and detection mechanisms to ensure reliable data transmission.

QAM signal is written as:

$$S_i(t) = A_i cos(2\pi f_c t + \theta_i) \;;\; \text{i} = 1,2,3,..\text{M} \tag{4.61}$$

Pulse shaping is usually used to improve the spectrum and for ISI control purpose in QAM. With pulse shaping, the QAM signal can be written as

$$S_i(t) = A_i p(t) cos(2\pi f_c t + \theta_i)$$

where, $A_i$ & $\theta_i$ are the amplitude and phase of the i-th signal of the M-ary signal, respectively and $p(t)$ is a smooth pulse define in the range [0, T]. Now $S_i$ can be rewritten as,

$$S_i(t) = A_{i1} p(t) \cos 2\pi f_c t - A_{i2} p(t) \sin 2\pi f_c t \tag{4.62}$$

$$\text{Here, } A_{i1} = A_i \cos\theta_i \,;\, A_{i2} = A_i \sin\theta_i \;\&\; A_i = \sqrt{A_{i1}^2 + A_{i2}^2}$$

Now QAM signal can be expressed as,

$$s_i(t) = s_{i1}\phi_1(t) + s_{i2}\phi_2(t)$$

where, $\phi_1(t)$ & $\phi_2(t)$ are basis functions and $s_{i1}$ & $s_{i2}$ contain amplitude and phase information which are described as follows,

$$s_{i1} = \sqrt{\frac{E_p}{2}} A_{i1} = \sqrt{\frac{E_p}{2}} A_i \cos\theta_i \quad \& \quad s_{i2} = \sqrt{\frac{E_p}{2}} A_{i2} = \sqrt{\frac{E_p}{2}} A_i \sin\theta_i$$

$$\phi_1(t) = \sqrt{\frac{2}{E_p}} p(t)\cos 2\pi f_c t, 0 \le t \le T \tag{4.63}$$

$$\phi_2(t) = -\sqrt{\frac{2}{E_p}} p(t)\sin 2\pi f_c t, 0 \le t \le T \tag{4.64}$$

Here, $E_p$ is the energy of p(t) in [0, T]. When there is no pulse shaping, that is, p(t) = 1 in [0, T], $E_p$ = T. The energy of the i-th signal is $E_i = \int_0^T S_i^2(t)dt \cong \frac{1}{2} A_i^2 E_p$

Average signal energy is given by $\frac{1}{2} E\{A_i^2\} E_p$.

If pulse shaping is not desired, the p(t) block will be absent. The data bit sequence is divided into n-tuples of n bits. There are $M = 2^n$ distinct n-tuples. Each n-tuple of the input bits is used to control the level generator. The level generator provides the I and Q-channel the particular sign and level for a signal's horizontal and vertical coordinates ($A_{i1}$, $A_{i2}$), respectively. The mapping from n-tuples to QAM points are usually Gray coded for minimizing bit errors. For square QAM, perfect Gray coding is possible. Digital synthesis techniques can be used to generate QAM signals. Each signal in the constellation can be stored as a set of samples and the data n-tuple is used as the address to obtain the samples. The samples are fed to a D/A converter whose output is the desired QAM signal. A QAM modulator diagram is also presented in Fig. 4.27.

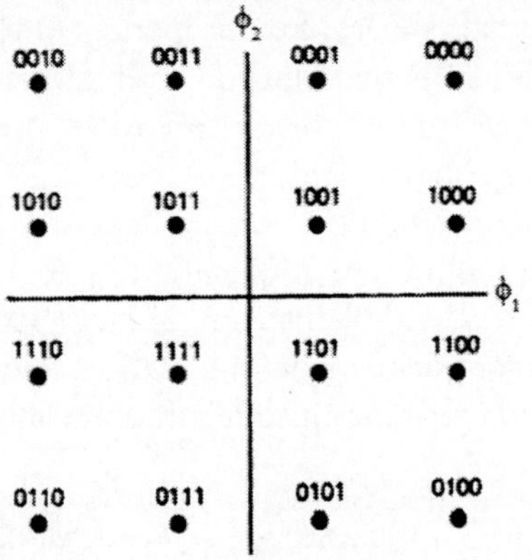


Fig. 4.26 QAM Constellation Diagram : $\phi_2$ is Quadrature component and $\phi_1$ is in-phase component.

## Minimum Shift Keying (MSK)

Quadrature Phase Shift Keying (QPSK) is a digital modulation technique that transmits data by changing the phase of two synchronized signals. In Offset QPSK (OQPSK), the I-channel and Q-channel data streams are staggered and directly modulated onto two orthogonal carriers. To create a Minimum Shift Keying (MSK) signal, each bit of the I(t) and Q(t) streams is weighted with a half period of a cosine or sine function with a period of 4T, where T is the bit period. The weighted signals are then modulated onto orthogonal carriers, resulting in an MSK signal given by the equation:

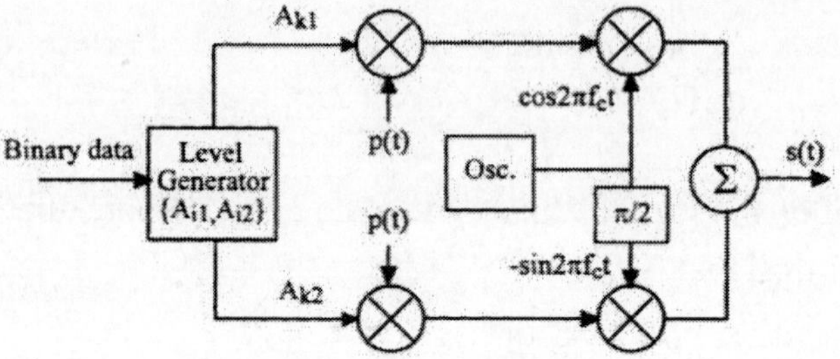


Fig. 4.27 QAM Modulator

$$S(t) = AI(t)\cos\left(\frac{\pi t}{2T}\right)\cos 2\pi f_c t + AQ(t)\sin\left(\frac{\pi t}{2T}\right) sin\, 2\pi f_c t \tag{4.65}$$

where, $f_c$ is the carrier frequency. The I(t) waveform represents the sample symbol stream, and each symbol occupies an interval of 2T. The weighting cosine waveform coincides with one symbol of I(t). The cosine-weighted symbol stream and the modulated I-channel carrier are obtained by multiplying the previous waveforms by the carrier signal, $\cos(2\pi f_c t)$.

Similarly, for the Q-channel, the Q(t) stream is delayed by T, and the weighting signal is a sine function. The sine-weighted symbol stream and the modulated Q-channel carrier are obtained similarly. The composite MSK signal is the sum of the modulated I-channel and Q-channel carriers.

Observing the composite MSK signal, several key properties emerge. First, the envelope is constant, providing a constant power waveform. Second, the phase remains continuous at bit transitions, avoiding abrupt phase changes present in QPSK or OQPSK. Third, MSK is essentially a Frequency Shift Keying (FSK) signal with two different frequencies, and its symbol duration is $2T$. These characteristics make MSK a robust modulation scheme, well-suited for applications where constant envelope and phase continuity are essential, such as in mobile communication systems and satellite links. The continuous phase property helps minimize inter-symbol interference and facilitates efficient use of bandwidth, making MSK an attractive choice for various communication standards. Understanding the waveform evolution in each stage of modulation provides insights into the unique features and advantages of MSK in digital communication systems.

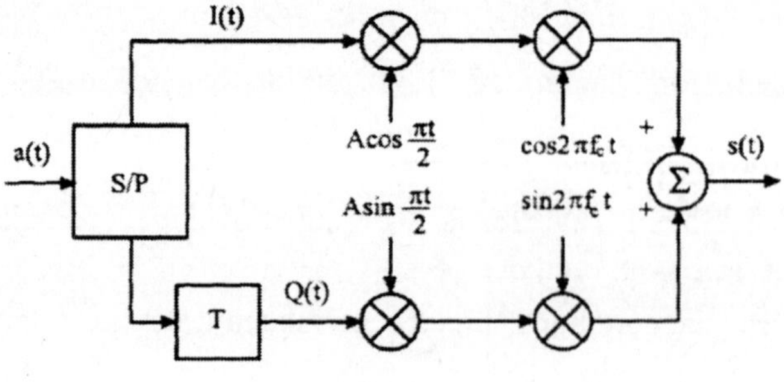


Fig. 4.28 MSK Modulator

Fig. 4.28 is the MSK modulator implemented as a sinusoidal weighted OQPSK. The data stream signal a(t) is demultiplexed into I(t) and Q(t) by the Serial-to-Parallel converter (SIP). The in-phase channel signal I(t) consists of even-numbered bits, and the quadrature channel signal Q(t) consists of odd-numbered bits. Each bit in I(t) and Q(t) has a duration of 2T. Q(t) is delayed by T with respect to I(t). I(t) is multiplied by $A\cos\left(\frac{\pi t}{2T}\right)$ and $\cos(2\pi f_c t)$. in the two subsequent multipliers in the I-channel. Q(t) is multiplied by $A\sin\left(\frac{\pi t}{2T}\right)$ and $sin(2\pi f_c t)$ in the two subsequent multipliers in the Q-channel. $A\sin\left(\frac{\pi t}{2T}\right)$ and $sin(2\pi f_c t)$ are obtained through $\pi/2$ phase shifters from $A\cos\left(\frac{\pi t}{2T}\right)$ and $\cos(2\pi f_c t)$, respectively. In the summer, the I-channel and Q-channel modulated signals are added to obtain the MSK signal. Previous discussion has shown that $A\cos\left(\frac{\pi t}{2T}\right)$ and $\cos(2\pi f_c t)$ need not be synchronized. Therefore Acos $\left(\frac{\pi t}{2T}\right)$ and $\cos(2\pi f_c t)$ can be generated by two independent-oscillators.

Using the two basis functions defined in the previous section, the MSK signal in the kth bit interval can be written as

$$s(t) = I_k\phi_I(t) + Q_k\phi_Q(t), \quad kT \le t \le (k+1)T$$

It can be shown that $\phi_I(t)$ and $\phi_Q(t)$ are orthogonal for fc, = n/4T, n integer ($n \neq 1$), over a period of T.

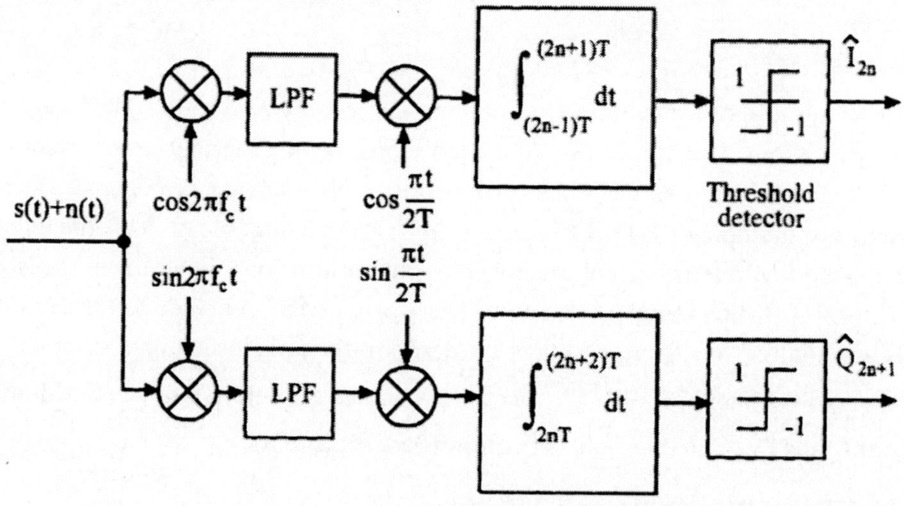


Fig. 4.29 MSK Demodulator

Since I(t) and Q(t) are orthogonal, the optimum coherent demodulation of MSK is very much similar to that of QPSK. Fig. 4.29 is the optimum coherent MSK demodulator (the method of obtaining the reference signals and bit timing will be discussed in the next section). Since each data symbol in I(t) or

Q(t) occupies a period of 2T, the demodulator operates on a 2T basis. We now denote symbols as ($I_k$, k = 0,2,4, ... and $Q_k$, k = 1,3,5, ...). For kth symbol interval, the integration interval in the I-channel is from (2n - l)T to (2n + l)T and in the Q-channel is from 2nT to (2n + 2)T, where n = 0,1,2, .... These intervals correspond to the respective data symbol periods. In I-channel the integrator output is:

$$\int_{(2n-1)T}^{(2n+1)T} s(t)\phi_I(t)dt$$

$$= \int_{(2n-1)T}^{(2n+1)T} [I_k\phi_I(t) + Q_k\phi_Q(t)]\phi_I(t)dt$$

$$= \int_{(2n-1)T}^{(2n+1)T} I_k\phi_I^2(t)dt, \quad \text{the second term vanishes due to orthogonality)}$$

$$= \int_{(2n-1)T}^{(2n+1)T} A^2 I_k \cos^2\left(\frac{\pi t}{2T}\right) \cos^2 2\pi f_c t dt$$

$$= \int_{(2n-1)T}^{(2n+1)T} A^2 I_k \frac{1}{2}\left(1 + \cos\left(\frac{\pi t}{T}\right)\right)\frac{1}{2}(1 + \cos 4\pi f_c t)dt$$

$$= \int_{(2n-1)T}^{(2n+1)T} \frac{1}{4}A^2 I_k \left[1 + \cos\left(\frac{\pi t}{T}\right) + \cos 4\pi f_c t + \cos\left(\frac{\pi t}{T}\right)\cos 4\pi f_c t\right] dt \qquad (4.66)$$

$$= \frac{1}{2}A^2 T I_k$$

Only the first term in the above integration in (4.66) produces a nonzero result. The integration of the second term is exactly zero. The integrations of the third term and the fourth term are exactly zero only when $f_c$, is a multiple of 1/4T (i.e., when the carriers of two channels are orthogonal). Therefore, we usually choose $f_c$, as a multiple of 1/4T. However, even if, is not a multiple of 1/4T, the integrations of the third term and the fourth term are not exactly zero; but they are very small in comparison with the first term for $f_c$, >> 1/T, which is usually the case. Therefore, we can conclude that the sampler output of I-channel is essentially $\frac{1}{2}A^2TI_k$ regardless of the carrier orthogonality. Similarly, we can show that the sampler output of Q-channel is $\frac{1}{2}A^2TI_k$. These two signals are detected by the threshold detectors to finally put out $I_k$ and $Q_k$. The thresholds of detectors are set to zero.

## Gaussian Minimum Shift Keying (GMSK)

There are two main ways in which GMSK modulation can be generated. The most obvious way is to filter the modulating signal using a Gaussian filter and then apply this to a frequency modulator where the modulation index is set to 0.5. This method is very simple and straightforward, but it has the drawback that the modulation index must exactly equal 0.5. In practice this analogue method is not suitable because component tolerances drift and cannot be set exactly. A second method is more widely used. Here what is known as a quadrature modulator is used. The term quadrature means that the phase of a signal is in quadrature or 90 degrees to another one. The quadrature modulator uses one signal that is said to be in-phase and another that is in quadrature to this. In view of the in-phase and quadrature elements this type of modulator is often said to be an I-Q modulator. Using this type of modulator the modulation index can be maintained at exactly 0.5 without the need for any settings or adjustments. This makes it much easier to use, and capable of providing the required level of performance without the need for adjustments. For demodulation the technique can be used in reverse.

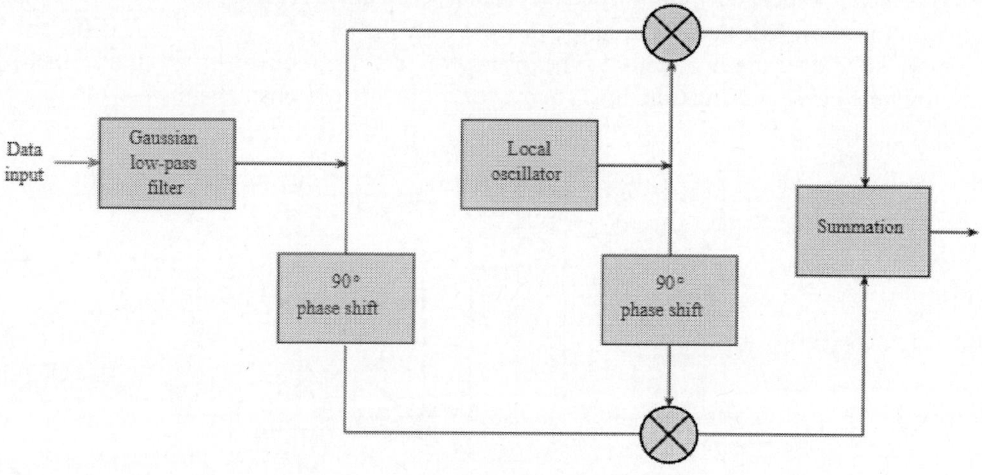


Fig. 4.30 GMSK Modulation

## 4.4 MULTICARRIER BASICS

Consider a bandwidth $B = 2W$ available for communication, where $W$ is the one-sided bandwidth, or, in other words, the maximum frequency. For a single carrier communication system, the symbol time $T$ is given as

$$T = \frac{1}{B} \tag{4.67}$$

basically, implying that symbols can be transmitted at intervals of $\frac{1}{B}$ seconds each. Therefore, the symbol rate is given as

$$\text{Rate} = \frac{1}{1/B} = B \tag{4.68}$$

Such a system is termed a single-carrier communication system. In such a system, a single carrier is employed for the entire baseband bandwidth of $B$. Therefore, roughly speaking, the symbols are transmitted as symbol $X(0)$ from $0 \leq t < T$, symbol $X(1)$ from $T \leq t < 2T$, and so on, i.e., roughly one symbol transmitted every $T = \frac{1}{B}$ seconds.

Consider now dividing the total bandwidth $B$ into $N$ sub-bands of bandwidth $B/N$ each as shown in Fig 4.18. Each subcarrier can now be represented by a subcarrier. Therefore, the subcarriers are placed at

$\ldots, -\frac{B}{N}, 0, \frac{B}{N}, \ldots$, as shown in the Fig. 4.31. For instance, consider the bandwidth $B = 256$kHz with $N =$ 64 subcarriers. The bandwidth per sub-band is equal to $\frac{256}{64} = 4$ kHz, which is also the frequency spacing between the subcarriers. We now implement a multi-carrier transmission system as follows. Consider the $i^{\text{th}}$ subcarrier at the frequency $f_i = i\frac{B}{N}$, with $-\left(\frac{N}{2} - 1\right) \leq i \leq \frac{N}{2}$. Let $X_i$ denote the data transmitted on the $i^{\text{th}}$ subcarrier. Then, the signal $s_i(t)$ corresponding to the $i^{\text{th}}$ subcarrier is given as

$$s_i(t) = X_i e^{j2\pi f_i t} = X_i e^{j2\pi i \frac{B}{N} t}$$

where $f_i$ is the $i^{\text{th}}$ subcarrier centre frequency, as described above, and $e^{j2\pi f_i t}$ is the $i^{\text{th}}$ subcarrier. The above equation shows the data modulation process over the $i^{\text{th}}$ subcarrier. The $N$ different data symbols $X_i$ are modulated over the $N$ different subcarriers with centre frequencies $f_i$. Hence, there are a total of $N$ data streams. Next, we illustrate the scheme for multicarrier transmission.

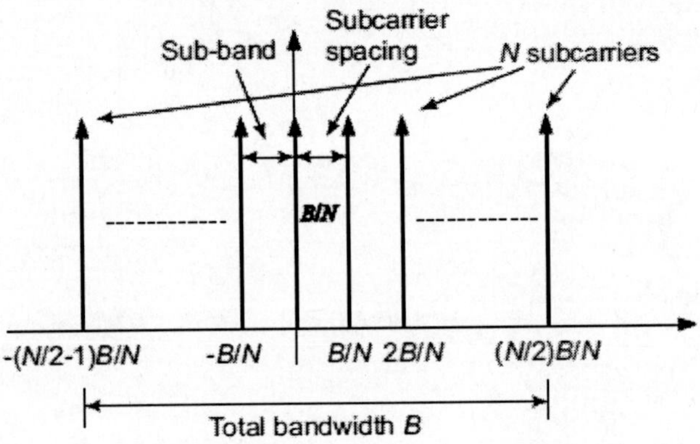


Fig. 4.31 Multi-carrier Concept

## 4.5 MULTICARRIER TRANSMISSION

Consider the different modulated signals $s_i(t)$ corresponding to the $N$ different subcarriers. These signals are then superposed at the transmitted to form the composite signal $s(t)$ given as

$$\begin{aligned} s(t) &= \sum_i X_i e^{j2\pi f_i t} \\ &= \sum_i X_i e^{j2\pi f_i t} \\ &= \sum_i s_i(t) \end{aligned} \tag{4.69}$$

This composite signal $s(t)$ is then transmitted over the wireless channels. Thus, $N$ different data streams are transmitted over $N$ subcarriers in parallel in this multicarrier system. At the receivers, the individual data streams have then to be isolated from the composite signal $s(t)$ above. This is accomplished as follows. Consider the signal $y(t)$ received as

$$y(t) = s(t) = \sum_{i} X_i e^{j2\pi f_i t} \tag{4.70}$$

For simplicity, to illustrate the demodulation procedure at the receiver, we have assumed noise to be absent above. We will consider the general case of a noisy received signal later. From the expression for the composite signal $s(t)$ *in* , it can be readily seen that the expression on the right-hand side is indeed the Fourier series respresentation $s(t)$, corresponding to the fundamental frequency $f_0 = (B)N$ and the various $X_i$ representing the Fourier coefficients. Indeed, all the frequencies $i\frac{B}{N}$ are multiples of the fundamental frequency $f_0 = \frac{1}{T_0} = \frac{B}{N}$. Therefore, to extract $X_l$, which is the Fourier coefficient corresponding to the frequency $f_l = lf_0$, one needs to follow the procedure similar to compute the Fourier series as

$$\begin{aligned}
f_0 \int_0^{T_0} y(t)\left(e^{j2\pi f_i t}\right)^* dt &= \frac{B}{N}\int_0^{\frac{N}{B}} \left(\sum_i X_i e^{j2\pi i \frac{B}{N}t}\right) e^{-j2\pi l \frac{B}{N}t} dt \\
&= \frac{B}{N}\sum_i \int_0^{\frac{N}{B}} X_i e^{j2\pi(i-l)f_0 t} dt \\
&= \underbrace{\frac{B}{N}\int_0^{\frac{N}{B}} X_l dt}_{i=l} + \frac{B}{N}\sum_{i\neq l}\int_0^{\frac{N}{B}} X_i e^{j2\pi(i-l)f_0 t} dt \\
&= X_l + \frac{B}{N}\sum_{i\neq l} X_i \underbrace{\int_0^{\frac{N}{B}} e^{j2\pi(i-l)f_0 t} dt}_{=0} \\
&= X_l
\end{aligned} \tag{4.71}$$

where we have used the fact that $\int_0^{T_0} e^{j2\pi(i-l)f_0 t} dt = 0$ for $i \neq l$, since this is basically integrating a sinusoid of frequency $(i-l)f_0$, which is a multiple of the fundamental frequency $f_0$ over the period $T_0$. Therefore, since there are an integer number of cycles of the sinusoid of frequency $(i-l)f_0$, this integral is 0. In fact, this basically implies that the different sinusoids $e^{j2\pi i f_0 t}$ and $e^{j2\pi l f_0 t}$ are orthogonal. It is this key property of orthogonality which helps extract the different streams $X_i$ modulated over the different subcarriers. This property of orthogonality can be summarized as

$$\int_0^{N/B} e^{j2\pi(i-l)\frac{B}{N}t} = \begin{cases} 0, & i \neq l \\ \frac{N}{B}, & i = l \end{cases} \tag{4.72}$$

Therefore, all the subcarriers other than the $l^{\text{th}}$ subcarrier are orthogonal to the $l^{\text{th}}$ subcarrier. Further, observe that multiplying with $\left(e^{j2\pi f_l t}\right)^*$ and integrating is basically coherent demodulation, i.e., demodulation with the carrier matched to the subcarrier frequency $f_l = l\frac{B}{N}$. Thus, $X_l$, the data modulated on the different subcarriers, can be conveniently recovered by coherently demoudulating with each of the subcarriers corresponding to $l = -\left(\frac{N}{2} - 1\right), \ldots, \frac{N}{2}$. The above scheme of transmission on multiple orthogonal subcarriers and the associated data recovery at the receiver is termed Multi Carrier Modulation (MCM). Also observe that the window of time associated with detection of this multicarrier signal is $\frac{N}{B} = \frac{1}{f_0} = T_0$, which is basically the time period of integration. Hence, MCM basically transmits $N$ symbols using $N$ subcarriers in a time period of $\frac{N}{B}$. The symbol rate is, therefore, $\frac{N}{N/B} = B$. Thus, the overall symbol rate in single carrier vs multicarrier systems is unchanged. The transmitter and receiver block schematics for this MCM system are shown in Fig. 4.32 and 4.33 respectively.

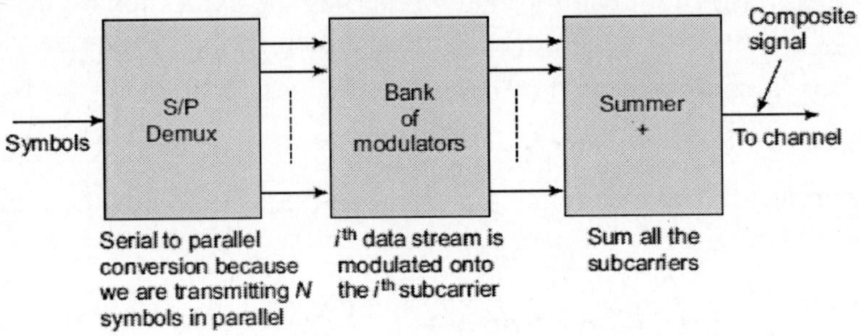


Fig. 4.32 Multicarrier modulation transmitter

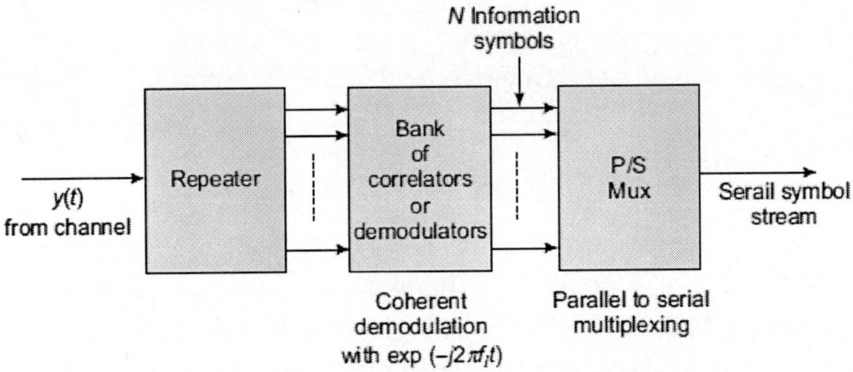


Fig. 4.33 Multi-carrier modulation receiver

It is very important now to note the following fact. Observe from (4.68) and the above rate for an MCM system. It is clear that the symbol rate in both these systems is exactly identical, i.e., $B$. The single-carrier system transmits each symbol in time $\frac{1}{B}$, while the MCM system transmits $N$ symbols in parallel in time $\frac{N}{B}$. What then is the advantage of an MCM system over the single-carrier system? To understand this, consider an example with a transmission bandwidth of $B = 1.024\text{MHz}$, i.e., 1024kHz. As seen in an earlier chapter, notice that this bandwidth $B$ is much greater than the coherence bandwidth $B_c$ which is typically around 250kHz, i.e., $B_c \approx 250\text{kHz}$. Therefore, since the transmission bandwidth $B \gg B_c$, the single-carrier system experiences frequency-selective fading and inter-symbol interference. However, consider an OFDM system with employs $N = 256$ subcarriers in the same bandwidth. The bandwidth per subcarrier is $B_s = \frac{1024}{256} = 4\text{kHz}$. It can be readily seen that the subcarrier bandwidth of 4kHz is significantly lower than the coherence bandwidth of 250kHz. Thus, since $\frac{B}{N} << B_c$, each subcarrier experiences flat fading. Hence, there is no inter-symbol interference in the data transmitted on any of the subcarriers. Thus, the most critical and key benefit of this MCM system is that through parallel transmission using multiple narrowband subcarriers, it eliminates the Inter-Symbol interference (ISI), thus avoiding distortion of the received symbols.

However, the above MCM system suffers from a significant bottleneck. Implementing the bank of $N$ modulators and $N$ demodulators with closely spaced subcarrier frequencies is an extremely challenging task. This was solved by the key idea proposed by Weinstein and Ebert in 1972, in the paper titled "Data Transmission by Frequency Division Multiplexing using the Discrete Fourier Transform". Both of them were engineers at Bell Telephone Laboratories. Their idea can be described as follows. Consider the MCM transmit signal $s(t)$. Observe that it is band-limited to the bandwidth $B$ (total bandwidth). Therefore, the Nyquist sampling rate is $B$ and the associated sampling time is $T_s = \frac{1}{B}$. The composite MCM signal given in (4.69). The $u^{\text{th}}$ sample at time instant $uT_s = \frac{u}{B}$ is given as

$$\begin{aligned} s(uT_s) = x(u) &= \sum_i X_i e^{j2\pi i \frac{BH}{NB}} \\ x(u) &= \underbrace{\sum_i X_i e^{j2\pi \frac{iu}{N}}}_{\text{DFT}} \end{aligned} \tag{4.73}$$

Observe from the expression above that the sample $x(u)$ is basically the Inverse Discrete Fourier Transform (IDFT) coefficient of the information symbols $X(0), X(1), \ldots, X(N-1)$ at the $u^{\text{th}}$ time point. Thus, the Inverse Fast Fourier Transform (IFFT) can be conveniently employed to generate the sample MCM signal. This scheme of generating the composite transmit signal through IDFT was proposed by Weinstein and Ebert in 1971. Thus, it drastically reduces the complexity of implementing an OFDM system since it eliminates the need for the bank of modulators corresponding to the different subcarrier frequencies. This technique, where the MCM signal is generated by employing the IFFT operation is termed Orthogonal Frequency Division Multiplexing, or OFDM. At the receiver, to recover the information symbols, one can correspondingly employ an FFT operation. Schematic figures of the OFDM transmitter and receiver with the IFFT and FFT blocks are given in figures 4.34 and 4.35 respectively.

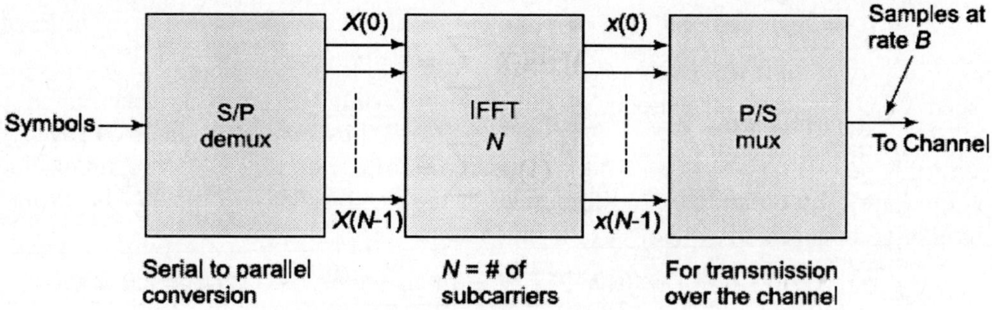


Fig. 4.34 OFDM transmitter schematic with IFFT

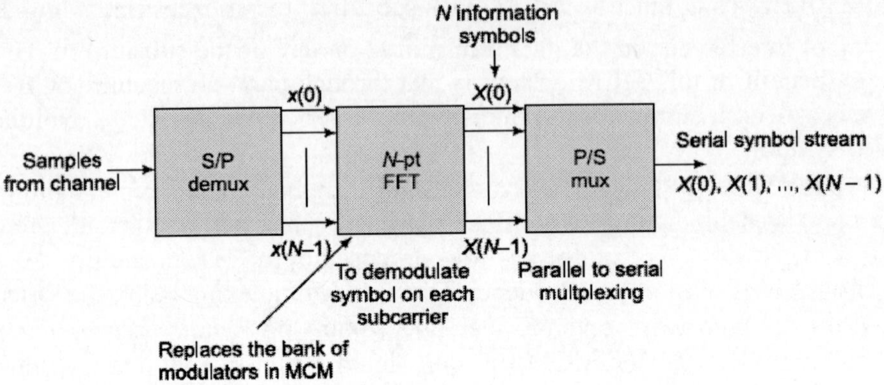


Fig. 4.35 OFDM receiver schematic with FFT

## 4.6 MULTICARRIER TRANSMISSION

In this section, we explain the concept of cyclic prefix, which is an important component of an OFDM system. Consider a frequency-selective channel modelled with channel taps $h(0), h(1), \ldots, h(L-1)$. Thus, the received symbol $y$ at a given time instant $n$ can be expressed as

$$y(n) = h(0)x(n) + \underbrace{h(1)x(n-1) + \cdots + h(L-1)x(n-L+1)}_{\text{ISI component}}, \tag{4.74}$$

from which it can be seen that the received symbol $y(n)$ at the time instant $n$ experiences inter symbol interference from the previous $L-1$ transmitted symbols. Consider two OFDM symbols as follows. Let $x(0), x(1), \ldots, x(N-1)$ denote the IFFT samples of the modulated symbols $X(0), X(1), \ldots, X(N-1)$, while $\tilde{x}(0), \tilde{x}(1), \ldots, \tilde{x}(N-1)$ denote the IFFT samples of the previous modulated symbol block $\tilde{X}(0), \tilde{X}(1), \ldots, \tilde{X}(N-1)$. Thus, the samples corresponding to these two blocks of OFDM symbols are transmitted sequentially as

$$\underbrace{\tilde{x}(0), \tilde{x}(1), \ldots, \tilde{x}(N-1)}_{\text{Previous block}} \underbrace{x(0), x(1), \ldots, x(N-1)}_{\text{Current block}}$$

Now, consider the received symbol $y(0)$ corresponding to the transmission of $x(0)$. This can be expressed as

$$y(0) = h(0)x(0) + \underbrace{h(1)\tilde{x}(N-1) + \cdots + h(L-1)\tilde{x}(N-L+1)}_{\text{ISI from previous OFDM symbol}}. \tag{4.75}$$

It can be seen from the above equation that the received symbol $y(0)$ experiences inter-symbol interference from $\tilde{x}(N-1), \tilde{x}(N-2), \ldots, \tilde{x}(N-(L-1))$. Thus, there is inter-OFDM symbol interference in this new OFDM system. The initial samples of the current OFDM symbol block are being subject to interference from the $N-1$ samples of the previous OFDM block. This is shown in Fig. 4.36. Similarly, the received symbol $y(1)$ is given as

$$y(1) = h(0)x(1) + h(1)x(0)\, \underbrace{h(2)\tilde{x}(N-1) + \cdots + h(L-1)\tilde{x}(N-L+2)}_{\text{ISI from previous OFDM symbol}}, \tag{4.76}$$

which can again be seen to experience inter-OFDM symbol interference from the previous OFDM block symbols $\tilde{x}(N-1), \tilde{x}(N-2), \dots, \tilde{x}(N-L+2)$. Let us now consider a modified transmission scheme as follows. To each transmitted OFDM sample stream, we pad the last $L_c$ symbols to make the transmitted stream as follows.

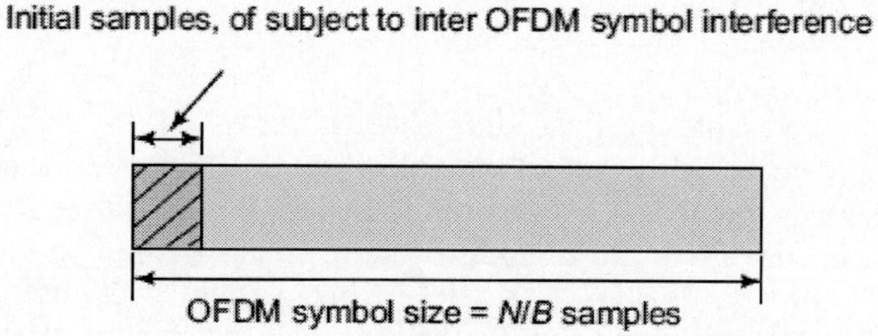


Fig. 4.36 Inter OFDM-symbol interference

Observe that we are prefixing the transmitted sample block $x(0), x(1), \dots, x(N-1)$ of the current block with the $L_c$ samples $x(N-L_c), x(N-L_c+1), \dots, x(N-1)$. Further, this prefix is cyclic in nature, since the same samples from the end of the block are being cycled towards the beginning. Therefore, this is known as the cyclic prefix and is an important aspect of OFDM systems. Consider now the received symbol corresponding to $x(0)$. This is given as

$$y(0) = h(0)x(0) + \underbrace{h(1)x(N-1) + \cdots + h(L-1)x(N-L+1)}_{\text{ISI from same OFDM symbol}} \tag{4.77}$$

The inter-symbol interference can be seen to now be from $x(N-1), x(N-2), \dots, x(N-L+1)$, if $L_c \geq L-1$. Thus, with the cyclic prefix of appropriate length, i.e., $L_c \geq L-1$, inter-OFDM symbol interference can be avoided and inter-symbol interference is restricted to samples from the same OFDM symbol. Therefore, the samples $y(0), y(1), \dots, y(N-1)$ are given as

$$\begin{aligned} y(0) &= h(0)x(0) + h(1)x(N-1) + \cdots + h(L-1)x(N-L+1) \\ y(1) &= h(0)x(1) + h(1)x(0) + \cdots + h(L-1)x(N-L+2) \\ &\vdots \\ y(N-1) &= h(0)x(N-1) + h(1)x(N-2) + \cdots + h(L-1)x(N-L) \end{aligned} \tag{4.78}$$

It can now be clearly seen that the output $y(n)$ is a circular convolution between the channel filter $h(n)$ and the input $x(n)$. This can, therefore, be expressed as

$$\begin{aligned} y(0) &= h(0)x(0) + h(1)x(N-1) + \cdots + h(L-1)x(N-L+1) \\ y(1) &= h(0)x(1) + h(1)x(0) + \cdots + h(L-1)x(N-L+2) \\ &\vdots \\ y(\mathrm{N}-1) &= h(0)x(N-1) + h(1)x(N-2) + \cdots + h(L-1)x(N-L) \end{aligned} \tag{4.79}$$

where $*N$ denotes circular convolution of modulo $N$. Therefore, the output $y$ can be written as

$$y = h * Nx \tag{4.80}$$

Therefore, taking the DFT of $y(n)$ at the output, we have

$$Y(k) = H(k)X(k), 0 \leq k \leq N-1 \tag{4.81}$$

where $Y(k), 0 \leq k \leq N-1$, denotes the $N$-point DFT of $y(n)$. Similarly, $X(k)$ denotes the $N$-point DFT of $x(n)$. Further, observe that the samples $x(n)$ have been generated as the IDFT of $X(n)$. Therefore, the DFT of the samples $x(n)$ yields back the original transmitted symbols $X(n)$. The coefficients $H(k)$ denotes the DFT of the zero-padded channel filter,

$$h(0), h(1), \ldots, h(L-1), \underbrace{0, \ldots, 0}_{(N-L)}.$$

Thus, observe that (4.69) represents the flat-fading channel across the $k^{\text{th}}$ subcarrier in the OFDM system. The quantity $Y(k)$ represents the output symbol, while $H(k)$ denotes the equivalent flat-fading channel coefficient. This holds true for each subcarrier $k$, i.e., for $0 \leq k \leq N-1$. Thus, the frequency-selective fading channel is converted into a group of narrowband flat-fading channels, one channel across each subcarrier. Observe that if a single carrier system was used, and the symbols $X(0), X(1), \ldots, X(N-1)$ were transmitted directly then the received symbol $y(n)$ would be given as

$$y(n) = h(0)X(n) + h(1)X(n-1) + \cdots + h(L-1)X(n-L+1) \qquad (4.82)$$

Each symbol $X(n)$ would experience inter-symbol interference of $L-1$ past symbols. Therefore, using this novel scheme of OFDM, we have been able to totally eliminate the inter-symbol interference arising out of the frequency-selective nature of the channel. The set of parallel flat-fading channels can be summarized by the expressions

$$\begin{aligned} Y(0) &= H(0)X(0) \\ Y(1) &= H(1)X(1) \\ &\vdots \\ Y(N-1) &= H(n-1)X(N-1) \end{aligned} \qquad (4.83)$$

This conversion of the frequency-selective wideband channel into $N$ narrowband flat-fading channels is shown schematically in Fig. 4.37. Also, the modified transmitter and receiver schematics with the blocks corresponding to the cyclic prefix are given in Fig. 4.38 and 4.39 respectively. Now, considering the noise at the receiver, the received symbol $Y(k)$ can be expressed as

$$Y(k) = H(k)X(k) + N(k) \qquad (4.84)$$

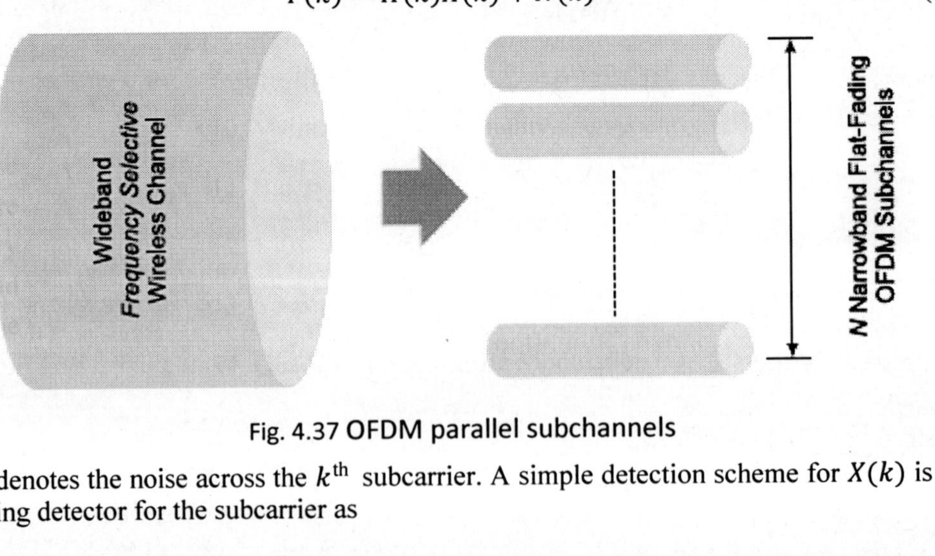


Fig. 4.37 OFDM parallel subchannels

where $N(k)$ denotes the noise across the $k^{\text{th}}$ subcarrier. A simple detection scheme for $X(k)$ is to use the zero-forcing detector for the subcarrier as

$$\hat{X}(k) = \frac{1}{H(k)}Y(k) = X(k) + \underbrace{\frac{N(k)}{H(k)}}_{\tilde{N}(k)} \quad (4.85)$$

Further, for a simplistic BPSK or QPSK-modulated transmission, the coherent or matched filter detector can be simply obtained by multiplying with $H^*(k)$, i.e., the complex conjugate of $H(k)$ as

$$H^*(k)Y(k) = |H(k)|^2X(k) + \underbrace{H^*(k)N(k)}_{N'(k)} \quad (4.86)$$

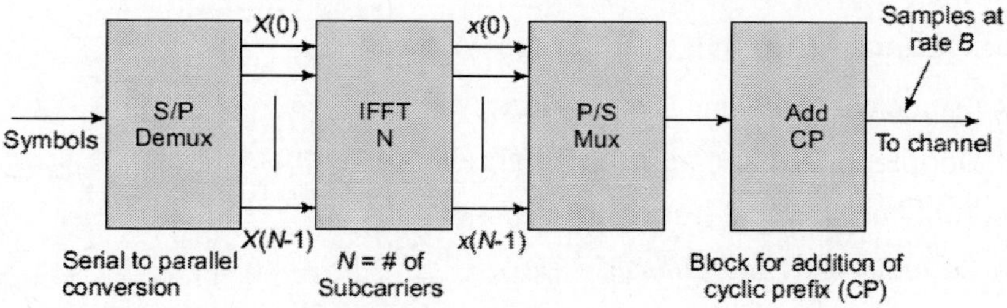


Fig. 4.38 OFDM transmitter schematic with CP

Also, one can employ the MMSE detector as

$$\hat{X}_{\text{MMSE}}(k) = \frac{H^*(k)}{|H(k)|^2 + \sigma_n^2}Y(k) \quad (4.87)$$

The above equation gives the MMSE receiver across the $k^{\text{th}}$ subcarrier in this OFDM system.

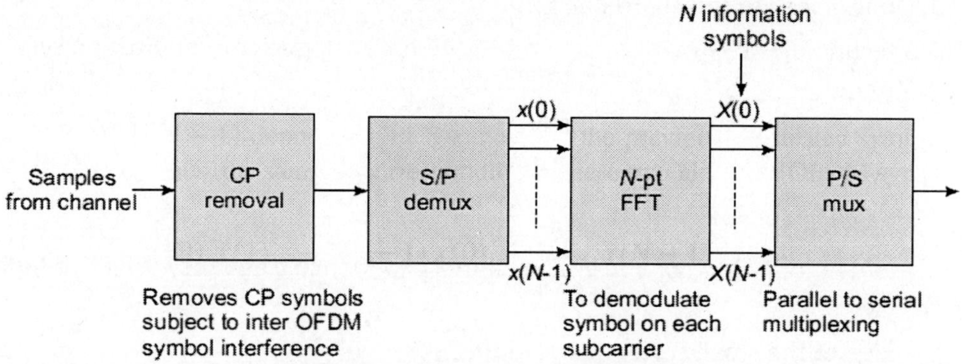


Fig. 4.39 OFDM receiver schematic with CP

## UNIT SUMMARY

Unit 4 focuses on multiple access techniques and modulation schemes, essential for efficient communication in wireless networks. The unit begins by explaining various multiple access schemes such as FDMA, TDMA, CDMA, and SDMA, detailing how these methods enable multiple users to share the same communication resources effectively. It then explores different modulation schemes, including BPSK, QPSK, and their variants like QAM, MSK, and GMSK. The concept of multicarrier modulation, particularly OFDM, is discussed to illustrate how these techniques enhance signal transmission and reception in complex communication environments.

The chapter addresses outage probability in selection combiners, specifically maximal-ratio combining, and extends to space diversity-on-transmit systems and basic considerations in Multiple-Input Multiple-Output (MIMO) systems. Digital modulation schemes are examined to understand signal encoding and transmission efficiency. Additionally, multicarrier basics and transmission methods are introduced, emphasizing their role in optimizing spectral efficiency and accommodating high data rates in modern communication systems.

## EXERCISE

### Multiple Choice Questions (MCQs)

1. In FDMA, spectral spreading is caused by:
    a) Doppler effect and adjacent channel interference
    b) Time division and frequency division.
    c) Code division and phase division.
    d) Guard bands and modulation techniques.
2. What happens to the modulated signal by changing the carrier frequency in FDMA
    a) It remains in the same frequency band.
    b) It can be placed in any frequency band.
    c) It is divided into multiple frequency bands.
    d) It is placed in the guard band.
3. Which technology is primarily based on FDMA for analogue communication systems
    a) GSM
    b) CDMA
    c) LTE
    d) AMPS and ETACS
4. In the context of FDMA, why might a channel experience frequency selective fading less often?
    a) Due to the small system bandwidth.
    b) Due to the use of guard bands.
    c) Because each user is assigned a unique frequency band.
    d) Because of the large system bandwidth.
5. What is a key advantage of TDMA's non-continuous transmission for any user?
    a) It allows for continuous channel estimation.
    b) It simplifies the Channel Estimation function.
    c) It eliminates the need for guard bands.
    d) It increases the frequency spectrum.

6. Why is synchronization required in TDMA for uplink channels?
    a) Because signals are transmitted with different power levels.
    b) Because signals are transmitted with different delays over different channels.
    c) Because signals use the same frequency bands.
    d) Because signals are continuously transmitted.
7. What can destroy both uplink and downlink time division orthogonality in TDMA?
    a) Guard bands.
    b) Intermodulation distortion.
    c) Multipath propagation.
    d) Narrow band fading.
8. What is one disadvantage of TDMA due to cyclic repeating time slots?
    a) Increased intermodulation distortion.
    b) Difficulty in frequency synchronization.
    c) The need for channel equalization on each cycle.
    d) Reduced bandwidth utilization.
9. What do orthogonal and non-orthogonal spreading codes in CDMA modulate?
    a) The carrier frequency.
    b) The information signal of a given user.
    c) The guard bands.
    d) The time slots for each user.
10. Why are non-orthogonal codes generally used in the uplink of a CDMA system?
    a) They are easier to synchronize.
    b) They require less bandwidth.
    c) Maintaining orthogonality and synchronization is complex.
    d) They are more efficient in downlink transmissions.
11. Which of the following modulation schemes is the most robust against noise and distortion?
    a) Amplitude Shift Keying (ASK)
    b) Frequency Shift Keying (FSK)
    c) Binary Phase Shift Keying (BPSK)
    d) Quadrature Amplitude Modulation (QAM)
12. In BPSK modulation, what phase shift represents a binary '0'?
    a) 0°
    b) 90°

c) 180°
d) 270°

13. What is the main disadvantage of using Amplitude Shift Keying (ASK)?
    a) High complexity
    b) Susceptibility to noise
    c) Low data rates
    d) Difficult implementation
14. Which digital modulation technique combines both amplitude and phase modulation?
    a) QPSK
    b) BPSK
    c) FSK
    d) QAM
15. What is the key difference between QPSK and DQPSK?
    a) DQPSK uses absolute phase values for encoding
    b) QPSK transmits two bits per symbol while DQPSK transmits one bit per symbol
    c) DQPSK uses phase differences between consecutive symbols
    d) QPSK is more robust to noise than DQPSK
16. What is the Bit Error Rate (BER) formula for BPSK modulation in an AWGN channel?
    a) $\frac{1}{2}\text{erfc}\left(\sqrt{\frac{E_b}{N_0}}\right)$
    b) $\text{erfc}\left(\frac{E_b}{N_0}\right)$
    c) $\frac{1}{2}\text{erf}\left(\sqrt{\frac{E_b}{N_0}}\right)$
    d) $\text{erf}\left(\sqrt{\frac{E_b}{N_0}}\right)$
17. How many bits per symbol does Quadrature Phase Shift Keying (QPSK) transmit?
    a) 1
    b) 2
    c) 4
    d) 8
18. Which aspect of digital modulation does the Gram-Schmidt orthogonalization procedure help with?
    a) Improving data rates
    b) Reducing noise susceptibility
    c) Generating basis functions
    d) Simplifying implementation

19. What is the key factor that makes QPSK advantageous for applications such as satellite communication and digital television broadcasting?
    a) High noise resistance
    b) Simple implementation
    c) Spectral efficiency
    d) Low power consumption
20. In the context of BPSK modulation, which of the following expressions represents the received signal y when a bit '1' is transmitted through an AWGN channel?
    a) $y = s_1 + n$
    b) $y = s_0 + n$
    c) $\mathrm{y} = s_1 \times n$
    d) $\mathrm{y} = s_0 \times n$

**Answers**

1. Doppler effect and adjacent channel interference

2. It can be placed in any frequency band.

3. AMPS and ETACS

4. Due to the small system bandwidth.

5. It allows for continuous channel estimation.

6. Because signals are transmitted with different delays over different channels.

7. Multipath propagation.

8. The need for channel equalization on each cycle.

9. The information signal of a given user.

10. Maintaining orthogonality and synchronization is complex.

11. Binary Phase Shift Keying (BPSK)

12. 180°

13. Susceptibility to noise

14. Quadrature Amplitude Modulation (QAM)

15. DQPSK uses phase differences between consecutive symbols.

16. \(\frac{1}{2} \text{erfc} \left(\sqrt{\frac{E_b}{N_0}}\right)\)

17. 2

18. Generating basis functions

19. Spectral efficiency

20. $y = s_1 + n$

## KNOW MORE

***For more information related to this topic scan the QR code.***

**OR**

***Type this link in your browser***

**https://nptel.ac.in/courses/117104115**

## REFERENCES


1. T. S. Rappaport, "Wireless Communications Prentice Hall PTR." New York, 1996.

2. J. H. Schiller, "Wireless and Mobile Communications." Handbook of Research on Ubiquitous Computing Technology for Real Time Enterprises. IGI Global, 2008.

4. Agrawal, Dharma P., and Qing-An Zeng, "Introduction to wireless and mobile systems." Cengage learning, 2015.

5. Halonen, Timo, Javier Romero, and Juan Melero, eds, "GSM, GPRS and EDGE performance: evolution towards 3G/UMTS." John Wiley & Sons, 2004

6. Richardson, Andrew, "WCDMA design handbook. Vol. 13." Cambridge: Cambridge University Press, 2005

# 5 RECEIVER STRUCTURE

## UNIT SPECIFICS

*We will be discussing the following aspects in this Unit:*

- *Introduction to receiver components and their functions.*
- *Different types of receivers and their operational principles.*
- *Mechanisms and structures of diversity receivers.*
- *Selection combining, maximal ratio combining, and equal gain combining.*
- *Structure and operation of rake receivers.*
- *Role in combining multipath signals to enhance reception quality.*
- *Linear equalizers, Zero Forcing Equalizer (ZFE), and Adaptive Decision Feedback Equalization (DFE).*
- *Methods to reduce intersymbol interference and improve data recovery.*
- *Principles and benefits of the Alamouti scheme.*
- *Implementation and performance analysis in wireless communication systems.*

*The practical applications of these topics are discussed to generate curiosity, creativity, and improve problem-solving capacity. The unit includes multiple-choice questions, short and long answer questions categorized according to Bloom's taxonomy, assignments through numerical problems, and a list of references and suggested readings for further practice.*

*QR codes are provided in different sections for additional supportive knowledge. After practical exercises, a "Know More" section offers supplementary information, highlighting initial activities, interesting facts, analogies, history, timelines, real-life applications, and case studies related to environmental, sustainability, social, and ethical issues.*

*Understanding receiver structures and enhancement techniques is crucial for designing reliable and efficient wireless communication systems. The concepts covered lay a foundational understanding of how receivers operate, the challenges they face, and the technological advancements to overcome these challenges. This knowledge is essential for appreciating the complexities of modern communication systems and contributing to innovative solutions in wireless communications.*

## RATIONALE

*This fundamental unit on mechanics helps students to get a primary idea about the transformation of scalars and vectors under rotation transformation and forces in nature. It explains Newton's laws and its completeness in describing particle motion. All these basic aspects are relevant to start the mechanics properly. It then explains clearly Newton's laws and its completeness in describing particle motion and the form invariance of Newton's second law as well as Newton's equations of motion in polar coordinates. All these are discussed at length to develop the subject. Some related problems are pointed out with an extension to cylindrical and spherical coordinates which can help further for getting a clear idea of the concern topics on mechanics.*

*Mechanics is an important branch of physical science that essentially deals with forces and energy and their effect on bodies. Mechanics started its journey by quantifying motion and then explaining it in terms of forces, energy and momentum. This permits one to analyze the operation of many day-to-day familiar phenomena around us. But at the same time it covers the mechanics of planets, stars and galaxies. Its practical applications are related to the construction, design, and operation of different type of machines and tools.*

## PRE-REQUISITES

*Basics knowledge of Mathematics &*

*Communication systems.*

## UNIT OUTCOMES

*After completion of this Unit, students will be able to:*

U5-O1: *Describe the basic architecture and components of receivers.*

U5-O2: *Explain the function and structure of diversity receivers.*

U5-O3: *Understand the operation of rake receivers and their role in signal combination.*

U5-O4: *Discuss various equalization techniques and their importance in signal recovery.*

U5-O5: *Analyze the transmit diversity using the Alamouti scheme and its impact on systems*

| Unit-5 Outcomes | EXPECTED MAPPING WITH COURSE OUTCOMES (1- Weak Correlation; 2- Medium correlation; 3- Strong Correlation) | | | | | |
|---|---|---|---|---|---|---|
| | CO-1 | CO-2 | CO-3 | CO-4 | CO-5 | CO-6 |
| U5-O1 | 3 | 2 | 3 | - | 2 | 1 |
| U5-O2 | 3 | 1 | 2 | - | 1 | 2 |
| U5-O3 | 3 | 1 | 2 | - | 2 | 2 |
| U5-O4 | 3 | - | 2 | - | 2 | 3 |
| U5-O5 | 3 | 1 | 2 | - | 2 | 3 |

## 5.1 RECEIVER

A receiver in the context of communication systems refers to a device or component that receives signals or messages sent from a transmitter. Its primary function is to decode the received signals and extract the intended information or data. Receivers are integral parts of various communication systems, including radio, television, telecommunications, and wireless networks.

### Functions of a Receiver

- **Signal Reception**: The receiver's main function is to detect and capture incoming signals, which may be transmitted over different mediums such as air (wireless), cables, or optical fibers.
- **Signal Demodulation**: Once the signal is received, it needs to be demodulated to extract the original information. Demodulation involves separating the modulated signal from the carrier wave and recovering the baseband signal.
- **Signal Decoding**: After demodulation, the receiver decodes the signal to extract the transmitted data or information. This decoding process may involve error correction techniques to ensure the accuracy of the received data.
- **Signal Amplification**: In many cases, the received signal is weak and requires amplification to bring it to a usable level. Receivers often include amplification stages to boost the signal strength.
- **Filtering**: Receivers may incorporate filters to eliminate unwanted noise and interference from the received signal, ensuring that only the desired information is extracted.

### 5.1.1 Receiver Structure

The receiver structure, in the context of communication theory, pertains to the arrangement or organization of components within a system designed to receive and process information. It is a fundamental aspect of any communication system, whether it involves interpersonal communication, telecommunications, or any other form of information exchange.

At its core, the receiver structure encompasses the set of devices, circuits, and algorithms tasked with extracting, interpreting, and possibly acting upon the transmitted signals or messages. These components work in concert to decode the incoming information, making it intelligible and relevant to the intended recipient.

One key element of the receiver structure is its sensitivity to incoming signals. It must be capable of detecting and capturing the transmitted information amidst any noise or interference that may be present in the communication channel. This often involves sophisticated filtering and amplification techniques to enhance the signal-to-noise ratio and improve the overall reliability of the received data.

Another crucial aspect of the receiver structure is its ability to decode and interpret the received signals accurately. This may involve demodulating analog signals, decoding digital data streams, or extracting specific features from the incoming information. Depending on the nature of the communication, the receiver may also need to perform error correction or data recovery procedures to ensure the integrity of the received message.

Furthermore, the receiver structure may incorporate various feedback mechanisms to optimize its performance and adapt to changing conditions. This could involve adjusting signal processing parameters dynamically or employing adaptive algorithms to enhance reception in real-time.

Overall, the receiver structure serves as the gateway through which information flows into a communication system, transforming raw signals into meaningful content for the recipient. Its design and operation play a critical role in the effectiveness and efficiency of the overall communication process.

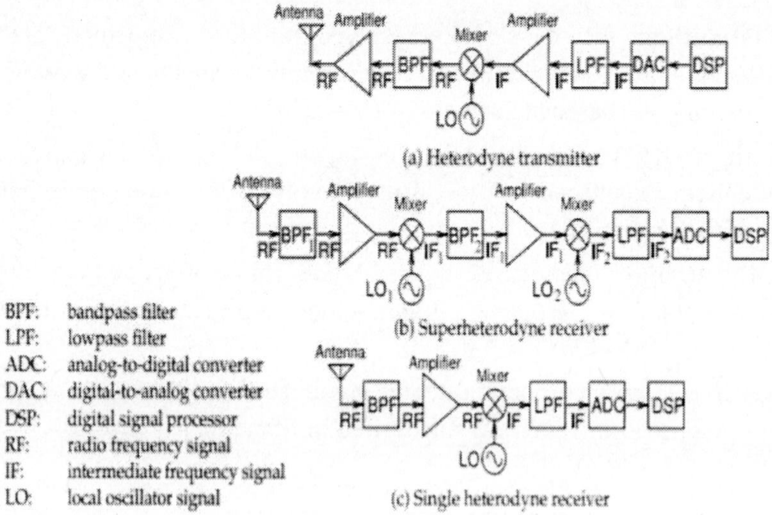


Fig 5.1 The Three Structures of a Receiver. This diagram illustrates the flow of signals through the various components of a receiver, from signal reception to data decoding and output. Each component plays a crucial role in the overall operation of the receiver, ensuring that the transmitted information is accurately received and processed.

### How the Receiver Works?

The receiver is a pivotal component in any communication system, responsible for capturing, processing, and interpreting incoming signals or messages. Its primary function is to extract the transmitted information from the communication channel and present it in a usable format to the intended recipient.

The process begins with the receiver's ability to detect and acquire the incoming signals. This often involves the use of antennas or other sensing devices designed to capture electromagnetic waves, acoustic signals, or other forms of communication depending on the medium employed. The receiver must be sensitive enough to discern the desired signal from any background noise or interference that may be present, utilizing techniques such as filtering and amplification to enhance signal clarity.

Once the signal is captured, the receiver proceeds to demodulate or decode it, depending on whether the transmission is analog or digital. In the case of analog signals, demodulation involves extracting the original information, such as voice or video, from the carrier wave. For digital signals, decoding entails converting the encoded data back into its original form using techniques like Pulse-Code Modulation (PCM) or phase-shift keying (PSK).

Following demodulation or decoding, the receiver may employ error correction mechanisms to ensure the accuracy and integrity of the received information. This can involve techniques such as Forward Error Correction (FEC) or Cyclic Redundancy Check (CRC), which detect and correct errors introduced during transmission, thereby improving the reliability of the received data.

Finally, the receiver presents the processed information to the recipient in a format that is comprehensible and actionable. This could involve converting analog signals into audio or video output for human consumption or forwarding digital data to a computer or other device for further processing. Additionally, the receiver may incorporate feedback mechanisms to adapt its operation based on the quality of the received signal or other environmental factors, optimizing performance in real-time.

In essence, the receiver serves as the gateway through which information flows into a communication system, transforming raw signals into meaningful content for the recipient. Its design and operation are crucial to the effectiveness and reliability of the overall communication process, enabling seamless exchange of information across diverse mediums and environments.

## 5.2 DIVERSITY RECEIVER

A diversity receiver is a specialized type of receiver used in communication systems to improve signal reliability and reduce the effects of fading and interference. It employs multiple antennas and signal paths to receive the same signal from different spatial or frequency locations. The primary function of a diversity receiver is to select the best-quality signal among the signals received by its antennas, thereby enhancing the overall reception performance.

### 5.2.1 Functions of a Diversity Receiver

- **Signal Reception Diversity**: The main function of a diversity receiver is to exploit the spatial or frequency diversity of the received signals. By using multiple antennas or receiving paths, it can receive the same signal through different propagation paths, such as direct and reflected signals or signals with different polarization.

- **Signal Selection**: The diversity receiver continuously monitors the quality of the received signals from each antenna or path. It selects the signal with the highest quality based on criteria such as signal strength, signal-to-noise ratio, or bit error rate.

- **Signal Combining**: Once the best-quality signal is selected, the diversity receiver combines the signals from different antennas or paths to create a single composite signal. This process helps mitigate the effects of fading, multipath propagation, and interference, resulting in improved signal reliability and robustness.

- **Switching Diversity**: Some diversity receivers employ switching diversity, where they rapidly switch between antennas or receiving paths based on the signal quality measurements. This switching mechanism ensures that the receiver always selects the best available signal at any given time.

### 5.2.2 Diversity Receiver Structure

The diversity receiver structure is a sophisticated arrangement employed in communication systems to enhance signal reliability and mitigate the effects of fading and interference. It operates on the principle of diversity reception, which involves using multiple independent reception paths to capture the transmitted signal. By leveraging diversity, the receiver can exploit the spatial, temporal, or frequency variations in the received signal to improve overall reception quality.

One common type of diversity receiver structure is space diversity, which utilizes multiple antennas placed at different locations to capture the same signal. By receiving the signal through multiple paths, the receiver can effectively mitigate the impact of fading caused by multipath propagation. In this setup, the receiver compares the received signals from each antenna and selects the one with the best quality for further processing.

Another type of diversity receiver structure is frequency diversity, which involves splitting the transmitted signal into multiple frequency channels and receiving them separately. Each frequency channel experiences different propagation conditions, allowing the receiver to select the channel with the least interference or fading for signal demodulation and decoding.

Temporal diversity is yet another approach, where the receiver samples the signal at different points in time. This can be achieved through techniques such as time-division multiplexing or by employing multiple receive antennas with slight temporal offsets. By capturing the signal at different moments, the receiver can mitigate the effects of fast fading or burst interference, improving overall reception reliability.

The diversity receiver structure can combine multiple diversity techniques to further enhance performance. For instance, a receiver may employ space diversity in conjunction with frequency or temporal diversity to combat a wide range of fading and interference scenarios effectively.

Overall, the diversity receiver structure represents an advanced approach to signal reception, leveraging the principles of diversity to improve reliability and robustness in communication systems. By incorporating multiple reception paths and exploiting variations in the received signal, diversity receivers can overcome the challenges posed by fading, interference, and other impairments, ensuring consistent and high-quality communication in diverse environments.

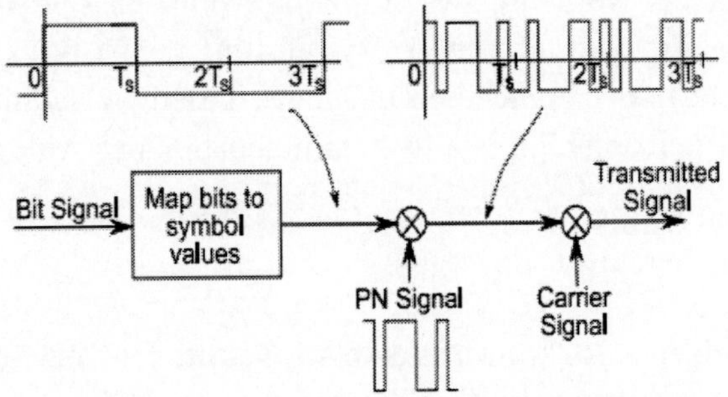


Fig 5.2: A DS-SS transmitter multiplies symbol values by the PN signal and cos(2πfct) to produce the transmitted signal.

## How Does the Diversity Receiver Works?

The diversity receiver represents an advanced strategy employed in communication systems to combat signal degradation caused by fading, interference, and other impairments. Its operation revolves around the principle of diversity, which involves utilizing multiple independent reception paths to capture the transmitted signal. By doing so, the diversity receiver can exploit spatial, temporal, or frequency variations in the received signal to improve overall reception quality.

At its core, the diversity receiver structure typically consists of multiple reception branches, each equipped with its own antenna or receiver. These branches operate in parallel, independently capturing the same transmitted signal from different vantage points, frequencies, or moments in time. This diversity of reception paths allows the receiver to overcome fading and interference effects that may affect individual paths, thereby enhancing signal reliability.

One common type of diversity receiver structure is space diversity, where multiple antennas are strategically positioned to receive the same signal. By capturing the signal through different spatial paths, the receiver can mitigate the effects of multipath propagation and fading caused by obstacles or reflections in the transmission environment. The received signals from each antenna are then compared, and the one with the highest quality is selected for further processing.

Frequency diversity is another approach, where the transmitted signal is split into multiple frequency channels, each received independently. Since different frequency channels may experience varying degrees of interference or fading, the receiver can choose the channel with the best quality signal for demodulation and decoding, improving overall reception performance.

Temporal diversity involves capturing the signal at different points in time, either by using multiple receive antennas with slight temporal offsets or through time-division multiplexing techniques. By sampling the signal at different moments, the receiver can mitigate the effects of fast fading or burst interference, ensuring consistent reception quality.

In essence, the diversity receiver works by leveraging the redundancy provided by multiple reception paths to improve signal reliability and robustness. By selecting the best-quality signal from among the diverse paths, the receiver can overcome the challenges posed by fading, interference, and other impairments, ensuring consistent and high-quality communication in a wide range of environments and conditions.

### 5.2.3 Selection Method

The selection method of receivers, also known as diversity selection or antenna selection, plays a crucial role in ensuring reliable communication in the presence of fading, multipath propagation, and interference. The selection method involves choosing the best-quality signal among the signals received by multiple antennas or receiving paths. There are several approaches to selection diversity, each with its advantages and disadvantages.

#### Maximal Ratio Combining (MRC)

In MRC, the received signals from all antennas are weighted according to their Signal-to-Noise Ratios (SNRs) or signal strengths and then combined. The weights are determined dynamically based on the instantaneous SNR of each received signal. This method optimally combines the signals to maximize the received signal power while minimizing the effects of noise and interference. MRC is particularly effective in environments with fading and multipath propagation but requires accurate channel state information for optimal performance.

#### Equal Gain Combining (EGC)

EGC involves combining the received signals from all antennas with equal weights, regardless of their individual SNRs. This method simplifies the combining process but may not fully exploit the diversity gain available in the received signals. EGC is more robust to variations in channel conditions compared to MRC but may result in suboptimal performance in highly dynamic or frequency-selective fading environments.

#### Selection Diversity

In selection diversity, the receiver continuously monitors the quality of the received signals from each antenna and selects the antenna with the highest-quality signal for further processing. This method is simpler than combining diversity techniques but may suffer from switching delays and may not fully utilize the diversity gain available in the received signals. Selection diversity is commonly used in systems where complexity and computational overhead are primary concerns.

**Switched Diversity**

Switched diversity combines the advantages of selection diversity and combining diversity by periodically switching between different antennas or receiving paths based on predefined criteria, such as signal strength or error rate. This method improves the reliability of the communication link by selecting the best available antenna or path at any given time. However, switched diversity introduces switching delays and may require additional hardware complexity.

**Hybrid Diversity Techniques**

Hybrid diversity techniques combine multiple diversity methods to leverage their respective strengths and mitigate their weaknesses. For example, a receiver may use MRC for combining signals from multiple antennas and switch between different antenna configurations based on channel conditions. Hybrid diversity techniques offer improved performance and robustness compared to individual diversity methods alone.

In summary, the selection method of receivers plays a crucial role in improving the reliability and performance of communication systems in diverse and challenging environments. By exploiting the spatial or frequency diversity of received signals, selection diversity techniques mitigate the effects of fading, multipath propagation, and interference, ensuring robust and reliable communication links. The choice of selection method depends on factors such as system complexity, computational overhead, and the specific characteristics of the communication environment.

**Maximal Ratio Combining (MRC)**

Maximal Ratio Combining (MRC) is a diversity combining technique used in communication systems to maximize the received signal power while minimizing the effects of noise and interference. MRC is particularly effective in environments characterized by fading and multipath propagation, where signals experience fluctuations in amplitude and phase due to reflections, diffraction, and scattering.

The method of MRC was first proposed by Kahn [10]. This method describes that signals from all of the M branches are weighted according to their individual signal voltage to noise power ratios and then summed. Consider Fig. 5.3 and observe that the individual signals must be co-phased before being summed and this generally requires an individual receiver and phasing circuit for each antenna element. Maximal ratio combining produces an output SNR equal to the sum of the individual SNRs.

The fundamental principle behind MRC is to weight each received signal according to its Signal-to-Noise Ratio (SNR) or signal strength and then combine them in a way that maximizes the overall received signal power. Unlike other diversity combining techniques, MRC takes into account both the amplitude and phase of the received signals, allowing for optimal combining even in frequency-selective fading channels.

In MRC, the received signals from multiple antennas or receiving paths are first amplified and phase-aligned before combining. The weights assigned to each signal are determined dynamically based on the instantaneous SNR of each received signal. Signals with higher SNRs are assigned higher weights, while signals with lower SNRs are assigned lower weights. This weighting process ensures that signals with better quality contribute more to the combined signal, while signals with poorer quality contribute less, thus maximizing the overall received signal power.

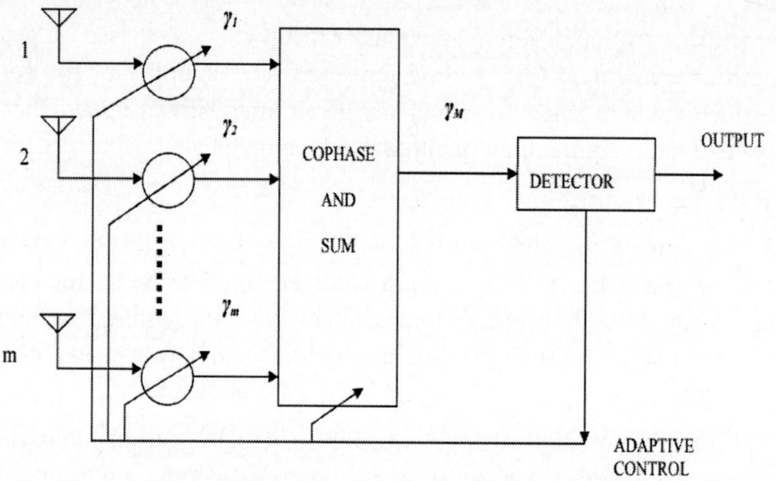


Fig 5.3: Maximal Ratio Combiner

Mathematically the combined signal y(t) in MRC can be expressed as the weighted sum of the received signals $x_i(t)$:

$$y(t) = \sum_{i=1}^{N} w_i x_i(t)$$

**where $N$ is the number of receiving antennas or paths, $x_i(t)$ is the received signal from the $i$-th antenna or path, and $w_i$ is the weight assigned to the $i$-th signal.**

The weights $w_i$ are typically computed using the instantaneous SNR of each received signal. One common approach is to set the weights proportional to the conjugate of the channel gains, normalized by the noise variance. This ensures that signals with higher SNRs contribute more to the combined signal. The weights are then adjusted dynamically as the channel conditions change over time.

One of the key advantages of MRC is its ability to achieve near-optimal performance in fading channels without requiring explicit knowledge of the Channel State Information (CSI). Unlike other diversity combining techniques such as Maximum Likelihood Combining (MLC), which rely on accurate CSI for optimal performance, MRC can adapt to varying channel conditions in real-time without requiring explicit feedback or channel estimation.

Overall, Maximal Ratio Combining (MRC) is a powerful diversity combining technique that effectively exploits the spatial diversity of multiple antennas or receiving paths to maximize the received signal power while mitigating the effects of fading, noise, and interference. Its simplicity, robustness, and near-optimal performance make it a popular choice in modern communication systems, including wireless networks, cellular systems, and satellite communication.

## 5.3 RAKE RECEIVER

The RAKE receiver is a sophisticated diversity combining technique used in spread spectrum communication systems, particularly in CDMA (Code Division Multiple Access) systems, to mitigate the effects of multipath fading and improve reception quality. Named after the garden tool used for gathering hay, the RAKE receiver collects multiple delayed versions of the received signal and combines them to reconstruct the original transmitted signal. The concept is based on the idea of exploiting multipath diversity to improve the robustness and reliability of communication links.

### 5.3.1 Functions of a RAKE Receiver:

- **Multipath Mitigation**: The primary function of a RAKE receiver is to mitigate the effects of multipath propagation, where signals take multiple paths due to reflections, diffraction, and scattering in the environment. Multipath propagation causes signal echoes to arrive at the receiver at different times, leading to intersymbol interference (ISI) and degradation in signal quality. The RAKE receiver leverages this diversity in signal paths to combat fading and improve reception quality.
- **Delay Estimation**: The RAKE receiver accurately estimates the delays between the different multipath components of the received signal. It achieves this by correlating the received signal with a set of delayed replicas of the transmitted signal, known as "fingers" or "taps." Each tap of the RAKE receiver corresponds to a different multipath component, and the delays are typically estimated using techniques such as maximum likelihood estimation (MLE) or matched filtering.
- **Finger Selection**: Once the delays are estimated, the RAKE receiver selects the most significant multipath components, or "fingers," for further processing based on their signal strengths or other criteria. This selection process ensures that the receiver focuses on the most dominant multipath components while ignoring weaker or less significant ones, reducing complexity and computational overhead.
- **Signal Combination**: After selecting the relevant multipath components, the RAKE receiver combines them to reconstruct the original transmitted signal. This combining process can take different forms, including Maximal Ratio Combining (MRC), Equal Gain Combining (EGC), or selection diversity, depending on the specific implementation and performance requirements.

### 5.3.2 RAKE Receiver Structure

The RAKE receiver structure is a sophisticated signal processing technique primarily used in wireless communication systems, especially in environments where multipath propagation and signal fading are prevalent. Named after the tool used in gardening, the RAKE receiver "rakes" through the received signal to capture and combine the multipath components effectively, thereby improving the overall reception quality.

At its core, the RAKE receiver consists of multiple correlators, each corresponding to a different time delay or path in the received signal. These correlators, often referred to as "fingers," are synchronized to the transmitted signal and aligned to capture the multipath components arriving at different times due to reflections or scattering in the transmission environment.

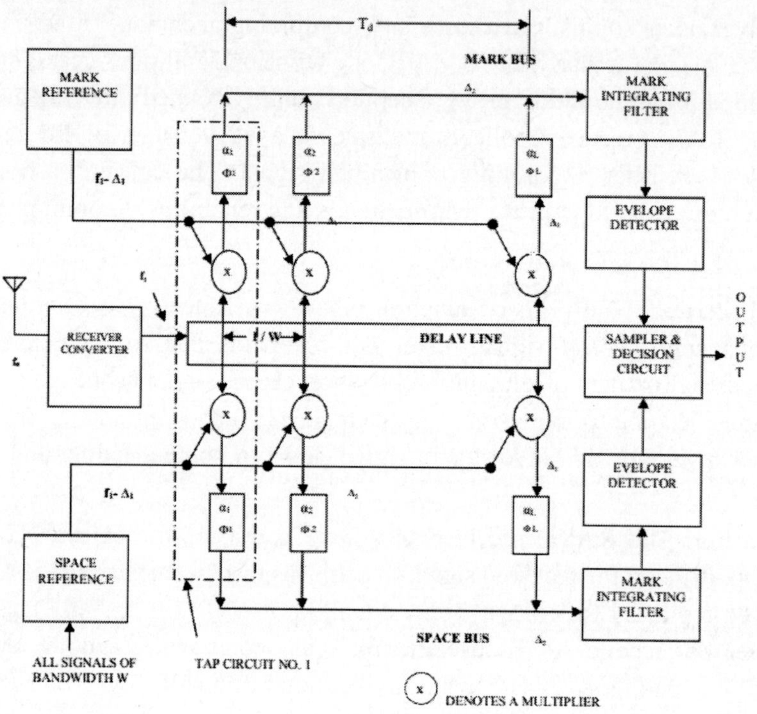


Fig 5.4 Simplified block diagram of Rake receiver. The f's and Δ's refer to center frequencies. The a's and Φ's are weightings and phase corrections, respectively based on path structure measurements.

The process begins with the reception of the transmitted signal, which typically experiences delays and phase shifts due to multipath propagation. The RAKE receiver employs a technique known as rake combining, where each finger correlates the received signal with a time-delayed version of the transmitted signal. By aligning the fingers to capture the various multipath components, the RAKE receiver effectively "rakes" through the signal to extract and combine the different arrivals.

Once the multipath components are captured by the fingers, the RAKE receiver combines them using techniques such as Maximal Ratio Combining (MRC) or Equal Gain Combining (EGC). These combining methods aim to maximize the Signal-to-Noise Ratio (SNR) of the combined signal, thereby improving reception quality and reducing the impact of fading and interference.

One key advantage of the RAKE receiver structure is its ability to exploit the diversity inherent in multipath propagation. By capturing and combining the multipath components, the RAKE receiver can effectively mitigate the effects of fading, improve signal reliability, and extend the communication range.

Furthermore, the RAKE receiver can adaptively adjust its finger positions and combining weights based on channel conditions, allowing it to dynamically optimize reception performance in real-time. This adaptive capability enhances the robustness of the receiver, ensuring reliable communication even in challenging environments with time-varying channel conditions.

The RAKE receiver structure represents a powerful signal processing technique for combating the challenges posed by multipath propagation and fading in wireless communication systems. By effectively capturing and combining the multipath components, the RAKE receiver enhances reception quality, improves signal reliability, and enables seamless communication in diverse and challenging environments.

Summarizing it all, let us define RAKE receiver as a radio receiver designed to encounter the effects of multipath fading. It does this by using several sub receivers each delayed slightly in order to make it coherent to the individual multipath components. In this process, each component is decoded individually and independently and at a later stage combined in order to make the most use of the different transmission Performance Evaluation of RAKE Receivers using Ultra wideband Multipath Channels characteristics of each transmission path. This could well result in higher signal to noise ratio, Eb/No, in a multipath communication scenario. The RAKE receiver is so named because of its analogous function to a garden RAKE, each finger collects bit or symbol energy similarly like tines on a rake collects leaves.

## 5.4 EQUALIZATION

Equalization is a signal processing technique used in wireless communication systems to mitigate the effects of distortion and interference introduced during transmission. The primary goal of equalization is to recover the original transmitted signal accurately despite the degradation it may have undergone.

In a wireless communication system, transmitted signals may experience various forms of distortion, such as amplitude and phase variations, multipath propagation, and frequency-selective fading. These distortions can cause inter-symbol interference (ISI), where symbols from one bit period interfere with symbols from adjacent bit periods, leading to errors in signal reception.

Equalization aims to counteract these distortions by applying corrective processing to the received signal. This involves manipulating the received signal in such a way that it matches the expected characteristics of the transmitted signal. By doing so, equalization helps to restore the original signal waveform and improve the accuracy of symbol detection at the receiver.

There are different types of equalization techniques, including linear and non-linear equalization methods. Linear equalizers, such as zero-forcing equalizers and Minimum Mean Square Error (MMSE) equalizers, operate based on linear filtering principles to minimize ISI. Non-linear equalizers, such as Maximum Likelihood Sequence Estimators (MLSE), use more sophisticated algorithms to optimize signal recovery.

Equalization plays a crucial role in various communication systems, including wireless communication, digital communication over wireline channels, and high-speed data transmission. It enables reliable communication by compensating for channel impairments and ensuring accurate signal detection, even in challenging transmission environments.

### 5.4.1 Linear equalizers

Linear equalizers are a type of signal processing technique used in communication systems to mitigate the effects of distortion, particularly ISI, which occurs when symbols from one bit period interfere with symbols from adjacent bit periods. Linear equalizers operate based on linear filtering principles to adjust the frequency response of the communication channel and compensate for the distortions introduced during transmission. .

Here's a detailed explanation of linear equalizers:

1. **Introduction to Equalization:** Equalization is essential in communication systems to ensure reliable and accurate transmission of data over a communication channel. In many communication channels, such as wired or wireless channels, the transmitted signal undergoes distortion due to factors like multipath propagation, frequency-selective fading, and variations in amplitude and phase.
2. **Need for Equalization:** Distortions in the communication channel can lead to ISI, where symbols overlap in time, making it challenging for the receiver to correctly detect and decode the transmitted data. Equalization helps mitigate ISI by compensating for the channel distortions, thereby improving the accuracy of symbol detection at the receiver.
3. **Linear Equalizers:** Linear equalizers are a class of equalization techniques that operate based on linear filtering principles. They adjust the received signal by applying linear filtering operations to counteract the effects of ISI caused by the communication channel.
4. **Working Principle:** The working principle of linear equalizers involves estimating the impulse response of the communication channel and then applying a corrective filter to the received signal. The corrective filter is designed to invert or compensate for the frequency response of the channel, effectively reducing ISI and improving signal recovery.
5. **Types of Linear Equalizers:** Linear equalizers can be categorized into two main types:
   i. **Zero-Forcing Equalizer (ZF):** ZF equalizers aim to completely eliminate ISI by inverting the channel response. However, they may amplify noise and lead to signal distortion, particularly in channels with frequency-selective fading.
   ii. **Minimum Mean Square Error Equalizer (MMSE):** MMSE equalizers minimize the mean square error between the transmitted and received signals. They achieve a balance between ISI suppression and noise enhancement by taking into account the statistical properties of the received signal and noise.
6. **Implementation:** Linear equalizers can be implemented using digital signal processing techniques. In practice, the channel impulse response is estimated using training symbols or pilot tones, and the equalizer coefficients are adapted iteratively using algorithms such as the least squares algorithm or the recursive least squares algorithm.
7. **Applications:** Linear equalizers are widely used in various communication systems, including Digital Subscriber Line (DSL) systems, wireless communication systems (e.g., Wi-Fi and LTE), and high-speed data transmission systems (e.g., Ethernet). They play a crucial role in ensuring reliable and high-quality communication by compensating for channel distortions and improving signal detection and decoding performance.

Overall, linear equalizers are fundamental components of modern communication systems, providing an effective means to mitigate ISI and enhance the reliability and performance of data transmission over communication channels.

### 5.4.2 Zero Forcing Equalizer (ZFE):

Zero Forcing Equalizer (ZFE) is a digital signal processing technique used in communication systems to mitigate the effects of intersymbol interference (ISI) caused by a dispersive channel. It's particularly effective in scenarios where the channel impulse response is known or can be estimated. The main goal of the ZFE is to eliminate ISI and recover the transmitted symbols accurately.

#### How Zero Forcing Equalizer Works:

1. Channel Model:
   i. In a communication system, transmitted symbols pass through a channel, which can distort the signal due to factors like multipath propagation, dispersion, and noise.
   ii. The received signal can be expressed as the convolution of the transmitted symbols with the channel impulse response, corrupted by additive noise.
2. ISI and Channel Inversion:
   i. ISI occurs when symbols from one bit period interfere with symbols from adjacent bit periods.
   ii. The ZFE aims to nullify the effect of ISI by inversely filtering the received signal with an estimate of the channel impulse response.
   iii. Mathematically, this involves dividing the received signal by the estimated channel response in the frequency domain, effectively canceling out the channel distortion.
3. Zero Forcing Criterion:
   i. The name "Zero Forcing" comes from the criterion that the equalizer attempts to achieve: forcing the intersymbol interference to zero.
   ii. By designing the equalizer to set the channel response to zero at the symbol sampling instants, it effectively removes ISI.
4. Implementation:
   i. The ZFE is typically implemented as a linear filter, often a Finite Impulse Response (FIR) filter.
   ii. The filter coefficients are determined based on the known or estimated channel impulse response.
   iii. Adaptive algorithms may be used to update the filter coefficients based on the received signal and the estimated channel response, improving equalization performance in varying channel conditions.
5. Trade-offs:
   i. While ZFE effectively eliminates ISI, it can also amplify noise and other distortions present in the received signal.
   ii. The choice of filter length and complexity is crucial, as longer filters provide better equalization but may introduce more noise amplification and computational complexity.

#### Advantages of Zero Forcing Equalizer:

1. Effective ISI Mitigation: ZFE is capable of completely eliminating ISI when the channel response is known or accurately estimated.
2. Simplicity: The concept of ZFE is relatively straightforward, making it easy to implement in digital communication systems.

3. Suitable for Known Channels: ZFE is particularly effective in scenarios where the channel characteristics are well understood or can be estimated reliably.
4. Limitations:
5. Noise Amplification: ZFE can amplify noise and other distortions present in the received signal, especially in channels with high noise levels.
6. Sensitivity to Channel Estimation Errors: Accuracy of channel estimation is crucial for ZFE performance. Errors in estimation can lead to degraded equalization.
7. Complexity: In scenarios with time-varying channels or changing characteristics, maintaining accurate channel estimates and adapting the equalizer can add complexity.

In summary, ZFE is a powerful technique for mitigating ISI in communication systems. It provides effective equalization by inversely filtering the received signal with an estimate of the channel response, aiming to force ISI to zero and recover transmitted symbols accurately. However, careful consideration of noise amplification, channel estimation accuracy, and computational complexity is necessary for practical implementation.

### 5.4.3 Adaptive Decision Feedback Equalization

Adaptive Decision Feedback Equalization (DFE) is a sophisticated digital signal processing technique used in wireless communication systems to combat Inter-Symbol Interference (ISI) caused by multipath propagation. It's an extension of conventional feedforward equalization techniques and offers improved performance by incorporating feedback from previously detected symbols. Adaptive DFE continuously adjusts its equalization parameters based on the received signal characteristics, making it particularly effective in dynamic and time-varying channel conditions encountered in wireless communications.

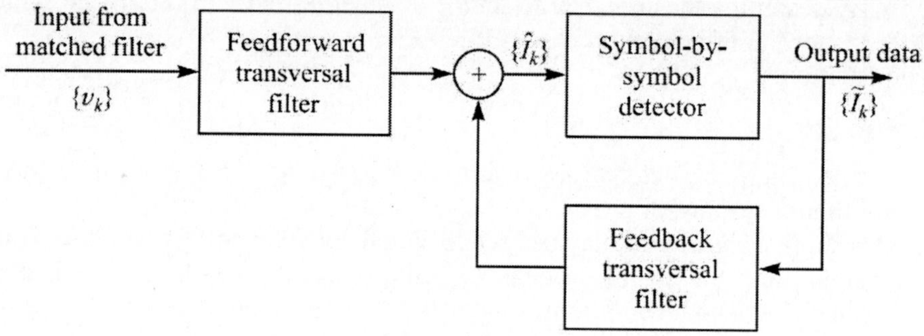


Fig. 5.5 Structure of decision-feedback equalizer.

where $I_k$ is the information symbol transmitted in the $k^{th}$ signaling interval and $\hat{I}_k$ is the estimate of that symbol at the output of the equalizer, and $\tilde{I}_k$are previously detected symbols.

## How Adaptive DFE Works:

1. Feedforward Equalization:

   Similar to conventional equalizers, Adaptive DFE employs a feedforward filter to mitigate ISI. This filter processes the received signal to minimize the effects of channel distortion.
2. Feedback Filtering:
   i. What sets Adaptive DFE apart is its inclusion of a feedback filter. This filter operates on previously detected symbols to further refine the equalization process.

   ii. The feedback filter takes the detected symbols, typically from a decision device or a slicer, and uses them to estimate the interference introduced by past symbols. This estimated interference is then subtracted from the current received signal.

3. Adaptation Mechanism:
   i. The key aspect of Adaptive DFE is its ability to adapt its filter coefficients based on the received signal characteristics.
   ii. Algorithms such as the Least Mean Squares (LMS) or Recursive Least Squares (RLS) are commonly employed to update the filter coefficients iteratively.
   iii. These algorithms use error signals derived from a comparison between the received symbols and the expected symbols to adjust the filter coefficients in a way that minimizes the overall ISI.
4. Joint Optimization:
   i. Adaptive DFE optimizes both the feedforward and feedback filters jointly to minimize the overall distortion introduced by the channel.
   ii. By considering both current and past symbols, Adaptive DFE achieves better performance compared to feedforward equalizers alone, especially in scenarios with severe ISI.
5. Convergence and Stability:
   i. The adaptation process in Adaptive DFE must strike a balance between convergence speed and stability.
   ii. Fast convergence is desirable to quickly adapt to changing channel conditions, but excessive adaptation may lead to instability and poor performance.
   iii. Careful parameter selection and algorithm design are necessary to ensure convergence and stability in practical implementations.

## Advantages of Adaptive DFE:

   i. Improved Performance: Adaptive DFE offers superior equalization performance compared to static equalizers, especially in channels with severe ISI and time-varying characteristics.
   ii. Robustness: By continuously adapting to changing channel conditions, Adaptive DFE maintains reliable communication links even in challenging environments.
   iii. Efficiency: Adaptive DFE optimizes both feedforward and feedback filters jointly, maximizing the utilization of available resources.

**Limitations:**

   i. Complexity: Adaptive DFE implementations are more complex than static equalizers due to the need for continuous adaptation and joint optimization of filter coefficients.
   ii. Computational Overhead: The adaptive algorithms used in Adaptive DFE require computational resources, which may be a limitation in resource-constrained systems.
   iii. Initialization: Proper initialization of Adaptive DFE is crucial for convergence. In some cases, it may require training sequences or pilot symbols to bootstrap the adaptation process.

In summary, Adaptive DFE is a powerful technique for mitigating ISI in wireless communication systems. By adaptively adjusting its equalization parameters based on received signal characteristics, Adaptive DFE offers improved performance and robustness in dynamic channel environments.

However, careful consideration of complexity, computational overhead, and initialization procedures is necessary for practical implementation.

### 5.4.4 Trasmit diversity-Alamouti scheme:

The Transmit Diversity-Alamouti scheme is a technique used in wireless communication systems, particularly in multiple-antenna systems, to improve the reliability of data transmission, especially in scenarios prone to fading and interference. It was introduced by Dr. Alamouti in 1998 and is widely used in various wireless standards like LTE and Wi-Fi [1]. The Alamouti scheme is based on the principle of spatial diversity, which exploits multiple transmit antennas to enhance signal robustness. The basic idea is to transmit two copies of the same data over two consecutive time intervals using two transmit antennas. This enables the receiver to effectively combat fading and interference by combining the received signals. The key advantage of the Alamouti scheme is its simplicity and effectiveness. By transmitting two copies of the data over different paths, the scheme achieves diversity gain, which improves the reliability of data transmission without requiring complex signal processing techniques.

Here's how the Alamouti scheme works with an example:

Suppose we have a transmitter with two antennas, Antenna 1 and Antenna 2, and a receiver with a single antenna.

1. At time instant 1, the transmitter sends data symbols $x_1$ from Antenna 1 and $x_2$ from Antenna 2 simultaneously.
2. At time instant 2, the transmitter sends $-x_2^*$ from Antenna 1 and $x_1^*$ from Antenna 2, where $x_1^*$ and $x_2^*$ are the complex conjugates of $x_1$ and $x_2$ respectively.

   We can represent the transmitted symbols at both time instants using matrices:

$$X_1 = \begin{bmatrix} x_1 \\ x_2 \end{bmatrix}, X_2 = \begin{bmatrix} -x_2^* \\ x_1^* \end{bmatrix}$$

3. At the receiver, the received signals are combined and processed to recover the transmitted symbols. We can represent the received signals at both time instants using matrices as well:

$$Y_1 = HX_1 + N_1, Y_2 = HX_2 + N_2$$

where,

- $H$ is the channel matrix representing the channel gains for Antenna 1 and Antenna 2,
- $N_1$ and $N_2$ are matrices representing the Additive White Gaussian Noise (AWGN) at the receiver.

To decode the transmitted symbols, the receiver combines the received signals $Y_1$ and $Y_2$. One common decoding technique is to use maximum likelihood decoding, where the receiver selects the transmitted symbols that maximize the likelihood of the received signals given the channel and noise conditions. The Alamouti scheme achieves diversity gain by exploiting the fact that the signals transmitted from the two antennas experience independent fading and interference. As a result, even if one of the signals suffers from deep fading or interference, the other signal can still be reliably received, leading to improved overall performance.

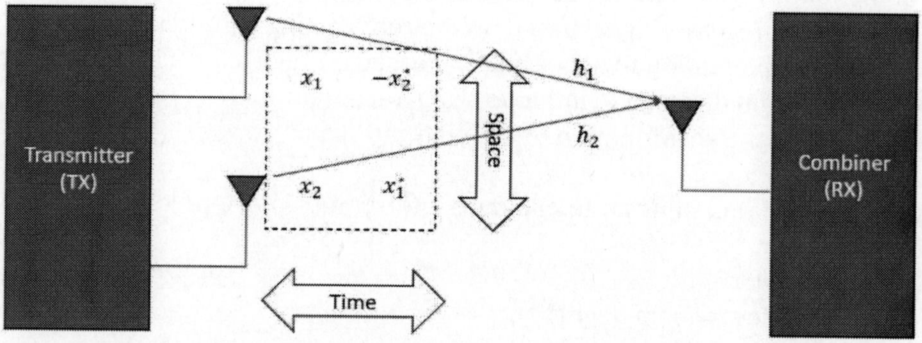


Fig. 5.6: Alamouti orthogonal space-time block c

## UNIT SUMMARY

Unit 5 explores fundamental aspects of receiver design and performance enhancement techniques. It begins with an overview of receiver structures, detailing their components and operational principles. The chapter then focuses on diversity receivers, discussing their functions, structures, and selection methods to mitigate fading effects and improve signal reliability. The Rake receiver is examined next, highlighting its role in combining multipath signals to enhance reception quality, along with its specific structure. Equalization techniques follow, including linear equalizers, the Zero Forcing Equalizer (ZFE), and Adaptive Decision Feedback Equalization (DFE), aimed at reducing intersymbol interference and improving data recovery. Additionally, the Transmit Diversity-Alamouti Scheme is discussed as a method to enhance diversity through multiple antennas. These topics collectively provide a comprehensive understanding of receiver architectures and strategies essential for robust signal reception in communication systems.

## EXERCISE

1. What is the purpose of equalization in communication systems?
   a) To amplify the received signal
   b) To minimize intersymbol interference (Right)
   c) To increase the transmit power
   d) To introduce noise into the received signal

2. Which equalization technique is used to mitigate the effects of multipath fading in communication channels?
   a) Alamouti scheme
   b) Adaptive DFE
   c) Line-ZFE (Right)
   d) MIMO

3. Which of the following best describes the Line-ZFE equalization technique?
   a) It equalizes the received signal based on the zero-forcing criterion (Right)
   b) It adapts the equalization filter coefficients based on the channel impulse response
   c) It utilizes transmit diversity to improve signal reception
   d) It applies a linear transformation to the received signal

4. In adaptive DFE, what is adjusted to minimize intersymbol interference?
   a) Transmit power
   b) Channel bandwidth
   c) Receiver filter coefficients (Right)
   d) Noise level

5. What is the primary advantage of the Alamouti scheme in wireless communication systems?
   a) Increased data rate
   b) Improved spectral efficiency
   c) Reduced multipath fading effects (Right)
   d) Enhanced security

6. Which of the following statements is true regarding the Alamouti scheme?
   a) It requires multiple antennas at the receiver only
   b) It doubles the data rate without requiring additional bandwidth (Right)
   c) It is only effective in narrowband communication systems
   d) It cannot be combined with equalization techniques

7. What does Alamouti encoding achieve in transmit diversity?
   a) Spatial multiplexing
   b) Spatial diversity (Right)
   c) Frequency hopping
   d) Time division multiplexing

8. How does the Alamouti scheme utilize multiple antennas at the transmitter?
   a) By transmitting the same data on each antenna
   b) By transmitting orthogonal symbols on each antenna (Right)
   c) By transmitting different data on each antenna
   d) By transmitting the data sequentially on each antenna

9. What is the primary limitation of the Alamouti scheme?
   a) High complexity
   b) Sensitivity to noise
   c) Requires precise channel knowledge
   d) Limited to two transmit antennas (Right)

10. Which technique is commonly used to combat fading and improve the reliability of wireless communication systems?
    a) Equalization (Right)
    b) Modulation
    c) Amplification
    d) Demodulation

## Answers

1. To minimize intersymbol interference
2. Line-ZFE
3. It equalizes the received signal based on the zero-forcing criterion
4. Receiver filter coefficients
5. Reduced multipath fading effects
6. It doubles the data rate without requiring additional bandwidth
7. Spatial diversity
8. By transmitting orthogonal symbols on each antenna
9. Limited to two transmit antennas
10. Equalization

### KNOW MORE

***For more information related to this topic scan the QR code.***

**OR**

***Type this link in your browser***

**https://archive.nptel.ac.in/courses/117/102/117102062/**

## REFERENCES

1. T. S. Rappaport, "Wireless Communications Prentice Hall PTR." New York, 1996.
2. J. H. Schiller, "Wireless and Mobile Communications." Handbook of Research on Ubiquitous Computing Technology for Real Time Enterprises. IGI Global, 2008.

# 6 MULTIPLE-INPUT MULTIPLE-OUTPUT

**UNIT SPECIFICS**

*We will be discussing following aspects in this Unit:*

1. *Introduction to MIMO:*

   *- Definition of MIMO and its significance in wireless communication.*

   *- Basic principles of MIMO communication.*

2. *MIMO System Model:*

   *- Mathematical representation of MIMO channels.*

   *- Parameters defining the MIMO system, such as the number of antennas at the transmitter and receiver, channel matrix, and modulation scheme.*

   *- Assumptions and considerations in modeling MIMO systems.*

3. *Space-Time Signal Processing:*

   *- Space-time processing techniques for MIMO systems.*

   *- Space-time coding schemes, including Alamouti coding, BLAST, and V-BLAST.*

   *- Diversity combining techniques to exploit spatial and temporal diversity.*

4. *Spatial Multiplexing:*

   *- Principles of spatial multiplexing and its advantages.*

   *- Spatial multiplexing techniques, such as vertical and horizontal beamforming, precoding, and Singular Value Decomposition (SVD).*

   *- Channel State Information (CSI) feedback and adaptive spatial multiplexing.*

*5. Diversity/Multiplexing Tradeoff:*

*- Explanation of diversity and multiplexing gains in MIMO systems.*

*- Tradeoff analysis between diversity and multiplexing gains.*

*- Practical implications of the tradeoff in MIMO system design and optimization.*

*6. Applications and Future Directions:*

*- Real-world applications of MIMO technology in wireless communication systems, such as 4G LTE, 5G, and beyond.*

*- Emerging trends and future directions in MIMO research and development.*

*- Challenges and opportunities in deploying MIMO in various communication scenarios.*

*In this chapter on MIMO, ranging from foundational concepts to advanced techniques and practical applications. Each subsection delves into specific aspects of MIMO technology, providing readers with a comprehensive understanding of the subject matter.*

## RATIONALE

*This unit on multiple-input multiple-output (MIMO) communication systems delves into the advanced wireless communication techniques that leverage multiple antennas at both the transmitter and receiver ends to enhance data throughput, reliability, and coverage. Understanding MIMO is crucial for appreciating its significant impact on modern wireless communication technologies, such as 4G LTE and 5G, which rely on these principles for improved performance. The chapter begins by introducing the basic principles of MIMO communication, establishing the foundation needed to understand its more complex aspects. It covers the mathematical modelling of MIMO systems, including key parameters and assumptions necessary for accurate system representation. The discussion then extends to space-time signal processing techniques, such as space-time coding and diversity combining, which are essential for optimizing signal robustness and mitigating interference.*

*Spatial multiplexing, a core concept in MIMO, is explored in detail, highlighting its advantages in increasing data rates without requiring additional bandwidth. The chapter also addresses the diversity/multiplexing trade-off, providing a comprehensive analysis of how to balance these gains to achieve optimal system performance. Practical applications of MIMO technology in current wireless systems are examined, demonstrating its real-world relevance and effectiveness. Future directions and emerging trends in MIMO research are also discussed, offering insights into ongoing developments and potential innovations.*

*In addition to theoretical concepts, the chapter includes practical sections on signal-to-noise ratio (SNR) estimation, bit error rate (BER) estimation, and outage probability estimation, equipping students with the tools to evaluate and improve MIMO system performance. An overview of related technologies such as GSM, EDGE, GPRS, IS-95, CDMA2000, and WCDMA contextualizes MIMO within the broader landscape of wireless communication.*

## PRE-REQUISITES

*Basic knowledge of Matrix manipulations and Linear Algebra & Communication Systems*

## UNIT OUTCOMES

*After completion of this Unit students will be able to:*

*U6-O1: Introduction to MIMO*

*U6-O2: MIMO System Model*

*U6-O3: Spatial Multiplexing*

*U6-O4: Diversity/Multiplexing Tradeoff*

*U6-O5: Applications and Future Directions*

*This table below need to be filled after discussion as marked with red.*

| Unit-6 Outcomes | EXPECTED MAPPING WITH COURSE OUTCOMES (1- Weak Correlation; 2- Medium correlation; 3- Strong Correlation) | | | | | |
|---|---|---|---|---|---|---|
| | CO-1 | CO-2 | CO-3 | CO-4 | CO-5 | CO-6 |
| U6-O1 | 3 | 2 | 2 | - | 1 | - |
| U6-O2 | 1 | 2 | 3 | 1 | 1 | - |
| U6-O3 | 2 | 2 | 3 | 1 | 1 | 2 |
| U6-O4 | - | 2 | 3 | 1 | 1 | 2 |
| U6-O5 | 3 | 3 | 3 | 3 | 3 | 3 |

## 6.1 INTRODUCTION

Multiple Input Multiple Output (MIMO) technology revolutionizes wireless communication by employing multiple antennas at both the transmitter and receiver ends. Unlike traditional Single-Input Single-Output (SISO) systems, MIMO exploits spatial diversity to enhance data throughput, improve reliability, and extend coverage. By transmitting multiple data streams concurrently over the same frequency band, MIMO significantly increases spectral efficiency. This is achieved through spatial multiplexing, where the multiple antennas exploit the spatial dimension to transmit independent data streams simultaneously. Additionally, MIMO systems benefit from spatial processing techniques, such as beamforming and spatial diversity, to combat fading and mitigate interference. The introduction of MIMO has paved the way for advanced wireless standards like 4G LTE, 5G, and beyond, enabling higher data rates, better spectral efficiency, and improved quality of service. MIMO technology finds applications in various wireless communication systems, including cellular networks, Wi-Fi, and point-to-point communication links. Its continued development and integration into emerging technologies promise to reshape the landscape of wireless communication, offering unprecedented performance and reliability in diverse deployment scenarios. Fig. 6.1 depicts a traditional MIMO system

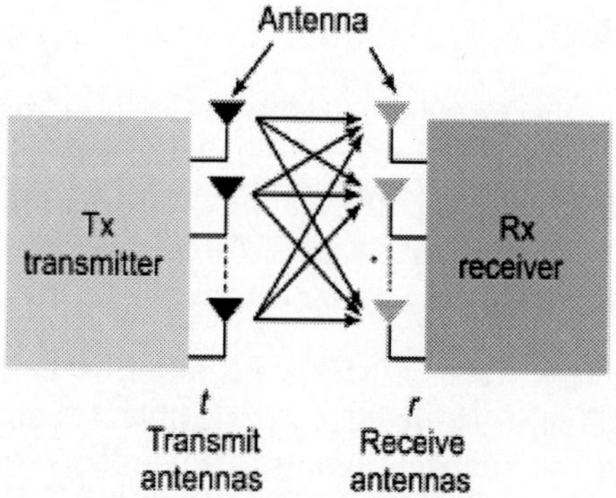


Fig.6.1 MIMO system

### 6.1.1 Basic principles of MIMO communication

The basic principles of Multiple Input Multiple Output (MIMO) communication lie at the heart of modern wireless communication systems, enabling higher data rates, improved reliability, and enhanced spectral efficiency. At its core, MIMO technology leverages multiple antennas at both the transmitter and receiver ends to exploit spatial diversity and multiplex multiple data streams simultaneously. Understanding the fundamental principles of MIMO communication is essential for grasping its significance and applications in various wireless communication standards and technologies.

1. Spatial Diversity
2. Spatial Multiplexing
3. Channel State Information (CSI)
4. Precoding and Beamforming
5. Diversity-Multiplexing Tradeoff

In conclusion, the basic principles of MIMO communication encompass spatial diversity, spatial multiplexing, channel state information, precoding, beamforming, and the diversity-multiplexing tradeoff. These principles form the foundation of modern wireless communication systems, enabling higher data rates, improved reliability, and enhanced spectral efficiency. By leveraging multiple antennas and sophisticated signal processing techniques, MIMO technology has revolutionized wireless communication and paved the way for advanced standards such as 4G LTE, 5G, and beyond. Understanding these fundamental principles is essential for designing, deploying, and optimizing MIMO systems in various communication applications.

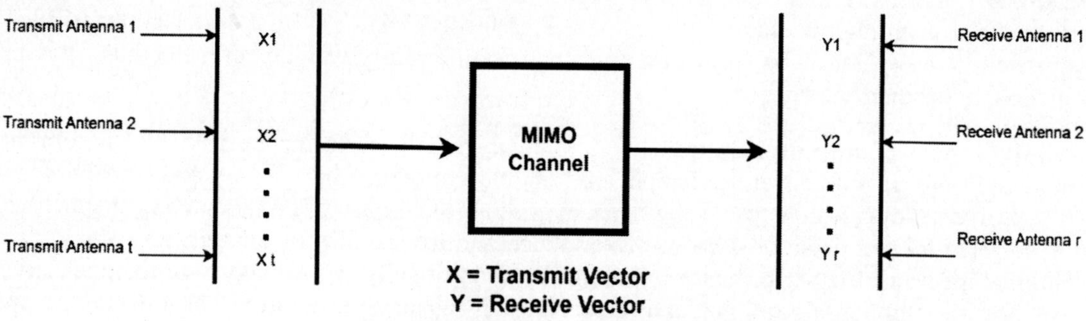


Fig. 6.2 MIMO Communication

### 6.1.2 MIMO System Model

The MIMO (Multiple Input Multiple Output) system model is a mathematical representation of a wireless communication system that incorporates multiple transmit and receive antennas. This model is essential for understanding the behavior and performance of MIMO systems and serves as the basis for designing and optimizing various MIMO signal processing algorithms and techniques. The MIMO system model typically includes the following components:

1. **Transmitter Antennas (Inputs)**: The MIMO transmitter is equipped with multiple antennas, denoted as $\boldsymbol{N_t}$. Each antenna emits its own signal, forming a vector of transmitted signals. This vector can represent symbols modulated onto carrier signals, data streams, or pilot signals used for channel estimation.

2. **Channel Matrix:** The channel matrix **H** represents the wireless channel between the transmitter and receiver in the MIMO system. It characterizes the propagation characteristics and spatial fading effects experienced by the transmitted signals as they propagate through the wireless medium. The channel matrix is typically represented as an $\boldsymbol{N_r} \times \boldsymbol{N_t}$ matrix, where $\boldsymbol{N_r}$ is the number of receiver antennas.

3. **Receiver Antennas (Outputs):** The MIMO receiver is equipped with multiple antennas, denoted as $\boldsymbol{N_r}$. Each antenna captures a portion of the transmitted signal after it has traversed the wireless channel. The received signals are combined to form a vector of received signals.

4. **Received Signal Vector:** The received signal vector **y** is a column vector representing the signals received at each antenna of the receiver. It is given by the matrix-vector multiplication $\mathbf{y} = \mathbf{Hx} + \mathbf{n}$, where x is the transmitted signal vector, **H** is the channel matrix, and **n** is the noise vector.

5. **Noise:** The noise vector **n** represents the additive noise introduced during signal transmission and reception. It typically follows a Gaussian distribution and is assumed to be uncorrelated across different antennas.

6. **Channel State Information (CSI):** Channel State Information refers to the knowledge of the wireless channel's characteristics at the transmitter and/or receiver. It includes information about channel gains, fading statistics, and spatial correlation. Accurate CSI is crucial for implementing advanced MIMO signal processing techniques such as beamforming, precoding, and spatial multiplexing.

7. **Feedback Channel:** In practical MIMO systems, the receiver may transmit feedback information to the transmitter regarding the channel conditions. This feedback is used by the transmitter to adapt its transmission strategy, such as adjusting transmit beamforming weights or selecting appropriate modulation and coding schemes.

The MIMO system model provides a framework for analyzing the performance of MIMO systems under various conditions, such as different channel environments, modulation schemes, and signal processing techniques. It enables researchers and engineers to evaluate the impact of factors such as channel fading, spatial correlation, and noise on system performance and to design efficient MIMO communication systems that meet specific performance requirements. Additionally, the MIMO system model serves as a basis for developing algorithms and protocols for channel estimation, beamforming, spatial multiplexing, and other advanced signal processing techniques employed in MIMO systems.

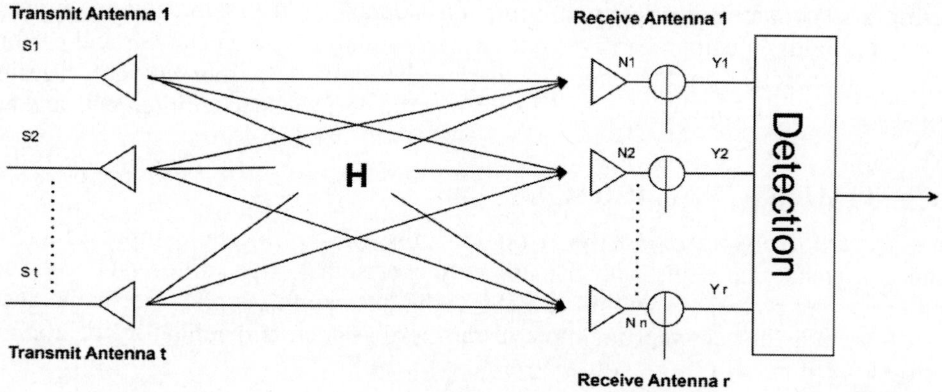


Fig. 6.3 MIMO System Model

### 6.1.3 Parameters Defining the MIMO System:

- Number of antennas at the transmitter (**Nt**): This parameter defines the number of antennas used for transmitting signals in the MIMO system.
- Number of antennas at the receiver (***Nr***): This parameter defines the number of antennas used for receiving signals in the MIMO system.
- Channel Matrix (**H**): As mentioned earlier, the channel matrix represents the wireless channel between the transmitter and receiver, relating the transmitted signals to the received signals.
- Modulation Scheme: The modulation scheme defines how information is encoded onto the transmitted signals. Common modulation schemes used in MIMO systems include QPSK (Quadrature Phase Shift Keying), 16-QAM (Quadrature Amplitude Modulation), and 64-QAM.

### 6.1.4 Assumptions and Considerations in Modelling MIMO Systems:

- **Flat Fading:** The model assumes that the channel response remains constant over the duration of a transmission symbol, simplifying the analysis of the system.
- **Line-of-Sight (LOS) and Non-Line-of-Sight (NLOS) Paths:** The model may consider both LOS and NLOS propagation paths, each with different characteristics such as path loss, delay spread, and multipath fading.
- **Channel State Information (CSI):** The model may assume that perfect or imperfect CSI is available at the transmitter and/or receiver. Perfect CSI implies that the transmitter and receiver have complete knowledge of the channel conditions, while imperfect CSI accounts for estimation errors and feedback delays.
- **Spatial Correlation:** The model may account for spatial correlation between the antennas at the transmitter and receiver, which affects the capacity and performance of the MIMO system.
- **Transmit and Receive Processing:** The model may incorporate various signal processing techniques such as beamforming, precoding, and spatial multiplexing to optimize the transmission and reception of signals in the MIMO system.

By considering these parameters, assumptions, and considerations, the mathematical representation of MIMO channels provides a comprehensive framework for analyzing the behavior and performance of MIMO systems in various communication scenarios. It serves as a foundation for designing and optimizing MIMO communication systems to meet specific performance requirements and application constraints.

## 6.2 SPACE-TIME SIGNAL PROCESSING

Space-Time Signal Processing (STSP) is a field within MIMO (Multiple Input Multiple Output) communication systems that deals with the processing of signals transmitted and received through multiple antennas over both space and time. STSP techniques aim to exploit the spatial and temporal dimensions of the wireless channel to improve the performance and reliability of communication systems.

### 6.2.1 Space-Time Processing Techniques for MIMO Systems

Space-time processing techniques encompass a variety of methods used to process signals transmitted and received through multiple antennas in MIMO systems. These techniques leverage the spatial and temporal dimensions of the wireless channel to enhance signal quality, increase data rates, and improve system reliability. Some common space-time processing techniques include:

- Spatial Filtering: Spatial filtering techniques, such as beamforming and spatial multiplexing, are used to enhance the Signal-to-Noise Ratio (SNR) at the receiver by adjusting the phase and amplitude of signals transmitted by each antenna.
- Temporal Processing: Temporal processing techniques exploit the time-varying nature of the wireless channel to mitigate the effects of fading and interference. These techniques include adaptive equalization, diversity combining, and error correction coding.
- Joint Space-Time Processing: Joint space-time processing techniques combine spatial and temporal processing to optimize the transmission and reception of signals in MIMO systems. These techniques include space-time coding, precoding, and space-time block coding.

### 6.2.2 Space-Time Coding Schemes

Space-time coding schemes are used to encode information onto the transmitted signals in MIMO systems, exploiting both the spatial and temporal dimensions of the wireless channel to improve reliability and data rate. Some common space-time coding schemes include:

- Alamouti Coding: Alamouti coding is a simple space-time block coding scheme that achieves diversity gain by transmitting two copies of the same data symbols over two consecutive time slots and multiple antennas. This scheme effectively combats fading and improves system reliability.
- Bell Laboratories Layered Space-Time (BLAST): BLAST is a spatial multiplexing technique that exploits the spatial dimension of the wireless channel to achieve high data rates. BLAST transmits multiple independent data streams simultaneously over multiple antennas, increasing the spectral efficiency of the system.
- Vertical-Bell Laboratories Layered Space-Time (V-BLAST): V-BLAST is an extension of BLAST that further improves spectral efficiency by employing linear precoding techniques. V-BLAST decomposes the data streams into layers and transmits each layer over a subset of antennas, exploiting the spatial dimension to achieve high data rates.

### 6.2.3 Diversity Combining Techniques

Diversity combining techniques are used to exploit spatial and temporal diversity in MIMO systems to improve system reliability and mitigate the effects of fading. These techniques combine multiple copies of the received signal to enhance the Signal-to-Noise Ratio (SNR) at the receiver.

Consider a MIMO system with $N_r$ receive antennas, each receiving a signal affected by fading and noise. Let $y_j$ denote the received signal at the j-th receive antenna, where i=1,2,.....,$N_t$ and j=1,2,...,$N_r$ . The received signals can be expressed as:

$$y_j = \sum_{i=1}^{N_t} h_{ij} x_i + n_j \tag{6.1}$$

where,

$N_t$ is the number of transmit antennas.

- $h_{ij}$ represents the channel coefficient between the *i*-th transmit antenna and the *j*-th receive antenna.
- $x_i$ is the signal transmitted from the *i*-th transmit antenna.
- $n_j$ is the Additive White Gaussian Noise (AWGN) at the *j*-th receive antenna.

Some common diversity combining techniques include:

- Maximal Ratio Combining (MRC): MRC combines the signals received from multiple antennas using weighted averaging, where the weights are chosen to maximize the SNR at the receiver. The combined signal $\hat{x}$ is given by:

$$\hat{x} = \sum_{j=1}^{N_r} \frac{h_{ij}^*}{\sqrt{\sum_{j=1}^{N_r} |h_{ij}|^2}} y_j \tag{6.2}$$

- Selection Combining: Selection combining selects the antenna with the highest received signal strength and uses its output as the final received signal. This technique eliminates the effects of fading on weaker antennas and improves system reliability. The combined signal $\hat{x}$ is given by:

$$\hat{x} = max_j |y_j| \tag{6.3}$$

- Equal Gain Combining (EGC): EGC combines the signals received from multiple antennas using equal weighting, regardless of the received signal strength. This technique provides diversity gain and improves system reliability in fading channels. The combined signal $\hat{x}$ is given by:

$$\hat{x} = \sum_{j=1}^{N_r} y_j \tag{6.4}$$

Space-Time Signal Processing encompasses a range of techniques and schemes used in MIMO communication systems to exploit the spatial and temporal dimensions of the wireless channel. These techniques and schemes improve system performance, increase data rates, and enhance reliability by leveraging the inherent diversity and multiplexing capabilities of MIMO systems.

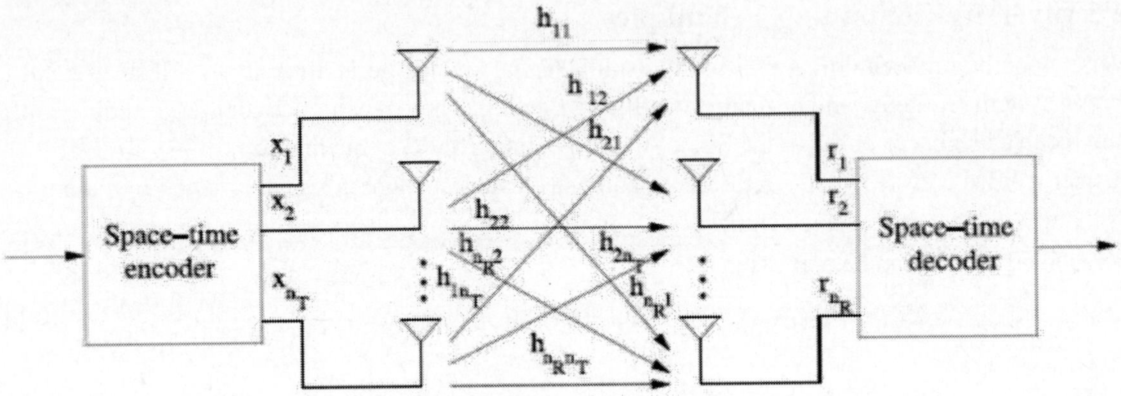


Fig. 6.4 Space-Time Signal Processing

## 6.3 SPATIAL MULTIPLEXING

Spatial multiplexing is a key technique used in MIMO (Multiple Input Multiple Output) communication systems to increase data rates by simultaneously transmitting multiple data streams over the same frequency band through different spatial paths. Unlike traditional Single-Input Single-Output (SISO) systems, spatial multiplexing takes advantage of the multiple antennas at both the transmitter and receiver to achieve higher spectral efficiency and throughput.

### 6.3.1 Principles of Spatial Multiplexing and its Advantages

Spatial multiplexing relies on the spatial diversity provided by multiple transmit and receive antennas to transmit independent data streams in parallel. Each transmit antenna sends a unique data stream, which is spatially separated and received by multiple receive antennas. By exploiting the spatial dimension of the wireless channel, spatial multiplexing enables simultaneous transmission of multiple data streams, effectively increasing the data rate without requiring additional bandwidth. The advantages of spatial multiplexing include:

- Increased Data Rates: Spatial multiplexing allows for the simultaneous transmission of multiple data streams, resulting in higher data rates compared to traditional single-antenna systems.
- Spectral Efficiency: Spatial multiplexing maximizes the utilization of available spectrum by transmitting multiple data streams over the same frequency band, improving spectral efficiency.
- Improved Robustness: Spatial diversity provided by multiple antennas helps mitigate fading and improve system reliability, enhancing the robustness of the communication link.

### 6.3.2 Spatial Multiplexing Techniques

Spatial multiplexing techniques aim to optimize the transmission of multiple data streams over multiple antennas in MIMO systems. Some common spatial multiplexing techniques include:

**Vertical Beamforming:** Vertical beamforming adjusts the phase and amplitude of signals transmitted by each antenna to direct them towards the intended receiver. This technique enhances the Signal-to-Noise Ratio (SNR) at the receiver and improves spatial separation between data streams.

Let $w_i$ denote the complex weight applied to the signal transmitted by the $i$-th transmit antenna. The transmitted signal $s_i$ from the $i$-th transmit antenna after applying vertical beamforming is given by:

$$s_i = w_i x_i \tag{6.4}$$

The received signal $y_j$ at the $j$-th receive antenna after vertical beamforming can be expressed as:

$$y_j = \sum_{i=1}^{N_t} h_{ij} w_i x_i + n_j \tag{6.5}$$

The optimization problem for vertical beamforming can be formulated as:

$$max_w \sum_{j=1}^{N_r} \left| \sum_{i=1}^{N_t} h_{ij} w_i x_i \right|^2$$

**Horizontal Beamforming:** Horizontal beamforming exploits the spatial diversity provided by multiple receive antennas to maximize the received signal power and mitigate interference from other sources. This technique improves the reliability and performance of the communication link.

**Precoding:** Precoding techniques optimize the transmitted signals' spatial distribution to maximize the achievable data rate and minimize interference. Precoding algorithms adjust the phase and amplitude of signals transmitted by each antenna based on The Channel State Information (CSI) to achieve optimal performance.

**Singular Value Decomposition (SVD):** SVD decomposes the channel matrix into its singular values and corresponding singular vectors, providing insights into the spatial characteristics of the wireless channel. SVD-based spatial multiplexing techniques exploit the spatial dimensions of the channel to maximize data throughput and achieve optimal performance. Here's a derivation of SVD in MIMO:

Consider a MIMO system with $\boldsymbol{N_t}$ transmit antennas and $\boldsymbol{N_r}$ receive antennas. Let **H** denote the channel matrix, which represents the wireless channel between the transmit and receive antennas. The channel matrix **H** can be expressed as:

$$\mathrm{H}=\mathrm{U}\Sigma V^H$$

where:

- **U** is an $N_r \times N_r$ unitary matrix containing the left singular vectors of H.
- **Σ** is an $N_r \times N_t$ diagonal matrix containing the singular values of H.
- **V** is an $N_t \times N_t$ unitary matrix containing the right singular vectors of H.
- $[]^H$ denotes the conjugate transpose operation.
- The SVD decomposition of **H** allows us to express the channel matrix as a product of three matrices, each representing different aspects of the channel:

1. **Left Singular Vectors (U)**: The columns of **U** represent the spatial signatures of the receive antennas. These vectors indicate the directions in which the received signals are most strongly correlated.
2. **Singular Values (Σ):** The diagonal elements of **Σ** represent the singular values of **H**, which quantify the strength of the channel's spatial modes. Larger singular values correspond to stronger spatial modes, indicating more significant signal power along those directions.
3. **Right Singular Vectors (V):** The columns of **V** represent the spatial signatures of the transmit antennas. These vectors indicate the directions in which the transmitted signals are most strongly correlated.

The SVD decomposition allows for several important insights and applications in MIMO systems:

- **Channel Capacity:** The singular values of **H** determine the channel capacity, with larger singular values indicating higher capacity along the corresponding spatial modes.
- **Beamforming:** The right singular vectors **V** can be used for transmit beamforming to maximize the received signal power at the receiver.
- **Receive Processing:** The left singular vectors **U** can be used for receive processing techniques such as matched filtering or zero-forcing to mitigate interference and improve signal detection.
- **Channel Estimation:** The decomposition provides a basis for estimating the channel matrix, enabling accurate channel estimation and feedback in MIMO systems.

### 6.3.3 Channel State Information (CSI) Feedback and Adaptive Spatial Multiplexing

Channel state information (CSI) feedback plays a crucial role in adaptive spatial multiplexing, where the transmitter adjusts its transmission strategy based on the current channel conditions. The receiver estimates the channel state and feeds back this information to the transmitter, enabling adaptive spatial multiplexing techniques to optimize the transmission parameters such as transmit beamforming weights, precoding matrices, and modulation schemes. By adapting to changing channel conditions in real-time, adaptive spatial multiplexing maximizes data rates and system performance, improving the overall efficiency of the MIMO communication system.

Spatial Multiplexing is a fundamental technique in MIMO communication systems that exploits the spatial diversity provided by multiple antennas to achieve higher data rates and spectral efficiency. By simultaneously transmitting multiple independent data streams over multiple antennas, spatial multiplexing enhances system performance, reliability, and throughput, making it a key enabler for next-generation wireless communication systems.

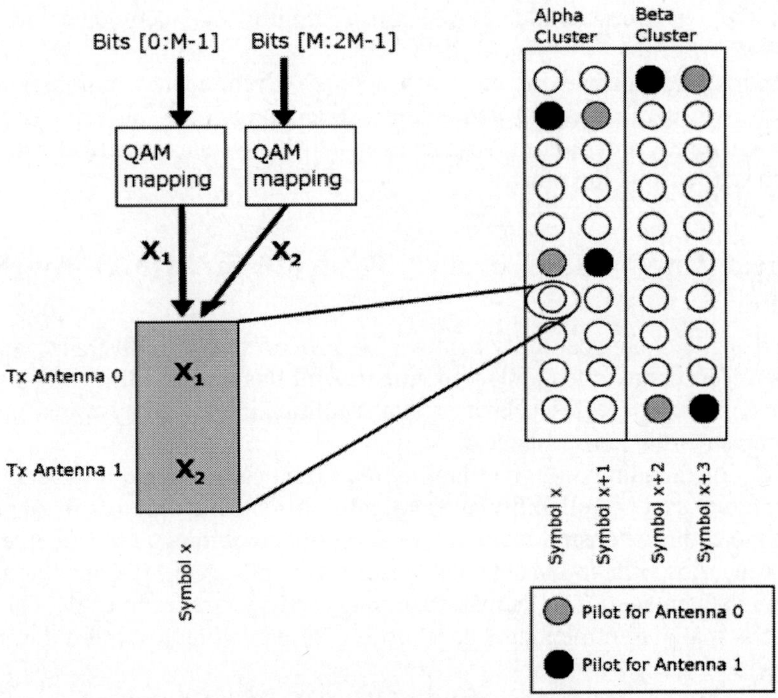


Fig. 6.5 Spatial Multiplexing

## 6.4 DIVERSITY/MULTIPLEXING TRADEOFF

The Diversity/Multiplexing Tradeoff in MIMO (Multiple Input Multiple Output) systems refers to the inherent tradeoff between diversity gain and multiplexing gain. This tradeoff arises from the different strategies used to exploit the spatial dimensions of the wireless channel for improving communication performance.

### 6.4.1 Diversity and Multiplexing Gains in MIMO Systems

Diversity Gain: Diversity gain refers to the improvement in communication reliability achieved by exploiting the spatial diversity provided by multiple antennas in MIMO systems. By transmitting redundant copies of the same data over different spatial paths, diversity gain helps mitigate the effects of fading and enhance system reliability.

Multiplexing Gain: Multiplexing gain, on the other hand, refers to the increase in data rate achieved by simultaneously transmitting multiple independent data streams over multiple antennas. Multiplexing gain exploits the spatial dimension of the wireless channel to achieve higher spectral efficiency and throughput.

### 6.4.2 Tradeoff Analysis between Diversity and Multiplexing Gains

The tradeoff between diversity and multiplexing gains arises from the limited resources available in the wireless channel, such as bandwidth, transmit power, and spatial degrees of freedom. Increasing diversity typically requires allocating more resources to transmit redundant copies of the same data, which reduces the resources available for transmitting independent data streams and achieving multiplexing gain.

Conversely, maximizing multiplexing gain may reduce the redundancy in transmitted signals, limiting the system's ability to combat fading and achieve diversity gain. As a result, there is a fundamental tradeoff between diversity and multiplexing gains in MIMO systems, where allocating resources to one gain comes at the expense of the other.

### 6.4.3 Practical Implications of the Tradeoff in MIMO System Design and Optimization

MIMO system designers must carefully balance the tradeoff between diversity and multiplexing gains based on the specific communication requirements and channel conditions. This involves selecting appropriate transmission strategies, such as spatial multiplexing, diversity combining, or a combination of both, to optimize system performance.

In scenarios with severe fading or high reliability requirements, prioritizing diversity gain may be more beneficial to improve system reliability and mitigate errors. This may involve employing techniques such as space-time coding, transmit diversity, or diversity combining at the receiver.

Conversely, in scenarios with ample channel capacity and less severe fading, maximizing multiplexing gain may be more advantageous to increase data rates and spectral efficiency. This may involve using techniques such as spatial multiplexing, beamforming, or precoding to exploit the spatial dimensions of the wireless channel.

Adaptive transmission schemes that dynamically adjust the tradeoff between diversity and multiplexing gains based on channel conditions and feedback information can further optimize MIMO system performance in real-time.

The Diversity/Multiplexing Tradeoff in MIMO systems highlights the delicate balance between diversity gain, which improves reliability by exploiting spatial diversity, and multiplexing gain, which increases data rates by exploiting spatial multiplexing. Understanding this tradeoff is crucial for designing and optimizing MIMO communication systems to meet specific performance requirements and maximize spectral efficiency while ensuring reliable communication in diverse channel conditions.

## 6.5 APPLICATIONS AND FUTURE DIRECTIONS

Applications and Future Directions of MIMO (Multiple Input Multiple Output) technology span a wide range of wireless communication systems, from current standards like 4G LTE and 5G to future technologies yet to be fully realized. Here's a detailed exploration of these points:

### 6.5.1 Real-world Applications of MIMO Technology

**4G LTE:** MIMO technology is a key enabler of 4G LTE networks, allowing for higher data rates, improved coverage, and increased spectral efficiency. LTE networks commonly employ 2x2 or 4x4 MIMO configurations to enhance performance, especially in urban and dense urban environments where multipath propagation and interference are prevalent.

**5G:** MIMO plays an even more significant role in 5G networks, which leverage massive MIMO configurations with hundreds or even thousands of antennas. Massive MIMO enables unprecedented levels of spectral efficiency, increased network capacity, and improved user experience by serving multiple users simultaneously in both time and space.

**Beyond 5G :** MIMO technology continues to evolve in future wireless communication systems, including beyond 5G (B5G) and 6G. These systems are expected to push the boundaries of MIMO technology further, with advancements such as terahertz communication, non-terrestrial networks, and intelligent reflecting surfaces (IRS) to improve coverage, capacity, and connectivity.

### 6.5.2 Emerging Trends and Future Directions in MIMO Research and Development

**Massive MIMO :** Research in massive MIMO focuses on improving the scalability, energy efficiency, and performance of massive antenna arrays. Techniques such as hybrid beamforming, massive MIMO with lens antennas, and distributed massive MIMO are being explored to overcome hardware constraints and deployment challenges.

**Millimeter Wave (mmWave) Communication :** MIMO technology is crucial for harnessing the potential of mmWave frequencies in future communication systems. Research in mmWave MIMO includes beamforming, channel modeling, and interference mitigation techniques to address the unique challenges posed by high-frequency bands.

**Machine Learning and AI :** Machine learning and artificial intelligence (AI) are increasingly being integrated into MIMO systems for optimization, self-configuration, and adaptive signal processing. Research in AI-driven MIMO includes intelligent beamforming, adaptive modulation and coding, and dynamic resource allocation to improve system performance and efficiency.

### 6.5.3 Challenges and Opportunities in Deploying MIMO in Various Communication Scenarios

**Hardware Complexity :** Deploying MIMO systems with a large number of antennas poses significant challenges in terms of hardware complexity, cost, and power consumption. Addressing these challenges requires advances in antenna design, signal processing algorithms, and integration techniques to enable cost-effective and energy-efficient MIMO solutions.

**Interference and Coexistence :** MIMO systems operating in crowded spectrum bands face challenges related to interference and coexistence with other wireless systems. Techniques such as interference cancellation, cognitive radio, and dynamic spectrum sharing are being explored to mitigate interference and improve spectrum utilization.

**Channel Estimation and Feedback :** Accurate channel estimation and feedback are essential for optimizing MIMO performance, especially in dynamic and time-varying channels. Research in channel estimation techniques, feedback mechanisms, and adaptive algorithms aims to improve reliability and efficiency in MIMO communication systems.

MIMO technology continues to drive innovation and advancement in wireless communication systems, from current standards like 4G LTE and 5G to future technologies beyond 5G and 6G. Emerging trends in massive MIMO, mmWave communication, machine learning, and AI are shaping the future of MIMO research and development, offering new opportunities to enhance performance, efficiency, and connectivity in diverse communication scenarios. However, deploying MIMO in real-world environments presents challenges related to hardware complexity, interference management, and channel estimation, which require innovative solutions and interdisciplinary collaborations to overcome.

## 6.6 SNR ESTIMATION

Without the loss of the generality of data security, faster data transmission is one of the most challenging prospects in digital data communications. Data can be either Analog or Digital, but computers only store data based on the binary sequence; hence, there is a need for digital-to-digital encoding (binary sequences generated by computer translated to sequences of voltage pulse which propagate through a wire). Transmission can occur using a Channel that can be either noiseless(ideal) or noisy (unwanted impairment), where two properties, 'Bandwidth' **(BW)** and 'Signal to Noise ratio' **(SNR)**, play a crucial role.**BW** of an Analog signal expressed in terms of frequencies, the faster a signal changes, the higher its maximum frequency is; hence larger the **BW** is. If the **'channel BW'** exceeds the **'signal BW'**, a signal transmission over the channel is successful, which implies that **BW** is directly proportional to the transmission rate. For a noiseless channel, Nyquist proposed a formula for predicting bitrate (**Bitrate =2×BW×log$_2$ L**, where **L** = no of signal levels), but in a real scenario channel is not always noiseless. Shannon proposed a formula for the capacity of maximum bitrate over a noisy channel (**Capacity=BW×log$_2$(1+SNR) bits/sec**; notice signal levels are missing here). **AGWN** (Adaptive Gaussian White Noise) is sometimes added with a signal to disturb the original signal where signal power must be greater than equal to noise power for near-perfect transmission. Otherwise, it leads to a bit of a flip. Hence, the bite error rate (**BER**) is under consideration, which has a direct impact on the throughput and efficiency of the channel. In Satellite communication, **AGWN** is used and does not suffer from impairments like fading, multipath and interference where noise is Gaussian because its amplitude can be modelled with a normal probability distribution where the **BW** is spectrally flat across the sampling, hence called **'white'** (equal spectral power level at all frequencies of the visible light spectrum). But before discussing **SNR** and its impact on transmission, we need to know what it is and how it affects the transmitted signal. Noise is the unavoidable random thermal fluctuation of our system that can't be expressed by an analytical function and requires statistical interpretation in terms of **'mean'** and **'variance'**. In a well-behaved system, the 'noise-mean' is zero; sometimes, it gets added or subtracted from our signal stochastically. Sometimes, 'noise-mean' is non-zero; the signal is 'biased', which is very easy to detect and remove, so it won't concentrate on noise and does not have any impact on the signal during transmission. To continue the discussion, one question arises: what about 'noise-variance' and how it affects signal transmission? The 'noise-variance' is its 'size'; when it is larger extremely difficult to distinguish both. We would like to make the 'noise variance' as small as possible. So, we can explain **SNR** as the ratio between the 'magnitude of the signal' and the 'variance of noise'. Low **SNR** means the noise is big, it is very hard to determine the magnitude of the signal and vice versa. **SNR** determines the recoverability of the transmitted signal. For example, to measure the **SNR** of an image, we need to find out the ratio between the mean of the pixel value and the standard deviation of the pixel values over a finite given neighbourhood'. In general, we formulate the **SNR** either in watts or volts **[$SNR_{watts}$= 10×log$_2$(signal/noise) or $SNR_{volts}$= 20×log$_2$(signal/noise)].** We can categorize **SNR** values in different ranges of values when a) **SNR** value ∈ [5db -10db], can't establish a connection, b) **SNR** value ∈ [10db -15db], can't establish a reliable connection, c) **SNR** value ∈ [15db -25db], establish poor connection, d) **SNR** value ∈ [25db -40db], establish a good connection e) **SNR** value ∈ [>41db], establish excellent connection. As a benchmark, we can say a good **SNR** must be greater or equal to 20db. Sometimes, **SNR** is also known as the ratio between the 'mean' of a signal and the 'standard deviation' of a signal. As a result, low **SNR** may cause high **BER**, so there is a very strong correlation between **SNR** and **BER**. Before exploring the connection, need to define the **BER** ratio that will be discussed in the next section.

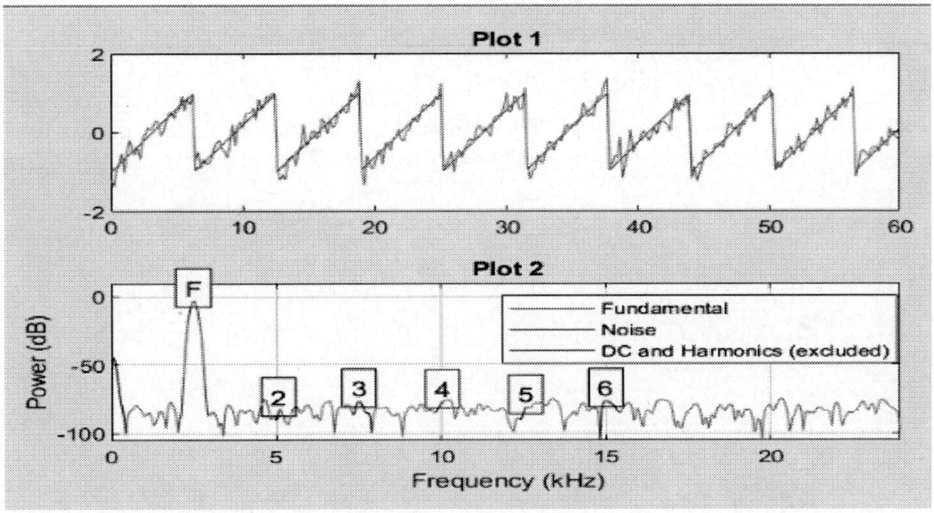


Fig. 6.6 SNR for AWGN

## 6.7 BER ESTIMATION

**BER** is a phenomenon caused due to low **SNR**, achieved during transmission. We can say alternatively that if the **SNR** is below some specified **threshold** (minimum **SNR** requirement), reliable transmission cannot take place over an underlined network architecture. This minimum requirement is called an **"outage"**. During transmission, how much **SNR** we can enrich is completely random, so we can only measure the amount of uncertainty in terms of "**outage probability**". The achieved **SNR** value defines the transmission possibility if it is greater than the **threshold**; channel noise is dominant by signal power (in decibels). From the previous discussion, we can argue (good SNR =20db) is the minimum requirement (**threshold**) for a reliable connection establishment, but the value of **thresholds** may change from context to context. So, **BER** is a ratio of the number of bits corrupted during transmission over the total number of bits transmitted. $10^{-11}$ **BER** can be explained as 1 error (bit flip) that can occur during transmission of 100,000,000,000 bits in a time interval. Our goal is to maintain **BER** as minimum as possible for effective transmission, which is the cause of the increase in throughput and efficiency. Any number of bits can corrupt during transmission, but which one can't predict follows a binomial distribution. As a result, we can conclude that larger signal power allows a system to maintain a minimum SNR over a long distance and vice versa. Alternatively, we can say that somebody willing to increase signal power may use lesser BW and vice versa. Shannon equation limits the communication rate imposed by SNR & BW. If there is no noise (noiseless, impractical in general), the SNR value tends to be infinite, and then the theoretical capacity of the channel is arbitrarily high. As a result, we can argue that factors affecting BER are Interference, increased transmitter power, reduced bandwidth, lower order modulation, etc. Now the question is how to reduce BER. Some useful techniques to tackle these problems need to be incorporated into our discussion, like 'channel coding', 'modulation', 'equalization', and 'error-detection & correction'. Cyclic Redundancy Check (CRC), Parity check and observation of Bit Interleaved Parity (BIP) and Probabilistic approach are used to estimate BER. Estimation of BER can vary from context to context. BER for polar NRZ, BPSK, and QPSK are probably the same. BER for different modulation scheme is shown in Fig. 6.7.

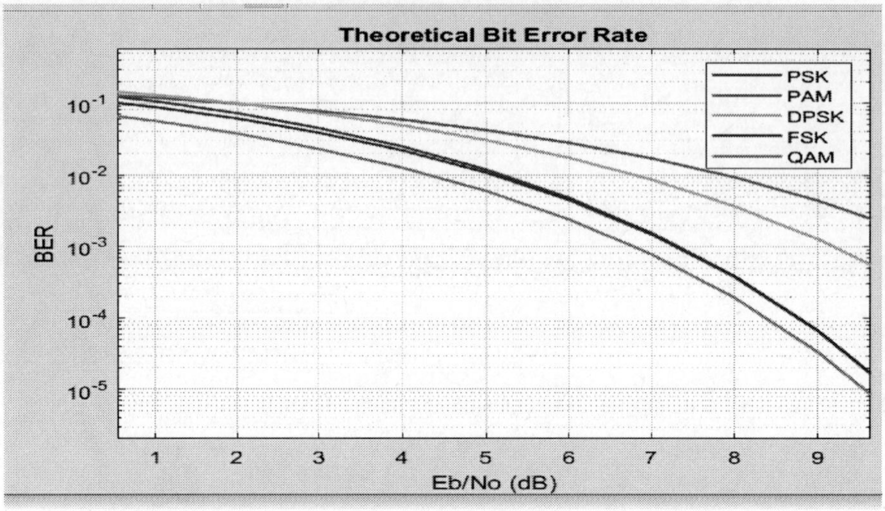


Fig. 6.7 BER for PSK, PAM, DPSK, FSK, QAM

The general formula for SNR and BER is given below.

$$\text{SNR} = \text{Signal power/Noise power} \quad (6.1)$$

$$= (E_b/N_0) \quad (6.2)$$

where $E_b$ = energy per bit & $N_0$ = noise spectral density.

The probabilistic theoretical bit error rate calculated as follows.

$$\Pr(\text{BER}) = \Pr(1) \times \Pr(0/1) + \Pr(0) \times \Pr(1/0) \quad (6.3)$$

Where Pr (1) = probability of transmitted bit is 1, Pr (0/1) = probability of received bit is 0 given that the transmitted bit is 1, Pr (0) = probability of the transmitted bit is 0, Pr (1/0) = probability of the received bit is 1, given that the transmitted bit is 0.

Also, a strong correlation exists among the BER, SNR and error functions(erf).

$$\text{BER} = (1/2) \times (1\text{-erf}) \text{ sqrt } (\text{SNR}) \quad (6.4)$$

$$= (1/2) \times (1\text{-erf}) \text{ sqrt } (E_b/N_0) \quad (6.5)$$

## 6.8 OUTAGE PROBABILITY ESTIMATION

Finally, we are going to discuss '**outage probability**'. But before discussion, we should know what we mean by the term 'outage'. When the communicating underlying channel is so **poor** (**SNR**< some specified **threshold** value) no scheme (**PSK, QPSK, BPSK**, etc.) can communicate reliably at a fixed data rate.'**path loss**' ,'**shadowing**' and '**fading**' are essential considerations for reasonable communication.'**path loss**' also called '**path attenuation**' is a continuous attenuation(signal power degradation) process over distance, as distance increases , '**path loss**' is also increases. In other words we can say signal power demises over distance ,as a result signal getting flat by loosing its power gradually some time reaches below to the minimum **SNR** requirement(**outage**),hence communication cannot possible further. Similarly '**Shadowing**' is another impairment over communication the received signal power fluctuates because of the obstacle exists on the propagation path between sender and receiver experienced in local mean power. Signals are coming form sender to receiver using (line of sight, the shortest distance) and non line of sight (multi path), so after reaching to the receiver end there is combined effect in either constructive or destructive manner due to time delay with respect to the source for multipath phenomenon. Finally talk about **'fading'** describes the strength and quality of **RF**(radio frequency/radio signal) fluctuate with respect to time and distance may due to 'atmospheric condition', 'movements of objects', 'multipath propagation' etc. There are majorly two categories of fading namely **'small scale'** fading and **'large scale'** fading. In **'small scale'** fading variation occurs in **short distance** (few meter *centimeter) is a* ***fast*** *(called small) process also called* ***'deep fade'*** *cause of interference and distortion of signal,only affects the symbols/*bits. Where as in **'large scale'** fading signal strength decreases over long distance (several kilometers) affects the entire signal, is a **slow** process (called large).**'path loss'** and **'shadowing'** is are the example of 'large scale' fading. But **'Multi delay spread'** is **'small scale'** fading happens when the transmitted signal takes multiple path to reach the receiver ,causing **ISI** (Inter Symbolic Interference) effect. Up to this point reader will acquire a bit idea over communication ,how different aspects affects the transmission over a communicating channel in terms of **'BER'**, **'SNR'** and **'Outage'**. Now we are going to describe mathematically described as follows.

$$\text{Path Loss, } (L) = 10 \times n \times log_{10}(d) + C \quad (6.6)$$

where L(path loss in db) , n=path loss component, d= distance between transmitter and receiver and C= constant for system losses.

Path loss in free space

$$(L) = (P_t / P_r) = \{(4\pi d) / (G_t G_r \lambda^2)\} \quad (6.7)$$

$$= \{(4\pi f d) / (G_t G_r C^2)\} \quad (6.8)$$

where $P_t$ = transmit power , $P_r$ = receive power ,$G_t$ = transmission antenna gain, $G_r$ = receiver antenna gain, $\lambda$ = wavelength, d = distance between transmitter and receiver ,C=speed of light = $3 \times 10^8$ meter per second respectively.

In a non-fade (thus fixed) radio channel the BER decreases rapidly as SNR increases whereas in a poor / fade state when BER = ½ , the SNR or SIR (Signal Interference Ratio) is sufficient to support reliable communication , the probability of being in this state is called 'outage probability'

In combined path loss and shadowing we have [Ref_1 , page 45]

$$(P_r / P_t)_{db} = 10 \times \log_{10} K - 10 \times \gamma \times \log_{10} (d / d_0) - \Psi_{db} \quad (6.9)$$

where $P_r$ = received signal power, $P_t$ = transmitter signal power, $\gamma$ = path loss exponent, $\Psi_{db}$ = Gaussian distribution of RV with mean = 0 and variance = $\sigma^2_{\psi\, dB}$. The path loss decreases linearly relative to $\log_{10}$ d with a slope of $10\gamma$ dB/decade.

So, outage probability , $p_{out}(P_{min}, d)$ under path loss and shadowing is the probability that the received power at a given distance d, Pr (d), falls below $P_{min}$ : $p_{out}(P_{min}, d) = p(Pr(d) < P\ min)$.

For the combined path loss and shadowing the outage probability [Ref_1, page 45-48] is as follows

$$p(Pr(d) \leq P_{min}) = 1 - Q[(P_{min} - (P_t + 10 \times \log_{10} K - 10 \times \gamma \times \log_{10}(d/d_0)) / \sigma_{\psi\, dB}] \quad (6.10)$$

**Analytical example worked out:**

1. Find the outage probability at 150 m for a channel based on the combined path loss and shadowing

assuming a transmit power of $P_t$= 10 mW and minimum power requirement $P_{min}$ = −110.5 dB m.

**Solution :**

We have $P_t = 10 \text{ mW} = 10 \text{ dB m}$.

$$p_{out}(-110.5\text{dBm}, 150\text{m}) = p(Pr(150\text{m}) < -110.5\text{dBm})$$

$$= P_{min} - (P_t + 10\times \log_{10} K - 10\times \gamma\times \log_{10}(d/d_0))$$

$$= 1 - Q[(-110.5 - (10 - 31.54 - 37.1 \log_{10}[150]) / 3.65)$$

$$= 0.0121$$

An outage probability of 1% is a typical target in wireless system designs.

## 6.9 GLOBAL SYSTEM FOR MOBILE (GSM)

The **Global System for Mobile (GSM)** emerged as a second-generation cellular system standard aimed at addressing the fragmentation challenges encountered by the initial cellular networks in Europe. **GSM** distinguished itself as the pioneer in specifying digital modulation, network architectures, and services, becoming the predominant 2G technology globally. Prior to **GSM**, European nations operated disparate cellular standards, hindering seamless consumer use across the continent. Originally conceived as a pan-European cellular solution, **GSM** offered a wide array of network services leveraging **ISDN** technology. Its unparalleled success has surpassed expectations, making it the prevailing standard for modern cellular and personal communications devices worldwide. By 2001**, GSM** boasted over 350 million subscribers worldwide. **GSM** services adhere to **ISDN** standards and are categorized into teleservices and data services. Teleservices cover typical mobile telephony as well as traffic originating from mobile or base stations. Data services encompass computer-to-computer communication and packet-switched traffic.

GSM made its debut in the European market in 1991. By the conclusion of 1993, numerous countries outside of Europe, spanning South America, Asia, and Australia, had embraced GSM along with its technically comparable variant, DCS 1800. DCS 1800 operates within the 1.8 GHz to 2.0 GHz radio bands, supporting the implementation of Personal Communication Services (PCS) as recently designated by governments worldwide.

The main objective of **GSM** was to establish a mobile phone network enabling users to travel across Europe while ensuring compatibility with **ISDN** and other **PSTN** systems for voice services. The original system specifications spanned over **5,000 pages**, and the addition of new services, particularly data services, has further expanded the specifications. Those acquainted with the **ISDN** reference model will notice numerous resemblances in acronyms, reference points, and interfaces. The standardization of **GSM** endeavors to incorporate as many elements from **ISDN** as feasible.

**GSM** represents a typical second-generation system, superseding the initial analog systems, albeit lacking the high global data rates promised by third-generation systems like **UMTS**. Initially rolled out in Europe, **GSM** operated within the frequency range of **890–915 MHz** for uplinks and **935–960 MHz** for **downlinks**, now commonly referred to as **GSM 900** to distinguish it from subsequent iterations. These include **GSM** at **1800 MHz** (1710–1785 MHz uplink, 1805–1880 MHz downlink), known as DCS 1800, and the **GSM** variant predominant in the **US** at **1900 MHz** (1850–1910 MHz uplink, 1930–1990 MHz downlink), termed **PCS 1900**. Additionally, two more GSM iterations exist: **GSM 400** proposes deployment within the frequency range of 450.4–457.6/478.8–486 MHz for uplinks and 460.4–467.6/488.8–496 MHz for downlinks, potentially replacing analog systems in sparsely populated regions.

A GSM system tailored specifically for railroad operations, known as **GSM-Rail** (GSM-R), has been implemented in various European countries (**GSM-R, 2002),** (ETSI, 2002). This system not only operates on dedicated frequencies but also offers a range of additional services unavailable in the public **GSM** network. **GSM-R** allocates **19 exclusive channels** for railroad operators, facilitating voice and data transmissions. Noteworthy features of **GSM-R** include emergency calls with confirmations, Voice Group Call Service **(VGCS)**, and **Voice Broadcast Service** (VBS). These **Advanced Speech Call Features** (ASCI) emulate functionalities typically found in trunked radio systems only. Calls within **GSM-R** are prioritized, with high-priority calls taking precedence over low-priority ones. Moreover, call setup times are remarkably short: emergency calls are established in less than 2 seconds, while group calls take less than 5 seconds. Calls can be directed to specific user groups based on location, function, or numerical criteria. However, the most sophisticated application of **GSM-R** lies in train, switch, gate, and signal control. Trains traveling at speeds not exceeding 160 km/h can autonomously manage gates, switches, and signals. Even when trains exceed 160 km/h (as many modern trains do, reaching speeds surpassing 300 km/h), **GSM-R** remains instrumental in maintaining control.

## 6.10 Enhanced Data Rates For Global Evolution (EDGE)

**EDGE** (Enhanced Data Rates For Global Evolution) was established as a global advancement path for GSM operators and, in the US, TDMA operators. It introduces the 8-PSK modulation on the GSM air interface for both packet-switched data (EGPRS - Enhanced GPRS) and circuit-switched data (ECSD - Enhanced CSD). This enhancement increases peak and average data rates and enhances network capacity. EGPRS supports data rates up to 59.2 kbit/s per time slot per direction (up to 473.6 kbit/s per 200kHz carrier), implements incremental redundancy (Hybrid Type II ARQ), introduces various modulation and coding schemes using GMSK and 8-PSK modulations, and introduces new link quality measurement parameters. These advancements enable precise link adaptation in varying channel conditions. ECSD offers data rates up to 43.2 kbit/s per time slot, significantly reducing the need for multiple time slots to increase data rates for circuit-switched data and addressing a key limitation of HSCSD: capacity. ECSD also supports fast power control.

## 6.11 General Packet Radio System (GPRS)

Shortly after the initial deployment of GSM networks in the early 1990s and the introduction of GSM data services, it became clear that circuit-switched bearer services were not ideal for certain applications with sporadic data transmission. Circuit-switched connections had long access times to the network and were charged based on connection time. In contrast, packet-switched networks did not reserve resources permanently but instead utilized a shared pool, which was more efficient for bursty applications. GPRS (General Packet Radio Service) was introduced to bring packet-switched bearer services to the existing GSM system. GPRS offered shorter access times to the network and billing based on the amount of data transmitted.

In the GPRS system, users could access public data networks directly using standard protocol addresses (such as IP or X.25) when their Mobile Station (MS) was connected to the GPRS network. The GPRS MS could utilize between one and eight channels over the air interface, depending on its capabilities, with channels dynamically allocated as needed for data transmission. Uplink and downlink channels were reserved separately in the GPRS network, allowing for MSs with varying uplink and downlink capabilities. Resource allocation in the GPRS network was dynamic, depending on demand and resource availability, and packets could be sent during idle times between speech calls.

The GPRS system supported both Point-To-Point (PTP) and Point-To-Multipoint (PTM) communication, as well as SMS and anonymous network access. The theoretical maximum throughput in the GPRS system was 160 kbps per MS, utilizing all eight channels without error correction.

## 6.12 Interim Standard-95 (IS-95)

A US digital cellular system based on CDMA, aimed at increasing capacity, was standardized as Interim Standard 95 (IS-95) by the US Telecommunications Industry Association (TIA). IS-95, like IS-136, was designed to be compatible with the existing US analog cellular system (AMPS) frequency band, allowing for cost-effective production of mobiles and base stations for dual-mode operation. Qualcomm introduced pilot production CDMA-AMPS dual-mode phones in 1994, and by 2001, there were over 80 million CDMA subscribers worldwide.

IS-95 enables each user within a cell to utilize the same radio channel, with adjacent cells also sharing the same channel, as it is a direct sequence spread spectrum CDMA system. This eliminates the need for frequency planning within a market. For a US cellular provider, each IS-95 channel occupies 1.25 MHz of spectrum on each one-way link, or 10% of the available cellular spectrum. To transition smoothly from AMPS to CDMA, a 270 kHz guard band (typically accommodating 9 AMPS channels) must be provided on each side of the spectrum designated for IS-95. IS-95 is fully compatible with the IS-41 networking standard.

Unlike other cellular standards, IS-95 adjusts the user data rate (though not the channel chip rate) in real-time based on voice activity and network requirements. It uses different modulation and spreading techniques for the forward and reverse links. On the forward link, the base station simultaneously transmits user data for all mobiles in the cell using a unique spreading sequence for each mobile, along with a pilot code transmitted at a higher power level, allowing all mobiles to use coherent carrier detection while estimating channel conditions. On the reverse link, all mobiles respond asynchronously and maintain a constant signal level due to power control from the base station.

The speech coder used in the IS-95 system is the Qualcomm 9600 bps Code Excited Linear Predictive (QCELP) coder. This vocoder detects voice activity and reduces the data rate to 1200 bps during silent periods. Intermediate user data rates of 2400, 4800, and 9600 bps are also used for specific purposes. Additionally, a 14,400-bps coder using 13.4 kbps of speech data (QCELP13) was introduced by Qualcomm in 1995.

## 6.13 CODE DIVISION MULTIPLE ACCESS-2000 (CDMA2000)

The International Telecommunications Union-Radio Communication (ITU-R) standardization sector developed specifications for International Mobile Telecommunications—2000 (IMT-2000), which significantly broadened the scope of service capabilities across various environments. IMT-2000 specifications were designed to enable the introduction of new capabilities and to ensure a smooth transition from the existing second-generation (2G) telecommunications infrastructure by the early 2000s. Third-generation (3G) telecommunications systems based on IMT-2000 specifications began to be deployed between 2000 and 2002. These 3G systems offer a wide range of telecommunications services, including voice, low- and high-bit-rate data, multimedia, and video, to mobile users through various types of mobile terminals in both public and private settings such as office areas, residential areas, and transportation networks.

The cdma2000 Radio Transmission Technology (RTT) is a wideband, spread spectrum radio interface utilizing CDMA technology to fulfil the requirements of 3G wireless communication systems. This RTT meets all the specifications outlined in the ITU circular letter and associated IMT-2000 documents. It satisfies service requirements for indoor office, indoor-to-outdoor/pedestrian, and vehicular environments. Additionally, the cdma2000 system will maintain backward compatibility with the existing cdmaOne (IS-95) standards family.

The cdma2000 system offers various implementation options to accommodate data rates (both circuit switched and packet switched) ranging from the TIA IS-95B-compatible rate of 9.6 kbps up to over 2 Mbps. This system provides carriers with maximum flexibility in making engineering.

The cdma2000 system offers flexible mobility options, supporting fixed wireless as well as speeds up to 300 mph. It uses a layered structure to integrate the lower two layers of the Radio Transmission Technology (RTT) into systems that implement various network standards. The system is backward compatible with TIA IS-95B signalling and call control models. Its extended upper layer signalling structure enables the support of advanced services like multimedia in an efficient manner. cdma2000 also supports 3G Wireless Intelligent Networking (WIN) services and complies with services defined by international standards organizations, providing a smooth transition from existing 2G TIA IS-95B technology.

## 6.14 Wideband Code Division Multiple Access (WCDMA)

Analog cellular systems are often termed first-generation systems, while the current digital systems like GSM, PDC, cdmaOne (IS-95), and US-TDMA (IS-136) are considered second generation. These digital systems have enabled wireless voice communications in many markets and are increasingly supporting services like text messaging and data network access, which are experiencing rapid growth.

Third-generation systems are designed for multimedia communication, enhancing person-to-person communication with high-quality images and video, and improving access to information and services on public and private networks through higher data rates and flexible communication capabilities. This evolution, along with ongoing improvements in second-generation systems, is creating new business opportunities for manufacturers, operators, and providers of content and applications on these networks.

WCDMA technology has emerged as the predominant third-generation air interface in standardization forums. It is specified in 3GPP (3rd Generation Partnership Project), a collaboration of standardization bodies from Europe, Japan, Korea, the USA, and China. Within 3GPP, WCDMA is known as UTRA (Universal Terrestrial Radio Access) FDD (Frequency Division Duplex) and TDD (Time Division Duplex), with the term WCDMA encompassing both FDD and TDD operations.

WCDMA employs a wideband Direct-Sequence Code Division Multiple Access (DS-CDMA) approach, where user data is spread across a broad bandwidth by combining the user information bits with quasi-random chips generated from CDMA spreading codes. To accommodate very high bit rates, up to 2 Mbps, WCDMA allows for variable spreading factors and the use of multiple codes simultaneously. The chip rate of 3.84 Mcps results in a carrier bandwidth of roughly 5 MHz. Compared to narrowband CDMA systems like IS-95, which have a bandwidth of around 1 MHz, WCDMA's inherently wider carrier bandwidth enables higher user data rates and provides performance advantages such as enhanced multipath diversity. Network operators can deploy WCDMA based on their operating licenses.

WCDMA enables highly variable user data rates, supporting the concept of Bandwidth on Demand (BoD). While the user data rate remains constant within each 10 ms frame, the data capacity among users can change from frame to frame. This rapid radio capacity allocation is typically controlled by the network to optimize throughput for packet data services. WCDMA operates in two modes: Frequency Division Duplex (FDD) and Time Division Duplex (TDD). FDD uses separate 5 MHz carrier frequencies for the uplink and downlink, while TDD shares a single 5 MHz band between the uplink and downlink. The uplink refers to the connection from the mobile to the base station, while the downlink is from the base station to the mobile. WCDMA supports asynchronous base stations, eliminating the need for a global time reference like GPS, as required in the synchronous IS-95 system. This simplifies the deployment of indoor and micro base stations since there is no need to receive a GPS signal.

WCDMA utilizes coherent detection on both the uplink and downlink, facilitated by pilot symbols or common pilot. While coherent detection is already used on the downlink in IS-95, its implementation on the uplink is new for public CDMA systems. This enhancement is expected to significantly improve coverage and capacity on the uplink. The WCDMA air interface is designed to accommodate advanced CDMA receiver concepts such as multiuser detection and smart adaptive antennas. These concepts can be deployed by the network operator as a system option to enhance capacity and/or coverage. In contrast, most second-generation systems do not include provisions for such receiver concepts, limiting their applicability or requiring their use under stringent constraints with only marginal performance gains.

WCDMA is intended to be deployed alongside GSM, allowing for seamless handovers between GSM and WCDMA. This capability leverages the existing GSM coverage to facilitate the introduction and expansion of WCDMA services.

## UNIT SUMMARY

Unit 6 provides a comprehensive exploration of advanced communication techniques. It begins with an introduction to MIMO communication, covering basic principles, the MIMO system model, parameters defining MIMO systems, and key assumptions in modeling. The chapter then delves into space-time signal processing techniques, including space-time processing and coding schemes, as well as diversity combining techniques crucial for enhancing signal robustness. Spatial multiplexing principles and techniques are discussed, emphasizing advantages and strategies for adaptive spatial multiplexing with Channel State Information (CSI) feedback. The diversity/multiplexing tradeoff in MIMO systems is analyzed, highlighting gains and practical implications for system design and optimization. Real-world applications and future directions in MIMO technology are explored, alongside challenges and opportunities in deployment across various communication scenarios. The unit concludes with discussions on SNR estimation, BER estimation, outage probability estimation, and an overview of GSM, EDGE, GPRS, IS-95, CDMA2000, and WCDMA technologies, illustrating the broad applicability and evolution of MIMO in modern telecommunications.

# EXERCISE

## Multiple Choice Questions (MCQs)

**1.** Which of the following is NOT a key aspect of MIMO systems?
a) Spatial multiplexing
b) Diversity gain
c) Frequency hopping
d) Space-time coding

2. What is the primary advantage of spatial multiplexing in MIMO systems?
a) Reduced power consumption
b) Increased data rate
c) Enhanced security
d) Improved battery life

3. Which tradeoff is critical in MIMO systems?
a) Power/bandwidth tradeoff
b) Diversity/multiplexing tradeoff
c) Speed/reliability tradeoff
d) Coverage/quality tradeoff

4. What does 'outage' refer to in performance measures?
a) A measure of average signal power
b) The probability that the system's performance falls below a certain threshold
c) The average bit error rate
d) The average symbol error rate

5. What does SNR stand for?
a) Signal-to-Noise Ratio
b) Signal Network Range
c) Symbol Noise Rate
d) Spatial Noise Ratio

6. What is measured by the average Bit Error Rate (BER)?
a) The percentage of correctly received bits
b) The percentage of incorrectly received bits
c) The power efficiency of the system
d) The average signal strength

7. Which system uses CDMA technology?
   a) GSM
   b) EDGE
   c) GPRS
   d) IS-95

8. Which of the following is a 3G technology?
   a) GSM
   b) EDGE
   c) GPRS
   d) WCDMA

9. Which technology is associated with the second generation (2G) of mobile communications?
   a) CDMA 2000
   b) GSM
   c) WCDMA
   d) IS-95

10. What does 'GSM' stand for?
    a) Global System for Mobile communications
    b) General Signal Modulation
    c) Global Satellite Mobile
    d) General System for Messaging

11. What is a key feature of EDGE technology?
    a) High-speed internet access
    b) Improved data rates over GSM
    c) CDMA-based modulation
    d) Enhanced voice quality

12. Which performance measure indicates the likelihood of an error-free transmission?
    a) Outage probability
    b) Average SNR
    c) Average symbol error rate
    d) Average bit error rate

13. What technology is GPRS associated with?
    a) Second generation (2G)
    b) Third generation (3G)
    c) Fourth generation (4G)
    d) Fifth generation (5G)

14. Which of the following technologies is known for using a wideband CDMA technique?
    a) GSM
    b) EDGE
    c) GPRS
    d) WCDMA

15. Which system was designed to support high data rates in mobile communications?
    a) GSM
    b) CDMA 2000
    c) EDGE
    d) IS-95

**Answers**

1. Frequency hopping
2. Increased data rate
3. Diversity/multiplexing tradeoff
4. The probability that the system's performance falls below a certain threshold
5. Signal-to-Noise Ratio
6. The percentage of incorrectly received bits
7. IS-95
8. WCDMA
9. GSM
10. Global System for Mobile communications
11. Improved data rates over GSM
12. Average bit error rate
13. Second generation (2G)
14. WCDMA
15. CDMA 2000

**KNOW MORE**

***For more information related to this topic scan the QR code.***

**OR**

***Type this link in your browser***

**https://nptel.ac.in/courses/117104115**

## REFERENCES

1. T. S. Rappaport, "Wireless Communications Prentice Hall PTR." New York, 1996.

2. J. H. Schiller, "Wireless and Mobile Communications." Handbook of Research on Ubiquitous Computing Technology for Real Time Enterprises. IGI Global, 2008.

4. Agrawal, Dharma P., and Qing-An Zeng, "Introduction to wireless and mobile systems." Cengage learning, 2015.

5. Halonen, Timo, Javier Romero, and Juan Melero, eds, "GSM, GPRS and EDGE performance: evolution towards 3G/UMTS." John Wiley & Sons, 2004

6. Richardson, Andrew, "WCDMA design handbook. Vol. 13." Cambridge: Cambridge University Press, 2005

# COURSE OUTCOME ATTAINMENT TABLE

Course outcomes (COs) for this course can be mapped with the programme outcomes (POs) after the completion of the course and a correlation can be made for the attainment of POs to analyse the gap. After proper analysis of the gap in the attainment of POs necessary measures can be taken to overcome the gaps.

**Table for CO and PO attainment**

| **Course Outcomes** | **Expected Mapping with Programme Outcomes** *(1- Weak Correlation; 2- Medium correlation; 3- Strong Correlation)* | | | | | | | | | | | |
|---|---|---|---|---|---|---|---|---|---|---|---|---|
| | **PO-1** | **PO-2** | **PO-3** | **PO-4** | **PO-5** | **PO-6** | **PO-7** | **PO-8** | **PO-9** | **PO-10** | **PO-11** | **PO-12** |
| **CO-1** | | | | | | | | | | | | |
| **CO-2** | | | | | | | | | | | | |
| **CO-3** | | | | | | | | | | | | |
| **CO-4** | | | | | | | | | | | | |
| **CO-5** | | | | | | | | | | | | |
| **CO-6** | | | | | | | | | | | | |

The data filled in the above table can be used for gap analysis.

# INDEX

## D



## E



## F



## G

**W**



**Z**